# THE BASICS

*Acting: The Basics* is a practical and theoretical guide to the world of the professional actor, skilfully combining ideas from a range of practitioners and linking the academy to the industry. It covers key areas such as:

- the development of modern drama and acting processes over the years
- the approach and legacy of acting pioneers and practitioners from around the world
- acting techniques and practicalities, including training, auditioning, rehearsing and performing for stage and screen.

Complete with a glossary of terms and useful website suggestions, this is the ideal introduction for anyone wanting to learn more about the practice of acting and the people who have advanced its evolution.

**Bella Merlin** is Professor of Acting at the University of California, Davis, as well as an actor and trainer. She has written a number of books on Stanislavsky.

# The Basics

**ACTING**
*BELLA MERLIN*

**ANTHROPOLOGY**
*PETER METCALF*

**ARCHAEOLOGY (SECOND EDITION)**
*CLIVE GAMBLE*

**ART HISTORY**
*GRANT POOKE AND DIANA NEWALL*

**THE BIBLE**
*JOHN BARTON*

**BLUES**
*DICK WEISSMAN*

**BUDDHISM**
*CATHY CANTWELL*

**CRIMINAL LAW**
*JONATHAN HERRING*

**CRIMINOLOGY**
*SANDRA WALKLATE*

**ECONOMICS**
*TONY CLEAVER*

**EUROPEAN UNION (SECOND EDITION)**
*ALEX WARLEIGH-LACK*

**FILM STUDIES**
*AMY VILLAREJO*

**FINANCE**
*ERIK BANKS*

**FOLK MUSIC**
*RONALD COHEN*

**INTERNATIONAL RELATIONS**
*PETER SUTCH AND JUANITA ELIAS*

**INTERNET**
*JASON WHITTAKER*

**ISLAM**
*COLIN TURNER*

**JUDAISM**
*JACOB NEUSNER*

**LANGUAGE (SECOND EDITION)**
*R.L. TRASK*

**LITERARY THEORY (SECOND EDITION)**
*HANS BERTENS*

**MANAGEMENT**
*MORGEN WITZEL*

**MARKETING (SECOND EDITION)**
*KARL MOORE AND NIKETH PAREEK*

**OPERA**
*DENISE GALLO*

**PHILOSOPHY (FOURTH EDITION)**
*NIGEL WARBURTON*

**POETRY**
*JEFFREY WAINWRIGHT*

**POLITICS (FOURTH EDITION)**
*STEPHEN TANSEY AND NIGEL JACKSON*

**THE QUR'AN**
*MASSIMO CAMPANINI*

**RELIGION (SECOND EDITION)**
*MALORY NYE*

**ROMAN CATHOLICISM**
*MICHAEL WALSH*

**SEMIOTICS (SECOND EDITION)**
*DANIEL CHANDLER*

**SHAKESPEARE (SECOND EDITION)**
*SEAN MCEVOY*

**SOCIOLOGY**
*MARTIN ALBROW*

**TELEVISION STUDIES**
*TOBY MILLER*

**THEATRE STUDIES**
*ROBERT LEACH*

# ACTING

# THE BASICS

bella merlin

Routledge
Taylor & Francis Group

LONDON AND NEW YORK

First published 2010
by Routledge
2 Park Square, Milton Park, Abingdon, Oxon OX14 4RN

Simultaneously published in the USA and Canada
by Routledge
270 Madison Avenue, New York, NY 10016

*Routledge is an imprint of the Taylor & Francis Group, an informa business*

Typeset in Bembo by Taylor and Francis Books
Printed and bound in Great Britain by TJ International, Padstow, Cornwall

*British Library Cataloguing in Publication Data*
A catalogue record for this book is available from the British Library

*Library of Congress Cataloging in Publication Data*
Merlin, Bella.
  Acting : the basics / Bella Merlin.
    p. cm. – (The basics)
  Includes bibliographical references and index.
  1. Acting. I. Title.
  PN2061.M395 2010
  792.02′8–dc22

                        2009040707

ISBN10: 0-415-46100-6 (hbk)
ISBN10: 0-415-46101-4 (pbk)
ISBN10: 0-203-85486-1 (ebk)

ISBN13: 978-0-415-46100-9 (hbk)
ISBN13: 978-0-415-46101-6 (pbk)
ISBN13: 978-0-203-85486-0 (ebk)

There are hardly any exceptions to the rule that
a person must pay dearly for the divine gift of creative fire.

Carl Jung (1875–1961)

Acting is the essential lubricant.

Marlon Brando (1924–2004)

For
Miles Anderson
whose acting is basically brilliant

# CONTENTS

Preface                                                           viii
Abbreviations                                                        x

**Introduction**                                                     1
1   'Mask or face?': A brief history of acting                       5
2   'I can do that!': Actor-training                                35
3   'You got the part!': Auditions                                  75
4   'Building a character': Rehearsal processes                     93
5   'Another opening, another show': Performance
    practices                                                      134
6   'Passing the baton': Eleven executors of acting                160

Glossary of terms                                                  209
Selected bibliography                                              217
Index                                                              222

# PREFACE

I was truly honoured to be asked to contribute to Routledge's acclaimed *The Basics* series. Writing this book has been both a pleasure and, indeed, a challenge, as there are so many wonderful actors, trainers, theorists and thinkers who could have featured – either at all or more prominently. As there simply isn't space to do them justice, I have homed in on the backbone of acting, if occasionally at the expense of some limbs and organs. However, the bibliography guides you towards other interesting *dramatis personae*, whom I hope you will visit. There are also numerous websites to be trawled. By simply Googling most of the practitioners and training programmes, you'll uncover a wealth of wisdom and opportunities. In order to keep a narrative flow going through the text, I only include the details of extended quotations, so do take note of the books cited at the end of each chapter and certainly in the bibliography.

While all those cited have been vital sources of information, *Acting: The Basics* would have been impossible to write without wholly integrating my original, practical research (on the stage, in front of the camera, in the studio and in the classroom). This book is aimed predominantly at the doer – the Actor – who uses their body, imagination, emotions and intellect to experience their learning as a truly transformative process and to embody their knowledge wholeheartedly. I encourage all students of acting – both in the Academy and in the Industry – to consider themselves 'practical researchers', not only into the nature of acting itself, but also into the working of human interaction.

I would like to thank the excellent editorial team at Routledge, including Andy Humphries, Katherine Ong, and not least Talia Rodgers, who is a constant source of inspiration and encouragement. The anonymous reviewers were also a vital source of thoughtful provocation and encouragement: thank you, whoever you were. All those with whom I've worked – actors, directors, teachers and students (chiefly at the University of California, Davis) – have (wittingly or unwittingly) provided invaluable insights. I particularly thank Phillip B. Zarrilli, Edward Kemp, Katya Kamotskaya and Jade McCutcheon for some great conversations, and Robert Ellerman for his inspiring and generous emails. My most heartfelt thanks go to Miles Anderson for his talent, wisdom, patience, and mental and physical nurturing, not to mention endless re-readings of endless re-writings.

Bella Merlin
info@bellamerlin.com
http://www.theatredance.ucdavis.edu

# ABBREVIATIONS

| | |
|---|---|
| ADR | Automated Dialogue Replacement |
| ATM | Awareness Through Movement |
| DOP | Director of Photography |
| GITIS | Russian Academy of Theatre Arts |
| LAMDA | London Academy of Music and Dramatic Art |
| MAT | Moscow Art Theatre |
| POV | Point of View |
| RADA | Royal Academy of Dramatic Art |
| SCOT | Suzuki Company of Toga |
| SITI | Saratoga International Theatre Institute |

# Introduction

This is a book about Acting. Not Drama. Not Theatre or Performance Studies. It's a book about the practice of acting and the people who advance its evolution. It combines information from various published sources with insights from my own experiences as a working professional and original material from fellow actors. The intention is to introduce you to an array of practitioners and thinkers who have shaped our craft, along with a range of insights into the challenges and experiences you'll possibly encounter on your way. In many ways, I lead you to the banquet table, so that you can choose whatever suits your taste buds.

In other words, this isn't a primer or 'how to act' book, because it's hard to learn how to act from a book. It's an art you discover experientially, by getting up and doing it, as it involves all aspects of your personality: your body, voice, imagination, emotions and psyche. That said, there are many ideas which *can* be shared through the written word. Hence *Acting: The Basics*. The contents of this book straddle both the Academy and the Industry, applying to you whether you're at a vocational drama school or a university studying Acting as part of a broader degree. (There may even be something for the seasoned professional.) So, I hope to share with you a desire to combine practical acting with intellectual curiosity, since – as a professional actor who also teaches in universities and drama schools – I believe there are so many exciting discoveries to be made by linking our own experience to the study of others. To which end, we begin with a historical overview.

## HISTORICAL CONTEXTS

Everything we do is an evolution of what has gone before, and it's both useful and important to understand the 'backstory', so that you can relate it to the present tense. So, let's start our journey by looking back at the development of acting over the last four hundred years during what's known as the 'modern' era. In Chapter 1 ('Mask or face?': A brief history of acting) I've contextualised how the pioneers peered at performance through different facets of the crystal, depending on whether they were actors, directors, philosophers or scientists. Between them, they evolved the kind of 'reality', with which we're familiar today in most stage and screen acting. We then canter through the centuries, resting at the highlights, with the selected bibliography at the end of the chapter drawing you to the great resources influencing this chapter.

## THE CORE NARRATIVE

*Acting: The Basics* then follows the arc of an actor's professional journey.

Chapter 2 ('I can do that!': Actor-training) investigates certain strategies for evolving your 'instrument'. We'll focus on breath, body, voice and imagination, turning to some major coaches who have emerged over the last few decades, predominantly (though not exclusively) in Europe and the USA.

Chapter 3 ('You got the part!': Auditioning) deals with one of the most stressful situations in which we find ourselves as actors, as all our talents are condensed into a very brief time-frame. Depending on the medium (theatre, television, film or commercials), the circumstances of the audition can be very different. We'll consider some of the challenges, along with a few strategies for alleviating the pressure.

Once you've clinched the audition and secured the job, the real work begins, and Chapter 4 ('Building a character': Rehearsal processes) forms the heart of this book. The chapter journeys from your first encounter with a script through to the theatre dress rehearsal or the television line run.

Having rehearsed the role and negotiated the medium in which you're working, the main part of your job is to give your performance, and Chapter 5 ('Another opening, another show': Performance practices) explores the art of doing your work publicly. The mental multi-tasking involved in performance is complex and varied, and we'll look in particular at acting for camera.

## THE PIONEERS OF CONTEMPORARY ACTING

In the final chapter – Chapter 6 ('Passing the baton': Eleven executors of acting) – I offer an overview of some key, pioneering practitioners from the last one hundred years. They've all impacted significantly on Western acting techniques and they feature prominently on drama syllabi. Whole books have been devoted to all of these people and their biographies are easily accessible on the Internet. So with each practitioner, I focus on one of their key texts, drawing out a number of nuggets (which you can begin to apply to your acting ethos) and a couple of cautions to bear in mind. In an ideal world, we'd all have the chance to work intensively with each practitioner's training. Since that's rarely possible, the snapshot insights into their books offered here are intended to provide you with a range of tools available as you develop your own unique acting voice, and to understand what you can take from the 'executors' without necessarily having the opportunity to take a full, years-long, training programme.

## 'THE EASY WAY IS THE RIGHT WAY'

There are hundreds of books on acting. Hundreds of teachers, directors, gurus and guides offering 'their' way – even '*the*' way – to act. My particular Anglo-Russian training was steeped in the ideas of Stanislavsky, Michael Chekhov and Jerzy Grotowski, and yet I believe a real technique is only as valuable as it is helpful. And so in my own acting work, I'm a magpie, stealing from whoever is useful given a particular character, director or medium. A bit of Brecht here, a morsel of Meisner there. Ultimately, all paths lead to Rome, and that Rome is something very simple: 'dynamic listening'. Dynamic listening is not just about hearing with your ears. It's also about listening to your partner's body and face, noting the changes in their energy and physical posture. In addition, it's about listening to yourself – your own body and your own emotional impulses.

Those impulses usually lead to words. And if you can listen to your own words and how those words impact both on yourself and your partner, as well as listening – and I mean *really* listening – to the words of the other actors, not to mention their moments of silence, then you can discover exactly what to *do* in the given circumstances of your character's life. And the *doing* is key. I'd go as far as to say that, by dynamically listening, you'll pretty much know how to *act*. Listen and respond. Act and react. Acting could be so easy!

Indeed, in 1967, the martial arts expert Bruce Lee (1940–73) devised a form which he called Jeet Kune Do: 'The way of the intercepting fist'. His aim was not to add more and more techniques on top of each other to create a new style, but rather to winnow out the extraneous. He wanted to free people from clinging to patterns or modes. For him, the 'extraordinary part' of Jeet Kune Do lay in its simplicity: 'There is nothing artificial about it. I always believe that the easy way is the right way. Jeet Kune Do is simply the direct expression of one's feelings with the minimum of movements and energy' (Lee 1971:24).

Lee could have been writing about acting, and I'd suggest there is no *one* acting system: if we enslave ourselves to a particular training or methodology, we can atrophy in our creativity. And, just like Jeet Kune Do, the extraordinary part of acting lies in its simplicity and economy, so that everything we do becomes a direct expression of our feelings.

# 'MASK OR FACE?': A BRIEF HISTORY OF ACTING

Acting processes have evolved enormously over the last four hundred years, but before we look specifically at the people who shaped that evolution, let's take a snapshot of some broader issues that influence acting, starting with our very basic human desires of 'being affective' and 'wanting witnesses' to our lives.

## WANTING WITNESSES

We come into this world alone. We leave this world alone. What a terrifying thought!

It's reassuring to know that somebody somewhere is bearing witness to our lives, hearing our stories and sharing our experiences. Be it best friend, boyfriend, cousin or cat – it's good to feel we're not alone. Maybe that's why so many of us head for the world of acting, where dozens, if not hundreds or thousands, of spectators actually pay to watch the stories we're telling. Being witnessed is a fundamental human desire that has found its way to becoming a massive, global industry.

## BEING AFFECTIVE

The desire to act isn't just about taking the spotlight: it's also about believing so much in what we're saying that we can influence our listeners. It's no surprise that the foundations of acting lie in religion (the sacred) and politics (the social), both of which have at their heart the power to be affective.

'Religion' covers a gamut of performance realms: from ancient rituals involving supernatural forces to medieval liturgical dramas. Impersonating another life-force has always been strongly connected with something magical, mysterious and inexplicable.

As for 'politics' and acting, the ancient Greeks had a particular interest in **oratory** (public speaking) and **rhetoric** (how you composed and delivered your speeches). The idea was that if you were a politician or a lawyer and you wanted to stir deeply a voting crowd or a deciding jury, then you yourself had to be deeply affected by your own words in the first place.

Whether you were sharing a story, or invoking religious characters, or making an impact through public speaking, the one component you always needed was an audience. Even an ancient ritual needed witnesses: if the gods didn't see your act of sacrifice, then the harvest might not grow.

## INFLUENTIAL FACTORS

There are a number of factors influencing how you take your audience on an imaginative and affecting journey, one of the most significant being the *space* you're in.

### THE INFLUENCE OF SPACE

Space is everything. The caveman round the campfire telling the story of his day's hunting would have used very different techniques from the masked chorus in a vast, Greek amphitheatre. Likewise, Robert De Niro (1943–) in an intimate two-shot uses different techniques from Michael Ball (1962–) in a West End musical. The dynamics of the space and the nature of the journey on which you're taking your audience significantly alter the physical and imaginative choices you make. In fact, several serious performance makers, including Rudolf Laban (1879–1958), Michel Saint-Denis (1897–1971) and Jacques Lecoq (1921–99) (all of whom we'll return to), were as interested in architecture as they were in art.

And the performance space itself may be determined by how much money you've got.

## THE INFLUENCE OF ECONOMICS

In 1887, when the Frenchman, André Antoine (1858–1943), set up his innovative *Théâtre Libre*, he was a gas company clerk; he had very little money and a tiny rehearsal space, so he used his own furniture and a bunch of talented amateurs. These economic restrictions – combined with Antoine's artistic vision – encouraged the kind of intimate acting that we're so used to seeing on television today. In stark contrast, the Russian, Konstantin Stanislavsky (1863–1938) was the son of a gold thread merchant, so he had ample capital to plough into the Moscow Art Theatre (MAT), which he founded in 1898 with Vladimir Nemirovich-Danchenko (1858–1943). Being able to afford impressive custom-built sets and embark on research trips to the relevant towns and museums affected naturalistic acting styles as much as Antoine's processes did, albeit in a completely opposite way.

And the literary movement of **naturalism** itself emerged from a dialogue with *science*.

## THE INFLUENCE OF SCIENCE

Here are two quick snapshots. In 1923, the MAT actor Richard Boleslavsky (1889–1937) gave a series of lectures in New York on Stanislavsky's 'system'. He declared that an actor must create a human soul on the stage with all its physical, mental and emotional aspects. At just the same time, Sigmund Freud's (1856–1939) theories of **psychoanalysis** were beginning to percolate throughout American society. Although Boleslavsky himself wasn't directly affected by Freud's influence, the American public – and its acting fraternity – were. Since acting and psychoanalysis both investigated a human being's inner workings, science and art inevitably intertwined.

And not for the first time: some years earlier, Charles Darwin's (1809–82) *Origin of Species* (1859) and *The Expression of Emotions in Animals and Man* (1872) sparked a flurry of responses in the arts. The 'father' of naturalism, the French novelist, Émile Zola (1840–1902), wrote complicated characters through which he examined the influence of our *heredity* (i.e. who we are as a result of our gene pool) and our *environment* (i.e. who we are as a result of our upbringing and experiences). The idea was that society makes us, and we in turn make society, and a part of that society is the theatre we create. Which brings us on to *politics* and its influence on acting processes.

## THE INFLUENCE OF POLITICS

Political theatre – and the particular demands it makes on an actor – has taken a number of forms over the last century: from the **invisible** and **forum** theatres of Brazilian practitioner, Augusto Boal (1931–2009) (where actors go out onto the streets and provoke social debate), to the anarchic clowning of Italian maestro, Dario Fo (1926–), to the eclectic internationalism of America's La MaMa, to the raw and inflammatory cabaret of German actor-writer, Frank Wedekind (1864–1918), to the **epic** plays of Bertolt Brecht (1898–1956), to the **verbatim** and **tribunal** dramas for which the Tricycle Theatre, London, has become famed in recent years.

Even in the realm of voice and dialect, politics has influenced performance styles. If you're based in Britain, you'll be used to the Geordie commentaries on the Channel 4 television show *Big Brother*, for instance. But fifty years ago, this would have been unheard of. It was only in the 1950s and 1960s that various social shifts in Britain spawned a school of acting where the regional accents and earthy **realism** of actors including Tom Courtney (1937–) and Albert Finney (1936–) replaced the typically crystal chimes of Edith Evans (1888–1976) and Laurence Olivier (1907–89). Which brings us on to *writers*.

## THE INFLUENCE OF WRITERS

The sweaty, 'working class' plays – including John Osborne's (1929–94) *Look Back in Anger* (1956) and Shelagh Delaney's (1939–) *A Taste of Honey* (1961) which rocked British theatre in the mid-twentieth century, not to mention the American director, Elia Kazan's (1909–2003) film version of Tennessee Williams' (1911–83) *A Streetcar Named Desire* (1951) with its tee-shirt bustin' Marlon Brando (1924–2004) – led to a new stage in the evolution of acting styles. This style was fleshy, earthy, sexy and extremely realistic.

A similar shifting of theatre's tectonic plates had happened half a century earlier, when the première of Anton Chekhov's (1860–1904) *The Seagull* (1896) failed dismally in St Petersburg. It was only thanks to Stanislavsky and Nemirovich-Danchenko, that Chekhov didn't give up playwriting altogether. Instead, the two directors painstakingly fathomed out Chekhov's **subtext**, and in so doing, they provoked a whole new style of acting. And the tectonic plates continue to shift. In their own way, American writers David Mamet (1947–) and Sam Shepard (1943–) challenge their performers through a combination of rhythm, theatricality and gritty, realistic characters – with more than a hint of the absurd. It comes as no surprise that they're both *directors* as well as writers.

## THE INFLUENCE OF DIRECTORS

As your acting career evolves, you'll discover that directors can influence your acting choices in all sorts of ways, both subtle and overt. As we'll see in Chapters 4 and 5, each director brings with them a whole set of unknowns for their actors: how they read a text; how they run a rehearsal period; how they collaborate with their cast; how they build a production; how they relinquish their hold once their main task is complete; and a vast range of other delicate operations. The relationship between director and actor is intimate, vulnerable, and delicious (when it goes well) and disorientating (when it goes awry). Every situation poses new conditions for you as an actor, which you then have to integrate into your creative process.

## THE INFLUENCE OF REHEARSAL AND PERFORMANCE

Not least of these conditions is the actual *length of the rehearsal period*. If you have as many months of rehearsal as some European companies, your strategy as an actor will be quite different from either a few weeks in theatre or a few minutes in television. The arc of your journey into the character is inevitably shaped by the amount of preparation time you have.

Then, of course, there's the *duration of the run*. From the 1850s onwards, extended runs became the norm. No longer were plays shown for only three or four nights. Indeed, I know of actors in the twenty-first century, who have stayed in West End shows for four consecutive years. The demands of recreating a role night after night on stage are quite different from maintaining a creative state during a number of takes for a film. Again, as we'll see in more detail in Chapters 4 and 5, each medium demands a variety of choices.

I've talked a lot about choices in this quick-fire glance at some circumstances that affect us as actors. But what exactly are those choices and how have they been handed down to us? In other words, who came up with the possible choices in the first place? Where were they based? Who were they writing for? What did they do for a living? The creators of modern acting theories were inevitably influenced by their *profession* and their *temperament*, or, as Zola might put it, by their *environment* and their *heredity*.

## THE INFLUENCE OF PROFESSION

Many of the major writers on acting – particularly in the nineteenth and twentieth centuries – were *actors*: David Garrick (1717–79), Benôit-Constant Coquelin (1841–1909), Stanislavsky, Michael Chekhov (1891–1955), Vsevelod Meyerhold (1874–1940), Uta Hagen (1919–2004), Jacques Copeau (1879–1949) and Louis Jouvet (1887–1951) to name but a few. They were *inside* the processes of creating a character and so they understood absolutely what our challenges are when we stand on a stage or face a camera.

On the other hand, the influential Denis Diderot (1713–84) was a *philosopher*. He was interested in all the arts, not just acting. Through his observations of artists at work in various media, he proposed ideas which have inflamed many debates about acting to the present day. The equally influential William Archer (1856–1924) was a *critic*, so his thoughts on acting stemmed from an objective, observational point of view, rather than a subjective, involved perspective.

Be they director, scholar, voice coach or educationalist, we'll see how the professional lens through which each individual looks at acting inevitably informs the training they propose. As indeed does their individual *temperament*.

## THE INFLUENCE OF PERSONAL TEMPERAMENT

This is something of a hot potato – especially for the American acting fraternity – but let's briefly take two key twentieth-century actor-trainers: Stella Adler (1901–92) and Lee Strasberg (1901–82). In her practice, Adler focused on Stanislavsky's idea of **action**, while her co-worker, Strasberg, highlighted **affective memory** (see 'The nature of emotions' later in this chapter). This led to two very different interpretations of Stanislavsky's 'system' evolving in the USA from the 1930s onwards. They were both actors, they were both teachers and both were concerned with developing nuanced acting. Yet one personality was drawn to rock-solid physical tasks, while the other personality was drawn to the more elusive, inner quality of those tasks. (See Chapter 6 for more details.)

From these brief snapshots, we can begin to see that, throughout history, a variety of circumstances – economic, scientific, artistic, political and personal – have affected acting processes. I've flagged up these influences because you'll spend your life as an actor being faced with an overwhelming number of books, courses, workshops, master classes and lectures. So it's worth your while remembering that both the occupation and the preoccupations of each 'master' (or 'mistress') are instrumental in how they put all their ideas together.

Holding that thought, let's turn our attention to the general contours of acting history and to some specific individuals.

## THE CLASSICAL ERA

### ARISTOTLE'S PLOT AND CHARACTER

We can't look at the modern era without casting a glance backwards towards ancient Greece. The philosopher Aristotle (384–22 BCE) was arguably the first serious analyst of drama, with his particular emphasis on 'plot' (i.e. a series of events). The plot – in other words, the story, or what happens to the characters – is the most important aspect of a drama; this is the play's *action*. Certainly, with Stanislavsky's later rehearsal practice of **Active Analysis** (see Chapter 4), one of the first things you do when you're analysing a play is identify the key events in each scene: 'What happens in this scene? Why did the playwright write this scene? How would the play's overall plot change if this scene wasn't here?' Time and again, we'll come back to the importance of action.

Secondary to 'plot' is 'character'. Aristotle proposed that each character should display a particular disposition or outlook, which is revealed to the audience by the action of the play. In other words, character is utterly dependent on action: if you don't carry out any actions, the audience will have no idea of your character. Again, this fits in very much with Stanislavsky's acting processes: once you've identified what the character *does* (in terms of inner, physical and verbal actions), you're in a far stronger position to make some sensible choices about interpreting the character.

Aristotle's fundamental ideas about character and action have had a huge influence on the development of acting theories to date, not least the technique of American coach, Sanford Meisner (1905–97). As we'll see in Chapter 6, Meisner focused mainly on what you do in response to other people, as that in itself reveals your character to the audience. Acting equals Doing. So: 'You know who I am by what I do. I *do*, therefore I am.'

## QUINTILIAN AND THE POWER OF ORATORY

Although it wasn't until the seventeenth century that discussion of acting really began to take shape in the West, thinkers initially turned to the ancient Greek philosopher Quintilian (c.35–c.100), especially his twelve-volume textbook called *Institutes of Oratory* (first published in Italy in 1470). Although Quintilian wrote for public speakers (such as lawyers and politicians), his words were just as applicable to actors. In fact, there were a number of key tools which you'll find now form the basis of most acting manuals, including imagination, breath, voice and physical gesture.

## IMAGINATION

Quintilian proposed that if you want to arouse a particular response in other people, then first of all you have to generate those feelings in yourself. Take any legal drama such as *JFK* (1991) or *The Verdict* (1982), not to mention *Rumpole of the Bailey* (BBC) or Shakespeare's Portia in *The Merchant of Venice*, and you'll see what he meant. It was the lawyer's job to use passionate rhetoric to incite their juries into seeing the world through the eyes of their victim or defendant. If the jurors can see just how dreadful the man's childhood was, they might understand why he shot the doctor. And the way to plant that world-view in the head of your listeners is by appealing to their *imaginations*, having first engaged your own.

## BREATH

Beyond imagination, Quintilian proposed there was a physical way of affecting your audience: through the power of your *breath*. Breath was the 'spirit of life' through which you could actually transport your soul into the body of another person. In other words, a very powerful speaker didn't just influence the *emotional* state of their listeners, they actually affected their *physiological* state. You know what it's like if your dad yells at you: his shallow breath and his raised voice begin to alter your own breathing pattern and you start to feel anxious. At the other extreme, physical comedians like Billy Connolly (1942–) or Robin Williams (1951–), with their vibrant energy and vigorous use of breath, can also affect us physiologically, as our breathing changes to a pattern of laughter.

## VOICE AND PHYSICAL GESTURE

Imagination and breath are inevitably connected to *voice*. As Quintilian points out, your voice responds naturally to the images you convey to your listener, just like an oboe sounds according to the way its reed is blown. In just the same way, your *physical gestures* should match your voice and imagination. To which end, Quintilian (among others) invented a host of gestural codes, which should be correlated to your words. Right arms were raised and left arms were lowered according to the point you were striving to make and the affect you wanted to have on your audience.

## THE POWER OF ACTING

Affecting others and being affected by your own emotions was powerful stuff, and Quintilian believed that the communication between a live performer and a live spectator could actually be dangerous. 'How can acting be *dangerous*?' you may well ask. Yet it's more relevant today than ever, with authorities such as the American

Academy of Pediatrics and the *British Medical Journal* concurring that there's a direct link in young people between watching violent movies and behaving violently themselves. As for actors, the complexities of 'affecting yourself' with another identity can also – in extreme cases – lead to the blurring of fact and fiction. In 1989, the Irish actor Daniel Day-Lewis (1957–) believed he saw his father's ghost while playing Hamlet at the National Theatre. So Quintilian's warning about the dangers of acting has some resonance, and history has proven that public speakers – both good guys and bad – are extremely powerful people. Just look at Barack Obama (1961–) and Winston Churchill (1874–1965), or Adolf Hitler (1889–1945) and Robert Mugabe (1924–).

As we turn to the modern era, it's useful to remember these classical influences: Aristotle's connection of action with character and Quintilian's ardent belief that, by feeling something yourself, you could infect your audience with that feeling.

## THE SEVENTEENTH CENTURY

### GALEN'S HUMOURS

At the heart of any actor-training system lies some kind of interconnection between your body, imagination and emotions. As we'll see in Chapter 2, a term often used is **psycho-physical**, meaning that our *inner* psychological realm and our *outer* physical body are completely in dialogue with each other. Our understanding of this in the West has largely come from our increased knowledge of science. Although the workings of our bodies and imaginations are still very magical and mysterious, they were even more so in the seventeenth century when the first serious debates about acting began to percolate.

At this time, there was a limited understanding of anatomy, and medicine was fairly primitive, with no real knowledge of the difference between the cardiovascular system and the nervous system. Unaware that our blood pumped around our bodies, scientists followed the teachings of another ancient Greek, the physician Galen (129–200).

Galen proposed that various organs in your body attracted one of four particular fluids or **humours**, which were then refined in those organs to help your body to expel waste. The four humours were: (1) blood (associated with your liver, and characterised by *sanguine* traits, such as courage, love and generosity); (2) yellow bile (associated with your gall bladder, and characterised by *choleric* traits such as anger, violence and vengefulness); (3) phlegm (associated with your spleen, and characterised by *phlegmatic* traits such as despondence, cowardice and calm); and (4) black bile (associated with your brain and lungs, and characterised by *melancholic* traits such as gluttony, laziness and thoughtfulness). If all the humours were balanced, you were in a state of *eukrasia*, and if there was an imbalance, you were in a state of *dyskrasia*. Ideally, you wanted to be 'eukrasic'.

## THE PASSIONS

The humours in your body would influence the kind of **passions** you experienced, and the passions themselves fell into two categories. *Concupiscible* passions were aroused when you really wanted something, in which case you might feel excitement or joy. *Irascible* passions were aroused when you wanted to avoid something, in which case you might feel anxiety or fear.

The word 'passion' comes from the Latin *patior*, meaning 'to suffer or endure'; so, if you felt passionate about something, it was thought you must be experiencing some kind of suffering. In which case, Quintilian's belief that acting is dangerous could be right: if you were *consciously* arousing your passions – i.e. acting – you could be putting your body and spirit through a potentially parlous process. An actor's job was made even more psychologically precarious by playwrights of the era writing deliberately big changes of passions into their plays, so that actors had to swing swiftly between huge and contradictory states.

The burning question then was: 'How do you control a passion, once you've provoked it?' After all, that's your job as an actor: you have to have your passions at your finger tips, as Hamlet stresses in what is probably one of the best known acting 'manuals' of the seventeenth century:

[I]n the very torrent, tempest, and, as I may say, whirlwind of your passion, you must acquire and beget a temperance that may give it

> smoothness. [ ... ] Be not too tame neither. But let your own discretion be your tutor. Suit the action to the word, the word to the action, with this special observance, that you o'erstep not the modesty of nature.
>
> (*Hamlet*, Act III, Scene ii)

So your passions must be engaged, and yet they must be aesthetically appropriate. Not too big, not too small. Which leads to more burning questions: 'How do you turn them on and off? Where's the tap? Where exactly are your passions located in your body?' Before science could answer that with any real authority, the possibilities had to be weighed.

## DESCARTES' DUALISM

One of the greatest influences on seventeenth-century thought was the French scientist and philosopher, René Descartes (1596–1650). A remarkable man in many ways, Descartes proposed that there were six primary passions: wonder, hatred, desire, love, joy and sadness. (Check out Ekman's basic emotions in Chapter 2.) Just like the primary colours, they could be mixed to make every other passion. Descartes set out to look at the fracture between our body and our mind, and in 1649 he produced *The Passions of the Soul* (*Les passions de l'âme*). His legacy became known as **Cartesian dualism**, referring to the dialogue between the two.

Descartes suggested that, in order to keep us alive, our body (the 'moving machine') responded to our sensory experiences of hunger, pain, heat, thirst and pleasure – the daily stimulants over which we had no control.

Our mind, on the other hand, was quite independent of our body and was purely involved with intellectual processes. And unlike the sensory experiences of hunger and pain, etc., we (supposedly) did have utter control over our mind.

Our mind resided in our body, like a 'ghost in the machine'. (This was a little like a driver in a car. Scientists had yet to consider that there might be an intermediary – i.e. the subconscious – which might be something like an automatic gearbox.) Our mind, therefore, *was* our personality, leading to Descartes' famous epigram: 'I *think*, therefore I am.'

## THE EIGHTEENTH CENTURY

### INTRODUCING PSYCHOLOGY

The eighteenth century saw a whirlwind of theatrical activity across Europe and America. It was the 'Age of Enlightenment', in which everything was questioned: religion, ethics, science, art. Added to which, there was a boom in the general public's literacy, so more people could read and, therefore, knowledge could spread much faster.

This expansion of knowledge affected acting in a number of ways. In 1749, the term **psychology** (as we understand it today) was introduced by the philosopher, David Hartley (1705–57) in his *Observations on Man, his Frame, his Duty and his Expectations.* Suddenly a spotlight was shone on the 'individual' and the way in which each of us evaluates the world, by comparing our past-tense memories with our present-tense experiences. In other words, no two interpretations of life can be the same, as none of us have had exactly the same experiences.

This raised even more questions about acting. If each person's responses were different, then each individual actor must be *completely* different. So, how useful as acting tools were the standardised, codified gestures in the oratory manuals? (Though, curiously, actors hung on to them tenaciously until well into the nineteenth century.) And how relevant or not were the broad brush-strokes of the four humours and the six passions?

### EMOTIONS AND SENSIBILITY

In fact, the passions were now superseded by 'emotions', which scientists discovered were physiological responses in our nervous systems, and because each person's physiology was different, then emotional responses would be different in every human being. They also discovered that the presence of an emotion in a person was more like a guitar string being plucked than an oboe being blown. In other words, emotions had reverberations: they didn't just vanish as soon as whatever provoked the emotion disappeared. Suddenly, it was clear how crazily unnatural it was for the seventeenth-century playwrights to take actors through vast and rapid mood swings all in one play: human emotions simply didn't operate like that. Of course, this discovery affected the kind of plays being written, and performances were no longer about actors putting themselves through their emotional paces, but rather about them revealing to the audience something of their own personal, moral fabric.

In fact, morality became a significant word in the eighteenth century, particularly with the development in art and philosophy of **sensibility**. Sensibility was your capacity to respond to sensations and to be receptive to the impressions around you. Do you weep when you see a baby bird on the pavement? Do you chuckle when you see a little child with its mother? To be swept along by sudden, strong emotions was a sign of your delicate, sensitive nature – and that was a noble and good thing. It was even suggested that the best love scenes were those where the actors really fell in love with each other.

## SAINTE-ALBINE AND THE SUBLIME

Before long, sensibility was applied directly to the art of acting, when in 1747, the French journalist, Pierre Rémond de Sainte-Albine (1699–1778) published his influential book, *The Actor* (*Le comédien*). For Sainte-Albine, there were three important qualities in a refined actor: *feeling* (to create the role), *intelligence* (to control the performance) and *charisma* (to inspire the audience through your personal fire or energy). Echoing the seventeenth-century theorists, he proposed that you still accessed powerful emotions in yourself in order to affect your audience as much as yourself. But, now (in the eighteenth century), the affect you were trying to create should be uplifting, so that you could take your spectators somewhere 'sublime'.

One of the ways to create a sublime experience was through 'irresistible weeping'. (As we'll see in Chapter 4, this has become the actor's scourge.) Across eighteenth-century society, you were considered to have a tremendously noble soul if you could weep in empathy with your fellow man – on the condition (insisted Sainte-Albine) that you also had the intelligence to control your emotions.

The actor who showed himself to be consummate in both controlling and arousing his sensibility was British actor David Garrick.

## GARRICK AND INTELLIGENCE

Garrick was a phenomenon. He brought to the Western stage a quality of realism previously unseen. He could read human beings with the same intelligence that he could read a play. In fact, he considered breadth of knowledge to be an essential tool for an actor, whether that was research-based knowledge or knowledge gained from simply observing other people. (Interestingly, this combination of research and observation became crucial for Stanislavsky in his evolution of acting processes.) Without that breadth of knowledge, Garrick believed it was hard to excel as an actor.

Garrick's intelligence was intuitive as much as intellectual, and in a truly revolutionary way, he recognised that your response to your emotions – i.e. your sensibility – often lies beneath the surface of your conscious thoughts. In other words, you don't consist of a controlling mind that tells your body what to do (i.e. the driver in the car) – there's an intermediary, over which you have no control; in fact, you may not even know about it. That intermediary became known as the **subconscious**. (At last – the automatic gearbox!)

Garrick's inherent genius was widely acknowledged. Apart from revolutionising the London stage during his years at the Drury Lane theatre, he's possibly best known for his appearances in the Paris salons of the early 1760s. His party piece was to stick his head repeatedly out from behind a screen, each time revealing a different passion, yet all the time seeming to be totally immersed in the emotions. There's no doubt from the descriptions of his performances at the time, he was a pivotal player in the evolution of acting. He seemed to mix seventeenth-century grand passions with a foreshadowing of twentieth-century emotional accessibility, and this mixture placed him at the absolute turning point of modern acting practice.

Significantly, Garrick's party piece captured the attention of the French philosopher, Denis Diderot, who has become one of the most significant writers on acting processes.

## DIDEROT AND THE PARADOX

Diderot was so taken with Garrick's acting that he wrote *Observations on a book entitled: Garrick or the English actor* (1770), in which he listed the qualities of a good actor as being: excellent judgement, calm observation of others, a subtle mind, and a keen skill for imitation applicable to all characters and roles, along with a bright imagination and an excellent memory.

Another of Diderot's books, *The Paradox of the Actor* (*Paradoxe sur le Comédien*) (1830) has proved extremely influential on acting theories, even though he himself wasn't an actor. Here, you'll find blue prints for components of Stanislavsky's 'system' (which appeared almost a century later), including 'emotion memory', 'dual consciousness', 'concentration of attention', 'solitude in public', the 'score' of a role, and the delicate balance of technique and spontaneity.

Diderot's main argument was that you may be overwhelmed by all sorts of emotions in the *preparation* of a role, but when it comes to the *performance*, you should remain calm, controlled and detached. Completely overturning Quintilian's belief that 'to move your audience, you yourself must be moved', he advocated that 'to move your audience, you yourself must remain controlled and certain of the journey upon which you're taking them'. And that was his paradox. Your genius as an actor was dependent upon your ability to go beyond your natural sensibility, and remain absolutely precise and flexible. If a play really was to transport an audience to a sublime place, there was no room for you to experience sudden, uncontrolled passions, or you would simply pull a production out of shape.

Diderot maintained that if you could train and condition both your physical and psychological 'muscle memories', you could present to the audience − as if for the first time − a performance you'd consciously honed and crafted. Here's another great paradox: the more you practise something, the more spontaneous you can appear. For Diderot, there was no mystery in acting. You weren't visited by a spirit stirring your soul; it was a craft for which you trained with the same discipline and discerning eye as a painter or a sculptor.

Some commentators have interpreted Diderot's words as encouraging rather cold, calculated performances. Again, I'd suggest that his theories aren't that far away from Stanislavsky's. Your job as an actor is to prepare a character that you can present to an audience or a camera with three-dimensionality and heartfelt commitment, in the knowledge that when the house-lights come up or the shout comes 'Cut!', you can step out of that character and get on with your life. And that professionalism requires training.

## AARON HILL AND 'PLASTIC IMAGINATION'

The eighteenth century saw the serious evolution of actor-trainers, not the least of whom was Aaron Hill (1685–1750), famed for his coaching of the actress Susannah Cibber (1714–66), one of Garrick's leading ladies at Drury Lane. Here we begin to see the real pay-offs of preparation and repetition. Hill filled Cibber's script with a filigree of margin notes for each line, word, movement, pause and intonation, guiding her through every moment of her life on stage. Audiences described her performances as incredibly natural, as if her sensibility 'flowed unprompted from her suffering heart'. And yet, each characterisation was built upon minute detail and total technique, stemming from what Hill called 'plastic imagination'. All the nuances of each passion were imprinted simultaneously on Cibber's brain and body. Like a musical score, her performances were charted and shaped to evoke the relevant responses from her audience at all the relevant times.

What Hill was really exploring was a kind of actor-training that harnessed both your inner realm (your capacity to generate emotions naturally) and your outer realm (your detailed observation of other people). Through constant repetitions, you could shape your natural responses with utter precision, while still being genuine and authentic. Hill's training was in direct opposition to the earlier seventeenth-century idea that actors were at the mercy of the passions which they had to evoke in performance.

## CLAIRON VS. DUMESNIL: TECHNIQUE VS. RAW TALENT

In fact, if you'd been around in eighteenth-century France, you'd have had the chance to see both styles of acting on display in the performances of actresses, La Clairon (Clair Josèphe Hippolyte Leris) (1723–1803) and Dumesnil (Marie Françoise Dumesnil) (1713–1803). While Clairon was technically accurate and could produce the same performance again and again, Dumesnil could fill herself with emotions that were so intense she almost seemed to forget herself. The flipside of her emotional performances was that she was generally considered inconsistent, and whether she'd have survived an eight-show-a-week, ten-month run is probably up for debate. (We'll come across another battle between two top European actresses when we reach the nineteenth century.)

Discussions about acting really heated up during the eighteenth century, with voices adding to the debate from all over Europe. German dramaturg Gotthold Lessing (1729–81) suggested that actors could generate *internal passions* by first of all executing *external actions*. (This argument pre-empted Stanislavsky's **Method of Physical Actions** by the best part of two hundred years.) The Italian playwright Antoine-François Riccoboni (1707–73) believed that actors should have a perfect knowledge of other people's hearts, while always remaining masters of their own. His actor-father, Luigi (1676–1753), offered this handy hint: you can't lay down dogmatic laws about acting because it's different for everyone. With so many theorists and practitioners offering advice, Riccoboni Senior's hint is very useful, especially as we step into the nineteenth century, which was prolific with scientific evolutions and artistic revolutions.

## THE NINETEENTH CENTURY

The impact of the nineteenth century was huge in terms of repertoire, acting styles, the rise of the director, the growth of the ensemble, and the consolidation of actor-training. All of these areas were influenced by an international cast of actors, directors, scientists, theorists and writers.

### DIRECTORS' THEATRE

There's a certain cyclical nature to the nineteenth century. Right at the start, we have indications of the growth of 'directors' theatre' in Johann Wolfgang von Goethe's (1749–1832) book, *Rules for Actors* (1803). His artistic vision involved dividing up the stage into squares like a chess board so that actors could be directed exactly where to stand and beautiful stage pictures could be created. (No doubt this began the practice of 'blocking' a play, where in effect directors move actors around the stage like chess pieces.) By the end of the nineteenth century, we see the well-formed 'directors' theatre' with which we're familiar today, where a director's aesthetic mark is stamped on a production.

## CELEBRITIES' THEATRE

That said, directors' theatre took a while to kick in, as the star system was rife across the continents. All the scientific and philosophical emphasis on individuality meant that actors gained acclaim for their temperaments as much as for their acting. Echoing the Clairon-Dumesnil tussle, a fiery battle blazed between the French actress, Sarah Bernhardt (1844–1923) and the Italian actress Eleonora Duse (1858–24). The public loved Bernhardt both for her flamboyant personality and her charismatic, exotic performances. The critics, however, found her interpretations sometimes rather weak and limited. Duse, on the other hand, avoided any public displays, channelling all her passions into her stage portrayals. The critics loved her, but her own physical and mental well-being suffered terribly.

## ENSEMBLES' THEATRE

The pendulum swing away from personality acting was towards the development of ensembles. They proliferated throughout the nineteenth century, with companies such as the German Saxe-Meiningen group (who were a tremendous influence on Stanislavsky in his vision of the MAT), as well as Antoine's *Théâtre Libre* and Otto Brahm's (1856–1912) *Freie Bühne*. Each company eliminated the gap between the 'star turn' and the other performers. Because the actors in an ensemble were fairly anonymous, the audience could watch a play and focus on what it was about, rather than who was in it. They could lose themselves in the narrative of the characters' lives, as they weren't suddenly jolted back into reality by the onstage arrival of a major celebrity.

## THE NATURALISTIC MOVEMENT

As ever, developments in science and the arts echoed each other. As we touched upon earlier, Darwin's publications coincided with

Zola's naturalistic novels such as *Thérèse Raquin* (1873), in which human beings were forensically put under the microscope. Zola studied the effect on their behaviour of their *heredity* (their gene pool) and their *environment* (their upbringing and social milieu). Right across the Western world, theatre writers such as Henrik Ibsen (1828–1906) in Norway, George Bernard Shaw (1856–1950) in Britain, August Strindberg (1849–1912) in Sweden, David Belasco (1853–1931) in America and Anton Chekhov in Russia, focused on domestic relationships and situations, including alcoholism, prostitution, mental illness, and a host of social vices. They created characters with psychological motivations and contradictory personalities, the like of which hadn't been seen in the music halls and vaudevilles which populated the Western stage. And as we've already noted, as soon as you have a new style of writing, you have to have a new approach to acting. And so **psychological realism** evolved, a style which forms the essence of most stage and screen acting today.

## PSYCHOLOGICAL REALISM AND THE ART OF EMPATHY

You could say that psychological realism centres on the idea of 'empathy'. What I mean by this is that, as an audience, you're invited to watch believable, motivated actions being carried out by three-dimensional actors, revealing psychologically complex characters. Through the logic and sequence of their actions, you're given an insight into why those characters behave as they do, and ideally you leave the theatre with a little more understanding about human behaviour.

For an audience to empathise with the onstage characters, the actors first of all have to go through a process of identifying – or empathising – with the roles, working out how those characters think and how they see the world. For actors to connect with their characters, they need to be open-hearted and to begin the process of characterisation, by first blotting out their own personalities and then by becoming the characters written by the author. So said one of the 'fathers' of realism, the Russian actor Mikhail Shchepkin (1788–1863).

Whether or not we can actually 'blot out our own personalities', what we see here is a subtle shift in the notion of 'transformation' or 'possession'. If the actors of the seventeenth century were anxious that, by arousing certain passions in their own souls, they'd become possessed by those passions, the actors of the nineteenth century were encouraged to 'vacate' themselves so that the character could 'inhabit' their bodies and imaginations. Writing about his performance as Oswald in Ibsen's *Ghosts* (1882), Antoine revealed that, 'after the second act I remembered nothing ... and shaken and weakened, I was some time getting hold of myself again after the final curtain had fallen' (cited in Goodall, 2002:178).

It's a challenge for any actor: 'How do I create a character using my own body, imagination, emotions and spirit, knowing that that creation has to *begin* at a certain time and *last* for a certain time?' And, as far as psychological realism is concerned, the nub of the challenge is the nature of our emotions.

## THE NATURE OF EMOTIONS

There were many investigations into the biology of emotions in the nineteenth century going far beyond Descartes' division into body and mind. To some extent, Darwin's *The Expression of the Emotions* put paid to the separation of head and heart, by indicating that both voluntary and involuntary muscle activities are involved when we're emotionally aroused. In other words, I might *voluntarily* clench my fist if I'm angry, but I can't do anything about my *involuntary* beating heart or sweaty brow. Essentially, the driver isn't driving the car.

From quite a different perspective, the French psychologist, Théodule Ribot (1839–1916) highlighted the way our body and mind interact when we're emotionally aroused. Working with his patients, he discovered that those, who wanted to get better and thought about positive things such as when they were healthy, recovered much faster than those who simply submitted to their illnesses. He also discovered that memories from their past could be conjured up if he stimulated their five senses of taste, touch, sound, smell and sight. Ribot referred to this process as 'affective memory'.

In the twentieth century, 'affective memory', 'emotion memory', 'emotional memory' and 'sense memory' were all commonly used as acting terms – and, indeed, they still are today. The idea behind all of these terms is that the images conjured up in your *mind* can be used to affect your *body*: you are physically and psychologically affected by your memory and imagination. One of the easiest ways of using these terms, I find, is to think of 'affective memory' as defining the overall process of accessing your present-tense emotions through your past-tense memories. And the two ways of doing that are through your **sense memory** (recalling the sensory details of an event) and your **emotion memory** (allowing those memories to affect your body, muscles, imagination, here and now in the present tense). (More on this in Chapters 4 and 6.)

These were fascinating discoveries, and pursuing the link between imagination-body-emotion was the British scientist and literary critic, George Henry Lewes (1817–78). G. H. Lewes was the first person to apply the principles of psychology directly to acting processes. He picked up on the eighteenth-century discovery that emotions had reverberations and he focused on the notion of 'subsiding emotions'. This term refers to the fact that our nervous system remains excited even after the stimulus has disappeared. So I'm still ecstatic with love for you, even though you've left the room. I'm still disappointed with my agent for not putting me up for the role, even though we put the phone down two hours ago. It's back to the plucked string metaphor: an emotion lasts, albeit decreasingly, even after whatever provoked it has vanished.

### KEAN AND SUBSIDING EMOTIONS

Lewes was particularly struck by this 'peculiarity' in the performances of Edmund Kean (1787–1833). Although Kean was renowned for extreme displays of tiger-like emotion and flashes of lightning, his 'instinct taught him what few actors are taught': that strong emotions express themselves 'in feebler currents' after the storm has abated (Lewes cited in Roach, 1993:187). That said, Kean left nothing to chance: he believed there was no such thing as impulsive acting, and his own performances were always carefully planned. Yet his use of subsiding emotions really moved acting ideas forward, highlighting that acting – just like being – is a *process*, rather than a series of fixed results such as those seen in Garrick's Parisian party piece.

## IRVING AND DUAL CONSCIOUSNESS

A celebration of acting technique is perhaps what characterises nineteenth-century developments the most: a technique which wasn't based on the codified gestures of classical oratory, but which connected the actor with seemingly heart-felt emotions. This balance between technique and emotion could be seen in the work of another great 'beast actor', Henry Irving (1838–1905). Renowned for fearsome characterisations, Irving openly accepted his use of **dual consciousness**, where an actor seems to be totally immersed in the emotional sweep of a scene, while at the same time they're being attentive to every technicality. For Irving, great acting was about giving the *illusion* of spontaneity, in which everything you manifest on stage looks as though it's pure accident, but all the time you have what Lewes called 'a mind in vigilant supremacy'.

## COQUELIN PICKS UP THE PARADOX

Dual consciousness was brought most sharply into focus by the French actor, Coquelin, in his classic book, *The Art of the Actor* (*L'Art du Comédien*) (1894). Here, Coquelin sets up the idea that, as an actor, you comprise two people. The first self (called 'Number One' in some translations) constitutes your mind and imagination, and basically it interprets the character you're working on: in other words, it's you as the instrumentalist. Meanwhile, the second self (called 'Number Two' in some translations) comprises your expressive body and voice: in other words, it's you as the actual instrument, bringing your interpretation of a character into being. Your first self is always in control of your second self, so that you never forget you're in front of an audience. They may *think* that you're distracted and affected by the scene, but all the time you know that, even though you're experiencing certain emotional charges, you're absolutely in control of the situation.

This is a subtle development of Diderot's *Paradox*. On the one hand, Diderot proposes that when you're *rehearsing* a role, you may get very caught up in the emotional world of the character, but by the time you come to *perform* it, you've refined it into something calm and controlled. (This corresponds to what Stanislavsky called the school of 'representation', where you give a very convincing portrayal of an emotion, but you know that you're not actually experiencing it.) Coquelin, on the other hand, seems to be suggesting that even in performance you can manifest all the aspects of the emotion, but as you do, you're almost sitting astride it, keeping it in check. You're *living* the emotion and *monitoring* it at one and the same time. Like the pianist who may seem lost in the concerto, but they still know they're in C sharp. (This corresponds to what Stanislavsky called the school of 'living the role', which means experiencing the fact you're *performing* as much as experiencing the role itself – otherwise you'd literally lose the plot.) (We'll look at this in more detail in Chapter 4.)

Despite all the discussions and practices from the seventeenth to the nineteenth century – even despite the early attempts of Aaron Hill and others to initiate some kind of comprehensive actor-training – it took until the twentieth century for acting to catch up with other art forms. But when it did – it did so big time!

## THE TWENTIETH CENTURY

In Chapter 6, we focus on some of the twentieth century's legendary actor-trainers – whom I've called the eleven executors of acting – so for the moment we'll consider just a few issues, including certain philosophies about acting, which range from *playing* to *purging*.

### ACTING AS PLAYING

Play came in a number of forms in the twentieth century, all of which had improvisation at their core. In terms of acting systems, you can see it in Stanislavsky's Active Analysis, Michael Chekhov's **feeling of ease** and Brecht's **Spaß** or 'fun'. In terms of catapulting actor-training right back into childhood play, you can see it in the exercises and writings of several practitioners across the globe (detailed in Chapter 2).

In various ways, actors were encouraged to use games and improvisations to find a naturalness, a spontaneity, a freedom, an absolute connection between their body, mind, word and imagination in the very moment of performance. (Stanislavsky called this 'a constant state of inner improvisation'.) This particular focus also threw up the *social* element of acting. Games (as playful, problem-solving structures) are our first experiments as small children in developing relationships and understanding how our own behaviour affects other people.

## ACTING AS PURGING

Acting as purging lies at the heart of works by Antonin Artaud (1895–1948) and Jerzy Grotowski (1933–99). In their own ways, they returned to the 'ritual' element of acting, the primitive and the sacred. In effect, they revisited the seventeenth-century belief that actors conjured up passions and physical states, which could then affect the bodies and minds of other people – like priests and shamans, rather than entertainers.

One of the fascinating paradoxes of twentieth-century acting is that, just as technology was having a major impact on theatre and cinema, certain practitioners were going back to the ancient, 'spiritual' aspects of being human. This created a curious tension between the mechanical and the mystical, the tangible and the intangible. These spiritual references included: Artaud's interest in the kabbalah (a mystic tradition which questions the origin and destiny of the soul, made sexy at the end of the century by pop star Madonna [1958–]); Michael Chekhov's interest in Rudolf Steiner's (1861–1925) **anthroposophy** (the belief in an inner spiritual world which you can access through self-development); and Grotowski's interest in G. I. Gurjieff's (c.1866–1949) esoteric writings (combining the mystical aspect of Islam known as 'Sufism' with Christianity, Buddhism and other religious doctrines). Not to mention Stanislavsky's own passionate interest in yoga and *prana* energy.

## MASK OR FACE?

The twentieth century was fascinated by personality, and psychology flourished under the particular influences of Carl Jung (1875–1961) and Sigmund Freud. Certainly, an eternal question plaguing most of us as actors at some point in our lives is: 'Do I transform my own personality into the character, or do I bring the elements of the fictional character into my own body and psyche?' Or as

William Archer might put it: 'Do I wear the character's mask or do
I show my own face?'

But what *is* our mask? What *is* our face? Who on earth are we?

This fascination with personality encouraged a peeling away of
the layers of who we *really* are versus who we *think* we are. In
actor-training especially, the mask was given renewed focus,
particularly in the hands of French actor-director Jacques Copeau.

## COPEAU AND SIMPLICITY

Copeau significantly shaped actor-training and rehearsal processes,
right up to the present day. He sought a simplicity and innocence
in his actors, emphasising their personal integrity and honesty. Like
others at the same time and across the globe, he included children's
games and improvisation in his training to help actors engage with
their spontaneous sense of creativity.

Copeau stripped away *social* masks by using *actual* masks, seeing
the literal, paper-and-glue mask as a means (paradoxically) of
revealing an actor's simple honesty. By wearing 'neutral' or 'noble'
masks (named after the ones used by eighteenth-century aristocracy
to hide their real identities), his actors found themselves curiously
liberated to become their open, direct selves. Again, it's a principle
we're still very familiar with: how often will the female of the
species spend hours putting on their make-up before going out to
greet the world? And what about tattoos? Could they possibly be a
kind of contemporary mask that helps the person sporting them feel
more confident, unique or exotic?

## SAINT-DENIS AND TEXT

Copeau's nephew, Michel Saint-Denis also made a huge impact on
present-day actor-training, founding several drama schools including the Old Vic Theatre School in London, the Juilliard School
Drama Division in New York, and the *Ecole Supérieure d'Art
Dramatique* in Strasbourg.

Saint-Denis explored the mask/face issue by focusing on the
actual playtext and how the playwright's words express the character's inner state. What a person says is just the tip of the iceberg of
what they really think and feel; by studying a character's words,

you can sense how the writer is directing you towards the play's inner realm. And it's not just *what* they say, but what they *don't* say that can reveal their inner world. With this in mind, Saint-Denis believed that the best-written scripts give us the greatest chance of penetrating the mask of a character, and so he worked extensively with Shakespeare's texts. Even though mastering classical language is challenging for any actor, you'll find that many British drama programmes still tackle Shakespeare in the first year of training, arguably following Saint-Denis' influence and his belief in Shakespeare as an actor's best teacher.

## ASPECTS OF THE MASK

The mask preoccupied many twentieth-century practitioners, each coming up with a slightly different perspective. Meyerhold saw the mask as a metaphor for the way you presented yourself in everyday life. For Michael Chekhov, total transformation into character was the actor's ultimate goal, and both he and Stanislavsky loved false noses, facial hair, wigs, make-up and padding: they turned their very own bodies into a physical mask. Grotowski went to the other extreme and saw the actor's task as one of self-revelation and self-penetration, and any mask you wore in performance was one created purely out of your own face, body and soul. Strasberg too investigated self-revelation and self-penetration, albeit through quite a different aesthetic: like Grotowski, he explored an actor's personal blocks and how you could shed your social defence masks to become emotionally 'free'.

Perhaps one of the most interesting takes on the mask is that of the French actor Louis Jouvet, a colleague of Copeau. Jouvet suggested that, in our everyday lives, we're always looking at our own social and professional masks to test which aspects of ourselves are 'authentic'. ('Authenticity' is a tricky word. I use it here to loosely mean: direct, sincere, without a hidden agenda.) He encouraged actors to consider what their *character's* social or professional masks might be. What was their character's 'secret'? For Jouvet, the idea of having a secret, of hiding behind some kind of invisible mask, was exactly what makes a character interesting. Building a role as far as Jouvet was concerned was, therefore, the absolute opposite of self-revelation or confession: you were constructing the character's (literally) hidden depths.

## THE TWENTY-FIRST CENTURY

Jouvet's idea of secret is playful and fascinating, with regard to *building a character* as well as *knowing yourself*. The twenty-first century is already riddled with conspiracy theories: Was Princess Diana murdered? What's the 'real' story behind the 9/11 plane crashes? Who shot Benazir Bhutto? We're a globe intrigued by cover-ups and confessions, the equal-and-opposite of which is: 'Who is authentic? Who can we actually believe?' Without being too bleak, twenty-first-century person-kind arguably has a hardened sense of cynicism.

### BEING AUTHENTIC

Cynicism and 'being authentic' are uneasy bed-fellows. One requires the thickening of skin; the other requires the peeling away of onion layers. In our cool culture, we have the opposite problem from our seventeenth-century acting colleagues. Their preoccupation was: 'How can you control and tame the passions you've unleashed in the process of performance?' Our preoccupation is: 'How can we be "thin-skinned" enough to access the relevant emotions in the first place?' As Joseph Roach puts it, the seventeenth-century anxiety was how to 'cap the gusher', while modern actors 'wonder where to drill' (Roach, 1993:218).

There's a great deal of exciting, scientific exploration going on into understanding our emotions, with pioneering work from psychologists including the American doctor, Paul Ekman (1934–), with his fascinating investigations into facial expression, awareness, compassion and emotions. Other areas of scientific research over the last few decades have focused on the way in which 'gut instinct' is becoming an increasingly acceptable way of assessing a situation, as we learn more about the neuro-peptides that carry information all around our bodies. We're now much more ready to accept the anatomy's own 'wisdom', with science proving that our bodies and our minds (or our consciousness) are biologically inextricable: human beings are innately psycho-physical. Inevitably, the more we discover about how we function as human beings, the deeper our questions about acting will probe.

Indeed, as I said in the Introduction, this is a book about acting – not drama or theatre or performances studies. There have been huge shifts in the kinds of performances being produced as we turn from the twentieth into the twenty-first century: in different arenas and contexts, you'll come across terms and styles including **post-modern** dramas, **post-dramatic** performances, fragmented multimedia, multi-narrative, physical, and experimental pieces, some of which you'll love and some of which will turn you off completely. However, the main acting style – with television and film clearly dominating the entertainment market – continues to be psychological realism. Whether it's *Dr Who* or *Nip/Tuck*, whether it's *The Green Wing* or *The West Wing*, whether it's vampires and superheroes, or gangsters and cops, audiences are used to a certain sense of belief in what they're seeing. The challenge for us as actors is to breathe that believability into all our scripts and characters, whatever the genre and whatever the medium.

Given that our instrument is a complex one, it requires a special kind of training that can take a number of different paths. So, now you've got an historical sense of how we've come to where we are, let's now head to the studio and do some actor-training.

## SUMMARY

In this chapter, we've looked at how the great thinkers and orators of the classical era influenced acting processes for several hundred years. As scientific knowledge of the human body developed across the centuries, so too did acting.

- The seventeenth century was characterised by the humours and the passions, with a dualism between body and mind.
- Eighteenth-century practitioners witnessed the development of psychology and sensibility, with actors requiring equal measures of intelligence and emotional accessibility.
- Nineteenth-century practitioners saw the emergence of naturalism, and the way in which imagination and memory work together to conjure up emotions. All the while, actors had to have a dual consciousness in performance, so that they could balance powerful passions with professional technique.
- Twentieth-century practitioners experienced an explosion in actor-training, with issues such as playing or purging, emoting or doing, and mask or face.

- Twenty-first-century practitioners are acknowledging the body's innate 'wisdom', with a multitude of different performance styles challenging us to use our resources in a diversity of ways.

## SELECTED READING

If you were to pick only three books to flesh out your understanding of contemporary acting processes, I'd suggest the following:

Jean Benedetti's *The Art of the Actor: The Essential History of Acting from Classical Times to the Present Day* (Methuen, 2005) is a very useful book, combining Benedetti's informed perspective as a practitioner with his longevity as a scholar and a teacher. He has collated all sorts of very useful primary material (often hard to locate elsewhere) in a book with wide margins specifically for note-taking.

Robert Gordon's *The Purpose of Playing: Modern Acting Theories in Perspective* (University of Michigan Press, 2006) is an extremely thorough analysis of acting strategies and practitioners in the twentieth century, with some nineteenth-century contextualising.

Joseph Roach's *The Player's Passion: Studies in the Science of Acting* (University of Michigan Press, 1993) is a terrific charting of the relationship between acting and scientific discoveries, which never becomes complex and always remains fascinating. (Areas of this chapter draw significantly on Roach's work.)

There are two series also worth visiting.

For easily accessible details of theatre movements through recent history, *Modern Drama in Theory and Practice 1, 2* and *3* by J. L. Styan (Cambridge University Press) are great value.

For pithy insights into a multitude of practitioners (many mentioned in this book), Routledge's *Performance Practitioners* Series (Routledge) are fantastic springboards into further reading if a particular individual excites you.

## USEFUL WEBSITES

www.nationaltheatre.org – their educational and archival sections are great.

www.whitman.edu/theatre/theatretour – for some wonderful images of ancient theatres.

www.theatredatabase.com – a whole range of articles, references and places to dip into.

# 'I CAN DO THAT!': ACTOR-TRAINING

## DO WE NEED IT?

Most of us have seen some reality TV show where a mum is plucked from the school canteen and launched onto the West End stage. And sportsmen and pop stars are regularly morphed into film actors. Which leads us to question, 'Can anybody act?' If the only required skills were walking, talking and looking right, then the answer could easily be yes. 'Then why bother training?' you may well ask. The answer is that the skills of acting actually go way beyond walking, talking and simply looking right.

The technical demands of incarnating a mighty stage role night after night, or knowing exactly how to hit your mark and reveal your innermost feelings to the lens of a camera – along with the challenges of interpreting and understanding all manner of characters from widely differing genres, styles and media – require skills far more extensive than most people credit. And although the 'dynamic listening' described in the introduction to this book might seem easy, in practice it's surprisingly tricky. Acting as an art has gradually been undervalued, and with it goes a misconception of what good actor-training entails.

## THE EVOLUTION OF ACTOR-TRAINING

Actor-training has a diverse history. Many Asian and oriental performance styles (including Indian **kathakali** dance or Japanese **Noh**
and **Kabuki** theatre) have what's known as 'vertical traditions'. That
means the skills and repertoire have been handed down for centuries from one generation to the next, and the training focuses on
students learning physical gestures that encode specific cultural and
social symbols. In Western actor-training, particularly Europe and
America, we tend to place more emphasis on individuality, with
students learning about the psychological and physical ways to
interpret characters, rather than inheriting a specific repertoire.

Western actor-training is very young compared with the ancient
heritage of the East. France was one of the first European countries
to establish any formal programme when, in 1786, the Royal
Dramatic School was founded in Paris. A hundred (or so) years later
in 1884 came the founding of what became known as the
American Academy of Dramatic Art. What we know now as
RADA – the Royal Academy of Dramatic Art – was the first
London theatre school to be founded in 1904. And two years later
Stanislavsky began the formal creation of an early acting 'system'.

Since then, actor-training has become increasingly inter-
nationalised. Cross-pollinations include the collaboration in the
1990s at the Saratoga International Theatre Institute (SITI) between
American director Anne Bogart (1951–), and Japanese director
Tadashi Suzuki (1939–). And at the University of California, Davis
(where I'm based at the time of writing), my own hybrid of Anglo-
Russian influences sits beside Shamanic journeying and African
dancing. Prior to this, I worked at the University of Exeter, UK,
with American actor-trainer Phillip B. Zarrilli, whose idiosyncratic
training features the Indian martial art **kalarippayatu**, alongside the
Chinese martial art **t'ai chi chuan**. As Zarrilli points out, you can't
really talk about the specifics of actor-training without looking at
the social and geographical contexts.

That said, essentially all actor-training has one fundamental purpose: to prepare young actors for the rigours and challenges of
acting a role. *How* you train will develop your ethos as an actor,
which in turn will impact on your professional practice for the rest
of your life.

## WHEN? HOW? WHY TRAIN?

There's no formula for when and how you train. Some children go to stage school at a very young age or find themselves as child stars in *Harry Potter* movies. It's usual in the UK for student actors to enter drama school or university between the ages of 18 and 22. In the USA, however, it can be quite a different story: many actors acquire their training through private teachers and coaches throughout the whole of their acting careers.

Whichever route we take, we all face one challenge not necessarily shared by other artists. We don't have a blank canvas or a cool block of marble or a neutral lump of clay as the starting point for our creative expression. Whatever our age and experience, our 'lump of clay' has already been half-molded and half-baked, with social, physical, cultural or personal peculiarities, which can act as obstacles to our creative flow: 'Am I talented enough? Am I pretty enough? Am I ethnic enough? Am I tall enough?' Or 'Am I so darn talented, nobody can teach me anything?' To address this accumulation of blocks, many training grounds begin with the principle of 'unlearning' or 'unconditioning'. We need to walk what Grotowski calls the *via negativa* (see Chapter 6) – the 'negative path' – where our first concern is to eliminate our personal blocks before we can acquire new skills.

'Unlearning' requires an awful lot of patience and humility: as human beings, we like the familiar, even if the familiar is not ideal. And, as we saw in Chapter 1, the key to all training – be it athletics, salsa dancing, playing the electric guitar – is repetition. Good actor-training includes constant repetition to re-programme our conditioned responses – and that process can make us feel vulnerable.

### VULNERABILITY AND THE NEED TO TAKE RISKS

One of the biggest difficulties we face as actors is how to be so relaxed in class or rehearsal or performance that we can respond openly and playfully to the task in hand. And the main obstacle to that openness is fear. Fear of not being good enough. Fear of 'getting it wrong' – which includes not being immediately brilliant in class, or not understanding what the director wants in rehearsal, or forgetting our lines in performance.

One tactic we use to deflect our fear is what Lee Strasberg calls 'anticipation': when we're working on a character, we anticipate where the dramatic moments are coming and grasp for the *result* of the emotional state rather than the *process* of interacting with the other actors. Yet what we end up doing is safe; it's prepared; it's rehearsed. It's dead …

One remedy for our fear is a healthy dose of what American actor-trainer Eric Morris calls 'irreverence'. Of course we must always be collaborative: we must always respect our colleagues and the script, but our choices can be intelligent and valid – *and* irreverent. Many situations presented in a drama are heightened human experiences – be they violent, or angry, or sexy, or frustrated, so we have to be 'grubby' with our sense of humanity. If we're too polite or guarded, we simply can't free ourselves to the extents to which we have to go. So we need to be open and vulnerable to every unexpected impulse.

This is where good actor-training comes in. It encourages us to stop worrying about whether or not we're getting things right, and invites us instead to embrace our creative vulnerability. Being vulnerable is about taking risks; it's about being playful and dangerous. That doesn't mean insulting our fellow actors, or falling off the stage, or trashing the camera. It doesn't mean not being serious about our craft. It means taking ourselves by surprise, not knowing exactly what we're going to do next, not 'anticipating', but rather walking the tight-rope of the moment and being irreverent towards ourselves. In Chapters 4 and 5, we'll see how great it is for our directors when we do take risks. It's in those moments of open vulnerability that we give ourselves the chance to listen dynamically and be visited by flashes of inspiration. And that's when acting really takes off and becomes as exciting as gladiatorial combat.

## WHAT NEEDS TO BE TRAINED?

So what do we have to do to allow ourselves to be so free? Basically: we need to get to know our selves – our 'instruments'.

The meat of this chapter looks at five particular aspects of your instrument: breath, body, voice, imagination and emotion. (These actually echo the basic components of Quintilian's oratory that we looked at in Chapter 1.) We'll also touch on the relevance of 'spirit' as a sixth aspect. For the purposes of this book, I've included the

Voice section here in 'Actor-training', with more detailed work on actual text featured in Chapter 4. Although Voice and Text go hand in hand, I've focused here on the exploration of sound, rather than specific words that unlock specific characters' thought processes.

I've drawn from a host of writings and training grounds, as well as personal experience, though the study is far from exhaustive. Given the excellent exercises available in specialist books (see the selected bibliography), I generally present attitudes and philosophies, rather than practical exercises. Inevitably, a book's structure means the information has to be presented to you in a linear form, whereas in reality, you'd be learning all these techniques simultaneously. Some of the material included here in 'Actor-training' could just as easily have gone into 'Rehearsal processes' or 'Performances practices', and vice versa. So as you work through these chapters, be aware that the division is somewhat artificial, but somehow the material has to be presented to you in a consumable form.

Before we start, a word of caution …

## THE NEED TO GO SLOW

Learning to act is inevitably slow, incremental and experiential. Those are big challenges to all of us today. Information and knowledge comes to us thick and fast – from the Internet, iPods, computers, sat-navs. As a 'Neomillenial learner', you're probably used to multi-tasking in your learning. If anything takes more than the minimal amount of time, it's already too slow – somebody else will have got there faster. Yet this rhythm of absorbing information is 100% antithetical to actor-training. I'm afraid you can't just download it onto your mental hard drive. You have to learn to act by doing it. And you can only embed that knowledge by repeating it and embodying it, until your instrument assimilates the new information.

What's curious is that, despite the fact that actor-training takes time, more and more people want to learn to act. More and more courses are opening and programmes are usually over-subscribed. So, there's clearly a hunger for self-expression which isn't keyboard- or cellphone-orientated, and for some kind of communication, which is direct person-to-person contact, unmediated by Twitter or Facebook or Skype.

So, given this hunger, let's get training.

## BREATH

### BREATH AS A REFLECTION OF INNER STATE

Your first task as an actor in a class, rehearsal or performance, is to be sure that you're in what Stanislavsky calls an appropriate 'inner creative state'. As we've already mentioned, that means being relaxed enough to respond playfully to your fellow actors and to be open to the environment in which you're working. The fear which gets in the way of our being relaxed usually manifests itself in some form of physical tension. British voice coach Cecily Berry points out that, although you actually need a certain buzz of adrenalin to excite your creativity, any undue physical tension can constrict your diaphragm. This inevitably affects your breathing, which inevitably affects not only how you speak in terms of audibility, but also how you connect with the outside world.

Yes, it's true. The way that you breathe reflects your actual relationship with the outside world. After all, if you didn't breathe, you wouldn't be here. It's an expression of your personality and your individuality; so people who speak very quietly or breathe very shallowly often reveal their fundamental fear of revealing themselves. Yet breath is the physical life of our thoughts. If we didn't take breath into our bodies – apart from dying – we wouldn't have any air to exhale through the various speech organs, so we wouldn't be able to form words and express ideas. How many times have you felt so much better for *voicing* the things that are going on in your head? To give vent to your anxieties or dreams – to let the breath pass through your vocal cords, tongue, teeth and lips, and to release yourself from the tricksy processes of your brain – is a vital part of your human survival. (Isn't that why people go to therapy?)

### BREATH AS A REFLECTION OF BODY-MIND INTEGRATION

Breath can integrate you in a simple and fundamental way. Phillip B. Zarrilli actually places breath as the means of overcoming the belief that there's any division between body and brain. Through simply focusing and mastering your breathing, you can attune yourself to the experience of body and mind being the same entity:

a **body-mind**. 'I *breathe*; therefore, I am.' (See 'The body' later in this chapter and the section on Eugenio Barba in Chapter 6.)

### BREATH AS A REFLECTION OF THE PROCESS OF ACTING

And breathing is at the very foundation of acting processes – both metaphorically and literally. *Metaphorically*, you *breathe in* the information from the playwright, and you *breathe out* the character as you slowly transform yourself into a role. *Literally*, you calm your mind and contact your body through deep inhalation and exhalation. In this way, you can strengthen your inner creative state and stay in a place where (in the words of movement educator Lorna Marshall) 'work can happen to you' and where you make your body 'available to yourself'.

Considering all these perspectives, it's easy to see why breathing frequently forms the first part of actor-training, and indeed the first part of an actor's daily warm-up. By beginning a warm-up with simple attention to your breath, you can begin to contact what Suzuki calls 'the stillness at the centre'. The purpose is not to become so relaxed that you're as limp as a wet rag, but rather to free yourself from the detritus and complexities of your daily self (which pays the rent and does the shopping) and to contact what Barba calls your **extra-daily self** (the self you use as a creative artist).

## THE BODY

### PHYSICAL PRECISION

For many of us, our relationship with our body can be uneasy. Yet it's a relationship we have to tackle head on in actor-training, because acting is an inescapably physical art. Our body becomes a site, a screen, a canvas, onto which we project a fictional character and onto which, as the audience watch us, they project a host of meanings.

According to psychologist Albert Mehrabian (1939–) (who has undertaken extensive research into nonverbal communication and 'silent messages'), we communicate most of the important information in our face-to-face dialogues through our bodies. When it comes to our likes and dislikes about something (in other words, our attitudes and feelings), Mehrabian maintains that we communicate that information in the following ratios : 55 per cent through our body (visual communication), 38 pre cent through our tone of voice (vocal communication) and only 7 per cent through the actual words we speak (verbal communication). If this is true, then our art of storytelling – which is all about face-to-face encounters – is certainly a physical one. Although we may start with the playwright's words, more than half our communication of the characters that we're playing is through our bodies. So if we're to be supreme storytellers, we have to be sure that we're in touch with every aspect of our physical expression, so that we can shepherd the audience towards the most appropriate reception of the dramatist's story. We have to be as physically precise as a keyhole surgeon. After all, we're surgeons of the soul.

Don't be put off by this degree of physical precision: it's actually very liberating. In my experience, nothing is more depleting for an actor (or an audience) than generalisation: blurred edges can kill the dynamism of our art. Being specific, on the other hand – finding the particularities of each character – not only makes our work exciting for us, but also renders each character completely unique and believable. Once you've developed and experienced a very precise way of working, I don't think you'll ever be satisfied with generalisations again: it'll feel like looking at the world through smeary spectacles. And the good thing is that this degree of physical precision can be learned.

Of course, we each have a unique body, so there's no *one* way to train our physicality. But there's arguably one overarching principle: we need to cast aside our preconceptions of what we think we can and can't do, and as Lorna Marshall says, 'invite our bodies to the party'.

## DIFFERENT TAKES ON PHYSICALITY

The recurring words which arise in body training are: stamina, flexibility, strength, co-ordination and awareness, though different practitioners have different ways of exploring these concepts.

Movement specialist Anne Dennis refers to three aspects of training: (1) Design (how do you move – for example, do you naturally lead from your pelvis or your chin?); (2) Intensity (how much tension does your movement use – for example, are you naturally very fluid or very taut?); and (3) Rhythm (what's the speed of your movement – for example, are you athletic or laid back?). American actor-trainer Robert Benedetti talks about the correlation of your Alignment (how you hold yourself) and your Physique (what exactly it is that you're holding). Indeed, legendary movement teacher Litz Pisk describes the shape of your body – your physique – as the actual boundary of your inner self. So how much space on the planet do you occupy as a psycho-physical being? What boundaries have you and Nature given yourself? Each of these three practitioners offers useful ways of thinking about your body objectively before you start manipulating and adapting it for different characters.

## THE BODY AS RESOURCE

Certainly as you work more and more psycho-physically as an actor, you'll find that you become your own incredible learning resource. By listening to your body, you'll begin to note the ways in which every aspect of your training impacts on your musculature – even (as Marshall points out) in your articulation class or your dialect work. How does a rolling New York accent *feel*? How does a lilting Southern Irish accent *feel*? How does 'Peter Piper picked a peck of pickled peppers' *feel*? Do you want to laugh? Do you want to kick ass? Do you want to woo every fair maid upon whom you should stumble? Every physical experience teaches us something about our personal vocabularies.

Given that our bodies are so full of information, we need to find ways of learning to hear them – and this we can do by developing flexibility, suppleness and responsiveness. There are numerous physical training techniques, two of which I briefly want to look at here, because they share a common feature: they were both inspired by their originators' own physical injuries.

## FELDENKRAIS TECHNIQUE

The **Feldenkrais Technique** was developed by Ukrainian scientist and judo instructor Moshe Feldenkrais (1904–84), when a knee injury that he'd incurred as a young man threatened him with a serious disability as he reached middle age. He set about studying human movement and came to the conclusion that the way we move and our image of ourselves are intricately connected. To change the former, we need to change the latter. Like other practitioners whom we've noted, Feldenkrais threw out the idea that there was any distinction between our bodies, minds and spirits, and he developed a movement technique which has subsequently evolved into two specific components.

The first, ATM, has nothing to do with cash withdrawals: it refers to **Awareness Through Movement®**. You're invited, through a series of verbal instructions from a trained practitioner, to become the spectator of your own body. As your awareness of your own body develops, you can consciously start to change the speed, rhythm and intensity of your activities. In this way, you are increasingly in control of your body and are awakened to how you can use it, rather than being the victim of your own, poor, physical carriage and locomotion.

The second evolution of the Feldenkrais method, **Functional Integration®**, involves the trained Feldenkrais practitioner using their hands to guide you through what Feldenkrais practitioner Dr Ralph Strauch refers to as a 'process akin to biofeedback'. This non-invasive contact helps you to adjust your habitual posture and re-train yourself to stand with a more healthy alignment.

## ALEXANDER TECHNIQUE

The second movement specialist to note here is Frederick M. Alexander (1869–1955), an Australian actor, who, in the 1890s, found himself constantly becoming hoarse in performance. Another advocate of the body–mind unity, he decided to take a good look at his own physicality. He discovered that the reason he suffered throat problems was because his whole vocal and breathing mechanisms were disrupted by muscular tension throughout his body, not least the very poor alignment of his head to his spine. He developed a system called the **Alexander Technique**, which he described as being 'for the control of human reaction' and for correcting all our unhelpful, habitual, neuromuscular activity. His technique looks at how we move, breathe, stay still and adjust our awareness, drawing particular attention to unusual activities such as sitting at the computer for hours, or lifting heavy boxes, or playing the cello.

It's curious to note that both Feldenkrais and Alexander developed their techniques because they themselves suffered physical afflictions. As we'll see in Chapter 6, Stanislavsky, Michael Chekhov, Stella Adler and Lee Strasberg all developed actor-training strategies based on their own difficulties or temperaments. How wonderful that other people's problems have benefited us all!

I've chosen to include two more movement specialists here in some detail, because they can be invaluable for actor-training and building characters. Although they were both dance practitioners, they provide some very useful ways of developing your understanding of your body – in relation to using the stage space and building a character.

## RUDOLF LABAN (1879–1958)

The Austro-Hungarian Rudolf Laban started out as a military cadet, became a dance student and then devoted his life to dance, choreography, composing, movement, architecture and design. His transition from marching to dancing is interesting, and his passion was the release of natural rhythms in the body, believing everyone could dance. He has connections with two of our 'executors' featured in Chapter 6, which are worth noting here: when Laban escaped Nazi Germany in 1936 to live in England, he established a dance company at Dartington Hall in Devon, where Michael Chekhov was also to spend time in exile from Russia. Then, during the Second World War, Laban's investigations at factories in Manchester revolutionised human movement and productivity in industry; as we'll see in Chapter 6, Meyerhold was also influenced by factory workers' efficiency.

## LABAN'S EIGHT BASIC EFFORTS

The invaluable tool you can take from Laban is his 'efforts of movement'. By watching people in everyday life, Laban reduced the vast array of human movements to eight, very simple, physical efforts: in fact, they're not only physical, they're extremely psycho-physical as they have definite psychological overtones. Each effort relates to three components: (1) Space (a movement's trajectory is either Direct or Flexible); (2) Time (a movement's flow is either Sudden or Sustained); and Weight (a movement's substance is either Strong or Light). The best way to understand how the eight efforts and the six qualities of movement combine is to try them out. Let's start with the six qualities.

Imagine for a moment you're throwing a number of objects to a partner, starting with a *dart*. As you throw the dart, you can feel its journey is Direct, Sudden and Light. The dart now becomes a large, sand-filled, *medicine ball*: as you throw the imaginary medicine ball, you can sense its path is Direct and Sudden like the dart, but its weight is Strong, rather than Light.

Now the medicine ball turns into a *feather*. You can feel the path of the feather is no longer Direct, as it catches on the breeze and crosses the space in an uncertain way – it's Flexible. Its journey through Time is now Sustained, rather than Sudden, as – unlike the dart or the medicine ball – you don't quite know when it's going to reach your partner. And obviously, the weight of the feather is Light, not Strong.

Finally, the feather turns into a *Frisbee*. Like the feather, the journey is Flexible, as the Frisbee is lifted on the breeze. Like the feather, the time it takes for the Frisbee to cross the space is Sustained. However, unlike the feather – which is very Light in its weight – there's something much more defined about the Frisbee's movement. It may not have the heaviness of the medicine ball, but there's a definite Strong quality to the way in which it cuts through the air.

Having got a sense of the six qualities of movement (Direct/Flexible; Sudden/Sustained; and Strong/Light), let's turn to the specifics of the **Eight Laban Efforts**.

The first Effort involves *Pressing*. Imagine you're trying to move a brick wall: the kind of effort involved would be *Direct*, *Sustained* and *Strong*. A Pressing kind of person is a social heavyweight: persistent, confident and uncompromising.

The second Effort involves *Gliding*. Imagine you're skating across a pond: the kind of effort involved is *Direct* and *Sustained* (like moving the brick wall), but this time the Weight is *Light*. A Gliding kind of person is still persistent, but would perhaps have a lightness of touch missing in the Pressing person.

The third Effort involves *Punching*. Imagine you're thumping a punchbag: the kind of effort involved is *Direct* and *Strong* (like Pressing), but this time the action is *Sudden* rather than Sustained. A Punching kind of person would possibly have a similar attack to the Pressing person, but a different kind of persistence, as there would be mini hiatuses between each of the onslaughts.

The fourth Effort involves *Dabbing*. Imagine you're typing up an assignment on a computer: the kind of effort involved is *Direct* and *Sudden* (like Punching), but this time the movement quality through Space is *Light*, rather than Strong as it is with the Punch. A Dabbing kind of person would possibly be focused and quite nimble, with a lightness of touch, lacking in the Punching person.

The fifth Effort involves *Wringing*. Imagine your whole body is a wet towel and you're wringing yourself out from the belly to the extremities: the kind of effort involved is *Strong* and *Sustained* (like Pressing), but this time the movement through Space is *Flexible* rather than Direct. A Wringing kind of person would probably be like a terrier with a bone: they just can't let go of an issue, and it squirms and churns round inside them with a force and an insistence that they can't ignore.

The sixth Effort involves *Floating*. Imagine you're lying on your back in the sea, or you're floating through the air on parachute ropes: the kind of effort involved is *Sustained* and *Flexible* (like Wringing), but this time the Weight effort is *Light* rather than *Strong*. A Floating kind of person might be a little airy and vague, but there's a sense that they'll probably get there in the end.

The seventh Effort involves *Slashing*. Imagine you have a vast piece of red silk hanging in front of you, at which you're slashing with a hefty sabre; the kind of effort involved is *Strong* and *Sudden* (like Punching), but this time the movement through Space is *Flexible* rather than Direct. As you slash your arm through the air, you'll feel the energy effort continue with a kind of dying fall, rather than the definite full-stop of the Punch. Try the two movements – Punching, then Slashing – and you'll inevitably feel the different Spatial quality as the energy either meets its target (Punch) or continues through the air (Slash). A Slashing kind of person would probably thrash out and expend far more energy than was actually needed to fulfil the task, like a child having a tantrum.

The eighth and final Effort involves *Flicking*. Imagine you've got fluff on your sweater and you're flicking it off: the kind of effort involved is *Sudden* and *Flexible* (like Slashing), but the Weight quality is *Light*. A Flicking kind of person might well be a shrug-the-shoulders, 'Yeah, whatever ... ' kind of fellow.

These eight Laban Efforts are invaluable tools in your actor's toolkit. Although they were initially focused on Modern Dance education, you can apply them to your own physical vocabulary as an actor. There are also a variety of ways you can apply them to work on a character. You could look at their personality type (is my character generally uncompromising/Pressing or full-on/Punching or obsessive/Wringing in the pursuit of their **objective**?). You could look at how they speak (is their rhythm staccato like a Dab or a Flick, or are their sentences fluid with a quality of Pressing or Gliding?). And you could look at their general flow of energy (does my character sustain their objective through to the end with the persistence of a Press or do they find themselves distracted or deflected with the quality of a Flick?). These physical efforts can unlock all sorts of psychological information for you as you work on characters and build your actor-training repertoire.

### MARY OVERLIE (1946–)

The second of the two dance-orientated physical trainings that I also find very useful when applied to actor-training is Mary Overlie's **Viewpoints**. Overlie is an American dancer and choreographer who, in 1976, began to devise the principles of her Six Viewpoints. The idea was to give actors more artistic authorship over their creations. (American director Anne Bogart has since developed them into what is now an extensively used actor-training system in the USA.) Overlie's original Six Viewpoints are Space, Shape, Movement, Time, Emotion and Story. You can use them in any order and swap them around as you feel fit. You don't necessarily need to use them to explore a ready-scripted character (though certainly Bogart's development of the Viewpoints does entail that), but they do provide you with a series of 'deconstructed languages' with which you can play. Let's look at how you might use the Viewpoints as you awaken your body's potential.

*Space* invites you to experience the room with the curiosity of a child. Where are the hot spots of the room? Where do you feel comfortable working? Where do you avoid? Through exploring the Space, you enhance your innate sense of architecture and how each part of the room can conjure up different feelings for you. (How often, when we're working in a studio or a rehearsal room, do we find our favourite chair, our safe corner, the area of the floor where we always want to do our warm-up?)

*Shape* is a language which you acquire through simply experiencing your body in Space, rather than learning a set of gestures like ballet or tap. Space and Shape work together, very much like a piece of clay and a sculpture. Each informs the other: I make this Shape in Space and I experience that new sensation. Having the Space gives me the possibility of making the Shape, and my Shape only means something because of the Space in which it's situated.

*Time* relates to **tempo-rhythm**, speed, impulse and the duration of a sequence. Overlie invites you to explore various re-structurings of Time, maybe 'crunch time', 'wrinkled time', or 'shattered time'. As with Space, it's the physical pleasure of exploring these imaginative understandings of Time that lie at the heart of the work: it's metaphorical as much as literal, it's physical as much as logical.

*Emotion* focuses on your actual presence as an actor. You open yourself up to the constant shifts in emotional experience, which are conjured up by your body actually moving in Space rather than being the cause or result of any particular narrative. This process is very psycho-physical: your body makes a movement which evokes a feeling. It's an inner-outer/outer-inner waltz. Working this way, you'll find that even inanimate objects can awaken an emotional response in you if you observe them precisely enough: pencils strewn across a table, a leather jacket slung over the back of a chair, a puddle of water in the middle of a playground. (There are real resonances here with Michael Chekhov's emphasis on imagination and Grotowski's physical *plastiques*.)

*Movement* provokes you to ditch the belief that your body must be tamed and ordered by the outside world. Instead, Overlie invites you to experience a sense of 'Original Anarchy', so that you can allow your body to move and respond to Space, Shape, Time, Emotion and Story in any way it wishes. You simply enjoy the spirit of being physically alive.

*Story* for Overlie is nothing more than 'an arrangement of information'. She discards any normal sense of logical, linear narrative, and tries to find a sense of Story that's as all-embracing as abstract art. Because you're working with Space, Shape, Time, Emotion and Movement, then at any moment, your exploration and physical experience of any one of these components might take your body's Story in a number of narrative directions. One moment you could be Hamlet on the castle battlements; the next minute your body could suggest to you that you're ploughing a field. Or your imaginative provocation might be more metaphorical, such as feeling haunted by uncertainty. You're completely free to follow whichever stimulus you please, until another takes over and excites your imagination.

These Six Viewpoints are so interwoven that you couldn't possibly work through them in a linear fashion, as each one spawns the next or feeds off the last. So Overlie describes them as working in a Matrix, which shifts according to where you are in the room and where your imagination or your emotional repertoire or your physical shape chooses to take you on a particular day. And moment by moment, the dominant Viewpoint will shift. (During my Scenic Movement classes in Russia, we underwent a very similar training, the roots of which lay in Michael Chekhov, Stanislavsky, Grotowski and clowning. So many of these different psycho-physical practices are interwoven, echoing similar inputs and outcomes.)

Both Overlie's Viewpoints and Laban's Efforts are ways of awakening your body and exploring the way it excites your imagination, and are both great tools to have in your kit.

## ANIMAL IMPROVISATIONS

The physical training of your body is ultimately about freeing yourself – from your social inhibitions, your imaginative blocks, and your physical tensions. Some practitioners use extensive mask work to help you find this freedom. Other practitioners incorporate animal exercises. Not so that you become adept at impersonating a dung beetle or a wildebeest, but in order to liberate you temporarily from your social constraints, to walk Grotowski's *via negativa* and to open yourself up to your inner impulses. Strasberg and

Grotowski both incorporated animal work into their training. Many of the forms adopted by Zarrilli from *kalaripyattu* use elephants, lions and cobras. The yoga sun salutation incorporates monkeys, dogs and swans. And indeed Grotowski's famous cat position finds its way into many an actor's physical warm-up.

Animal improvisations allow you to explore 'ordered transgression': for once, you don't have to be well-behaved, as you're stepping outside normal, social modes of behaviour. That said, you don't lose control in some kind of sociopathic way; you simply allow energy to flow through your body, particularly through those joints and muscles where you find it's frequently trapped or blocked. For Lecoq, this kind of liberating, physical education is vital for us as actors, as our job is to inhabit a world of illusion. So we need to access that almost primitive state, where we can leave behind all our cultural history and the imprint of our personality, and free ourselves to enter wholeheartedly a land of make-believe.

Animal exercises can be incredibly fun and liberating. And they're useful for tapping into our innate sense of play. (See 'Imagination' later in this chapter for more on play.)

A crucial aspect of training our body is to remind us that one of the most physical activities in which we engage is, in fact, speaking.

## THE VOICE

### HOW THE VOICE EVOLVED

It's interesting to note that the muscles we use to make speech – our lungs, tongues, teeth, lips and mouth – were originally created for other basic functions, such as breathing, swallowing, chewing and tasting. As human interactions became more complex and nuanced, the human desire to create particular sounds, which had specific meanings attached to them, caused those muscles to evolve from pure survival organs into organs of communication. Although we can have a strong sense of who we are without being able to speak, in many respects our voices have become a significant way of defining who we are. As South African voice specialist Roy Hart (1926–75) once described it, our voice is the manifestation of our psyche, 'psyche' meaning 'breath/blood' or 'soul'. Certainly, the desire to express ourselves vocally is an instinctive response to our basic needs: I'm hungry – I yell – my mother feeds me. I'm tired – I yell – my mother puts me to bed. It's a direct equation: I have a need, I make a noise, my need is fulfilled. In expressing those needs freely, a small baby has no trouble in shrieking its lungs to capacity without any contortion of its vocal cords or lack of breath support.

As we grow up, however, we find the equation between need and noise no longer equates. It's a terrifying moment when we discover as small children that the strategy we've always used, no longer works. Somehow 'Be quiet! Stop shouting! Shut up!' have become the responses to our expressions of need. And certain conditions are now attached: 'If you're a good girl, you can have a candy bar.' 'Big boys don't cry, so stop it.' As we learn to speak in our early years, we have to take in a huge amount of information. Not only do we discover that the word 'cup' is the thing that we get our milk in or that the word 'hot' alerts our mother to the fact that our milk is scalding our mouth, but we also discover that we have to be cunning to really fulfil our needs. 'Daddy, if I promise to go straight to bed, can I watch *Hannah Montana* first?' Voice and speech, in other words, don't have as direct a relationship as at first we thought they did.

Robert Benedetti reminds us that the root of the word 'personality' is 'per sona' – 'through sound'. In fact, speaking is utterly psycho-physical, in that it's the expression of your self through the musculature of your body. Therefore, good voice and speech training accesses your *inner life*, as well as building flexibility, strength and stamina into your vocal apparatus.

Perhaps three of the best-known vocal coaches in English-speaking actor-training are the American Kristen Linklater, and the two British tutors Cecily Berry and Patsy Rodenburg. Although others have followed extremely potently in their footsteps (including Catherine Fitzmaurice and Barbara Houseman), the overview of Voice training that I offer below is drawn from the writings and work of these three significant women. All their books provide excellent exercises in all areas of voice and text development. So, rather than repeat those here, we'll address some broader aspects of vocal training.

## VOCAL RELAXATION

Three things are needed to produce sound: (1) your breath; (2) the striking of your vocal cords in your larynx; and (3) the vibrations of those cords in the resonating areas of your body. (See 'Resonators' and 'Articulation' later in this chapter.) Voices like to be heard; roars of pain, hunger, sorrow, delight are natural and instinctive. Yet the way in which we speak is hugely affected by our upbringing; the kind of environment we knew; whether or not we were encouraged as children to speak; and whether or not we were listened to and valued for our opinions. As we become more socially aware, we build up blocks which scupper the release of our free voice. Those blocks might be physical (e.g. we carry tension in the larynx), psychological (e.g. we're aware of our self-image), emotional (e.g. we're afraid of showing how we feel), intellectual (e.g. we're afraid of sounding stupid), or aural (e.g perhaps we have hearing difficulties which impede the way we produce sound).

To tackle these issues, many voice tutors place physical relaxation and breathing right at the start of their vocal programmes (echoing the sequence of actor-training in general). Linklater, for example, concentrates the first four weeks of her training on what she calls 'the touch of sound': this includes relaxing your body so that it can respond to the different emotional vibrations of the sounds you make. Relaxation strategies focus on your spine, jaw, tongue, soft palate and pharynx. Indeed, Berry considers the lips as the 'portal' of language and the 'jaws' as the gates, so she devotes time to relaxing both of these areas, again allowing your breath to flow freely into your voice.

## SOUND AND EMOTION: THE ROLE OF THE DIAPHRAGM

In conjunction with relaxation, vocal training also focuses on strengthening all your intercostals muscles in (what Linklater calls) the 'breathing gym'. This includes your ribcage and diaphragm. She describes the diaphragm as a 'trampoline' on which you can bounce sounds, enjoying the dynamism of breath on muscle and the play of sound through your mouth. The activity of your diaphragm can be very emotional: as a muscle, it's extremely exercised by the vibrations of sound involved when you howl with laughter or wail with tears. Anatomically, it's situated very close to the **solar plexus**, which is a bunch of nerve endings between the spine and the stomach. These nerve endings receive as much information about our environment as the brain does: the brain may *process* that information, but the solar plexus actually *receives* it. So this part of your body intricately connects sounds and emotions, and their experience and expression. Don't be surprised if simple vocal training unlocks big emotions within you.

## RESONATORS

Along with vibrations and their emotional frequencies around your body, you have the actual resonators or 'chambers' of sound. They are your mouth (including your teeth); your chest (the main cavity); and your stomach. There are also various places around your head, including the sinus resonators (across your cheek bones); the nasal resonators (down the bridge of your nose); and the skull resonators (of which there are three: forehead, top and back of head). Sometimes the sinus, nasal and forehead resonators are referred to as your 'mask'. 'Getting the sound behind the mask' creates a bright, lively resonance, and stops you pulling your voice down into your throat.

Rodenburg suggests that, if you expand your awareness of your resonating chambers, you can start to broaden your vocal range. You can also sense where different vowels and consonants sit most comfortably in your body and how that feels. A resonant voice is full of substance: it holds a certain energy, which ignites a desire in your listener to hear what you have to say. A deep, warm sound taps into your stomach and chest, while a thinner, reedier sound draws on your nasal and sinus resonators. With practice, you can play upon yourself like a musical instrument, daring to step out of your usual voice into unknown territory.

Working on the resonators is a big task. Linklater spends about six to eight weeks on activating what she calls the 'resonating ladder', before moving on to speech itself and its articulation.

## ARTICULATION

How you create words corresponds directly to how you communicate ideas. There are ten general areas in your mouth used to articulate sound: (1) two lips; (2) the tip of your tongue; (3) your teeth; (4) the front blade of your tongue; (5) the upper gum ridge; (6) the middle of your tongue; (7) the roof of your mouth; (8) the back of your tongue; (9) the back of your hard palate; and (10) your soft palate. Once you start to break speech down into its bits, you realise how much activity and co-ordination goes into saying: 'Two pints of lager and a packet of crisps, please' or 'A hazelnut frappacino with room for cream, please', and much of that work is done by the tongue. You only have to bite your tongue on a toffee or scald it on a coffee for you to realise just how invaluable a muscle it is.

There are only 26 sounds in the English alphabet, excluding diphthongs (where two or more 'pure' vowels are elided together to form another sound, like 'miaow'). Through a combination of those 26 vowels and consonants, we convey all manner of commands, demands, desires, explanations, questions, confessions, obsessions and greetings. Vowel sounds are natural to us: the baby's instinctive expression is through open vowels, mainly 'aaaah'. Consonants, on the other hand (as Berry points out), close us down. But it's this closing down of the air from our mouths that actually gives meaning to the sounds that come out. Remember the last time you had an injection at the dentist and part of your mouth was numbed with anaesthetic? How difficult was it to form sharp consonants and how tricky was it for people to understand what you were saying?

Vowels are formed by your lips and tongue molding different shapes out of the air you expel from your mouth. Consonants are formed when two of your articulation points meet or almost meet – say, the middle of your tongue and the roof of your mouth, or the blade of your tongue and the back of your front teeth – so that they either stop the flow of air completely or (in the words of Linklater) they 'interrupt or modify' the flow of breath and sound.

## THE SENSATIONS OF SOUND

The point of articulation training is not only for you to develop a heightened sense of the muscularity of your words and the energy involved in speaking precisely. It's also to develop an imaginative flavour for different sounds. Michael Chekhov was passionate about the sensory, sensual quality of words. He was heavily influenced by Rudolf Steiner, whose series of lectures – *Speech and Drama* (1924) – presented the speaking of a text as an art form in its own right. Following Steiner's vein of thought, Chekhov encourages you to connect every vowel and consonant with an image or sensation. He believed that articulation work could only teach you how to speak artistically and expressively if you penetrated the deep, rich content of each syllable and letter. You have to feel the 'living soul' of every sound. For example, Chekhov found the letter 'b' was closed, reticent, defensive, whereas an 'l' offered life and growth, a sense of opening up. (Try them and see how it feels.) Most importantly, he incites you to feel the difference between vowels (which he connects with the different, inner states of a human being) and consonants (which he connects with the outer world and the shaping of events).

The more you allow yourself to play with sounds, the more you'll experience their imaginative, sensory quality. Words are not just intellectual and head-bound.

## LETTING GO

If you've followed a structured voice training, involving physical relaxation, freeing the breath, expanding the resonators, awakening the articulators, and sensing the imagery of sounds and words, you should now have a growing sense of freedom about using your voice. To build on this, Rodenburg suggests you should swear and scream and shout and laugh a lot. Indeed, when I was playing Susannah Cibber in April de Angelis's *A Laughing Matter* (2003), there was a scene in which I had to scream at the top of my voice. When I asked Rodenburg how to do this for eight shows a week during a five-month run in the vocally unforgiving space of the National Theatre's Lyttelton auditorium, she said, 'Enjoy yourself! It's a great opportunity – you've got permission to scream every night! Just smile. Raise your soft palate. Relax your tongue – and give it some!'

Ultimately, voice training is geared towards one goal: allowing your human voice to be a reflection of a character's whole being, taking pleasure in the visceral connection of words to body. And at the heart of this discovery is the actor's vital tool: imagination.

# IMAGINATION

Imagining is highly psycho-physical: you only have to watch the twitching of a dreaming dog to realise how physical our imaginations can be. There are a number of ways of stimulating and training the imagination. In Chapter 4, we'll look at the techniques of breaking down a script and analysing thoughts. For now, we'll focus on how we can exercise the imagination through play, improvisation and games.

## THE VALUE OF PLAY

The imagination loves to play, and the paradox is (as British director, Peter Brook [1925–] points out) that the less you give it, the happier it is. How many children unwrap their Christmas presents and then play with the box? Play involves learning in real time. There's no future 'skill' towards which it's geared: the present-tense discovery *is* the experience.

In his inspirational book *Free Play: Improvisation in Life and Art* (1990), the musician and composer, Stephen Nachmanovitch suggests that the best education systems tap into the close relationship between play and exploration. You'll find that watching children interacting with each other can be extremely revealing for you as an actor. Children show us the vitality of play for learning about social interaction and evolving as human beings.

One of our biggest frustrations as actors is that once upon a time we all had the innate ability to play: we all conjured up intricate and absorbing worlds into which we entered without any fear of self-censorship. And yet as we grow older and seek the approval of others – our parents, peers, teachers, directors, critics – we push our intuitive ability to spontaneously react further and further away. As 'success' becomes increasingly important, the less connected we are to our imaginations. Result overshadows process, and we find our inner judge becoming more and more vociferous. And yet, we cannot simultaneously *play* and *judge*: they're contradictory impulses. It's like trying to open and shut the door at the same time: playing is open and receptive, while judging is critical and selective.

Of course, play takes us back to the issue of vulnerability. Although we may know the rules of whatever game we're playing, we don't know its outcome. So we have to take a risk and improvise.

### 'INTUITION IN ACTION'

Nachmanovitch describes improvisation as 'intuition in action'. Improvising and being spontaneous are very closely connected: when we're being spontaneous, we're showing our *true* selves, rather than our *socialised* selves. Often in life, our intuitive selves come to the fore in a crisis or emergency, where our survival instinct kicks in and takes over from any 'trained' self or persona. You know what it's like when someone forgets their lines onstage – every atom of your intuitive being kicks into action.

### 'BEING IN THE MOMENT'

Another phrase connected with this degree of bold living is 'being in the moment', a term that came into common usage in the 1960s from psychology when 'being in the moment' was a primary key to self-realisation and self-actualisation. Here's an example of *not* 'being in the moment': I walk into my flat, I put my keys on the mantelpiece, I open my mail, I feed the cat, I decide to go out again – and I can't for the life of me remember where I put the keys. 'In the moment' of putting my keys on the mantelpiece, my thoughts were preoccupied with what was in the mail and if the cat was in the house.

When referring to acting, I personally find the phrase unhelpfully vague. To some extent, we're always 'in the moment' in that the past and the future don't *actually* exist. So, how can we be anything *but* 'in the present-tense moment'? However, when it is applied to acting, the phrase loosely refers to the actor's concentration of attention being focused on the action in hand. Are you in fact a second ahead of your partner, remembering your next line? Or are you thinking about your agent sitting on the tenth row and did they bring that important casting director? Where exactly is your point of attention? (And as we'll see in Chapter 5, a certain openness to the audience is actually a vital part of dynamic listening.)

### THE NATURALNESS OF IMPROVISATION

Following your intuition, being spontaneous and 'in the moment': these are highly desirable states for the actor. So, how can they be trained? Answer: through improvisation and games.

Many actors are terrified of improvisation, instantly blocking themselves with thoughts of 'Will I be funny? Entertaining? Good enough? Or just plain boring?' These fears instantly reveal the presence of that dreaded inner judge. They also reveal that you're worried about talking, playwriting, creating an amazing narrative full of sparkling and funny dialogue. These are not your concerns: the point of using improvisation exercises is to encourage dynamic listening. You can turn your attention off yourself and onto your partner, happy in the knowledge that you don't actually know what you're going to do or say next – because you don't actually know what *they're* going to do or say first to provoke your response.

There's really no point in being afraid of improvisation, since we're all doing it 24/7 anyway. We never really know what we're going to do or say in a situation, and we certainly can't guarantee what anyone else is going to do or say. Every day is a constant improvisation, and yet most of us seem to conduct our daily lives without too many hiccups.

### TAKING FROM YOUR PARTNERS: LIVE AND INANIMATE

There are of course strategies for dealing with theatrical improvisations so that you can train a sense of spontaneity and 'being present'. Essentially – as with all acting – your onstage partner is a huge source of inspiration as you constantly take cues and hints from what they do. (As we'll see in Chapter 6, Stanislavsky's notion of 'limitless attention to your partner' is at the heart of Meisner's training method.)

Your partner needn't actually be another human being. It can be the space: so, if there are real doors, windows, chairs or columns, use them. Really open a door and see what's out there. Really look through a window and watch the weather. By keeping in touch with the reality around you, you create your own sense of trust in what you're doing in the improvisation. Trust is crucial: you just have to trust yourself and your partner that something necessary and truthful will always arise 'in the moment' of encounter if you really listen and respond to each other, rather than convincing yourself that you have to impose something funny or eccentric or witty on the improvisation.

Perhaps one of the most useful strategies with improvisation is to understand that there are no mistakes: whatever you do will be appropriate if you listen to yourself and your partner. In improvisation, you can't go wrong if you simply listen, trust and keep it real – especially if you play the game. Indeed, games are a vital part of developing a 'constant state of inner improvisation'. Let's take a brief look at four key names associated with the use of theatre games in twentieth-century actor-training, and how they formalised their ideas of improvisation.

## VIOLA SPOLIN (1906–94)

American-born Viola Spolin was in many ways the originator of theatre games as a method of actor-training, and her book *Improvisation for the Theatre* (1963) has been an invaluable resource for actors, teachers and students for nearly fifty years. Her understanding of the importance of theatre games began as a student at Northwestern University, USA, in the 1920s. Through her exploration of games, folk-dance and traditional storytelling, Spolin began to craft her book in 1945. The significant points of her philosophy were that games were fundamentally social, as a group of people agreed upon certain rules and then (within the boundaries of those rules) embarked upon certain transactions – sometimes competitive.

Acting, for Spolin, was about being human and embracing our humanness, and her games focused on (1) orientation to the space; (2) acting with the whole body; (3) refining awareness; (4) emotion; and (5) character.

The first of those – orientation to the space – is great, in that Spolin really understood the value of 'where'. (As we'll see in Chapter 3, this is one of Stanislavsky's **Six Fundamental Questions**, when working on **given circumstances**.) If you really embrace the given circumstance of *where* your improvisation is taking place, you'll never run out of stimuli. In the head-teacher's office, you've got wall-charts and filing cabinets and term schedules and revolving desk chairs. On the top of a mountain, you've got boulders to trip over, thistles to sit on and grasses to bring on your allergies, not to mention the view of the reservoir down below and the elderly woman who has just dived into it. In the dentist's waiting room, you've got leaflets on plaque and braces and gingivitis; you've got magazines with the latest celebrity gossip; you've got the children's table in the corner with building bricks and plastic cars – all sorts of things to distract you from the impending molar extraction.

### CLIVE BARKER (1931–2005)

The impact of theatre games really kicked off in the UK in the 1950s and '60s, and two of the seminal practitioners were actors. The first, Clive Barker, worked with the pioneering director Joan Littlewood (1914–2002) at the Theatre Workshop in London's East End. Self-confessedly not a natural actor, Barker found himself struggling with certain aspects of physical movement and, if anyone drew attention to the problem, it inevitably grew worse. So he turned to theatre games as a way of distracting from the movement itself. In so doing, he indirectly drew his fellow actors towards exploring balance, weight and mobility, as instinctively as children do when they climb a tree or race across pebbles. Many of the games were very simple, from tag, to playing ball, to contact and trust exercises, to variations of games like Blind Man's Bluff. Barker found that these games released natural, emotional energy in his actors and free, uninhibited movement. From this relaxed perspective, they were able to correct their physical problems without even thinking about them.

Barker's work became particularly significant in the 1970s and '80s as university theatre departments grew in the UK, and he himself spent many years as a lecturer at the Universities of Birmingham and Warwick. His book *Theatre Games* (1977) has become a standard text.

### KEITH JOHNSTONE (1933–)

Keith Johnstone rose to prominence at a similar time to Barker. Also an actor, he was invited by director William Gaskill (1930–), to London's Royal Court Studio in 1963 to head some workshops exploring ideas that Saint-Denis had introduced from France. The whole emphasis of the work was to teach through doing, and – as with Barker's *Theatre Games* – Johnstone's book *Impro* (1979) has become an invaluable resource in theatres and drama schools.

*Impro* follows four main strands: (1) Status (in which Johnstone explores how every movement of your body alters the space you occupy, sending subliminal messages to other people. Remember Mehrabian's 55% physical communication?); (2) Spontaneity (in which one of the most useful concepts is 'accepting' what your fellow actor proposes to you in an improvisation, rather than 'blocking' their suggestions and stopping the scene from evolving. So if I say, 'Hello, Mum', you can't say, 'I'm sorry – who are you?'); (3) Narrative skills (involving exercises to develop your imagination and storytelling); and (4) Masks and Trance (in which Johnstone playfully builds on Saint-Denis' mask work).

## AUGUSTO BOAL (1931–2009)

Creating just as big an impact as his North American and European colleagues is Brazilian performance maker and 2008 Nobel Peace Prize nominee, Augusto Boal. Boal used games as a means of opening our eyes (as both actors and non-actors) to our social interactions. Taking theatre as a form of knowledge and a means of transforming society, Boal created a series of games and exercises – called 'gamesercises' – aimed specifically at provoking people's senses. He suggested that, by reawakening your senses, you can reawaken your engagement with the world around you and stimulate your ability to transform your social situations.

Themes of Boal's games include: (1) 'Feeling what we touch'; (2) 'Listening to what we hear'; (3) 'Seeing what we look at'; (4) 'The memory of the sense'; and (5) 'Dynamising several senses'. As with Barker, Johnstone and Spolin, the games are very simple, but in their simplicity lies their complexity as they operate on many different levels. And as the title of his seminal book suggests – *Games for Actors and Non-Actors* (1992) – the games are as relevant to everyday life as they are to actor-training, and they raise profound questions about how we depend on each other socially. As Copeau suggested (see Chapter 1), games teach us to think and act spontaneously, so that our actions are a living response to our thought processes. In other words, theatre games help us get out of our heads and into our bodies; at the same time, we develop a whole host of transferable skills in a deep and transformative way. Those skills include ensemble interaction, collaboration, communication, confidence, imaginative strategising, and physical contact. Actor-training is relevant to people way beyond the realm of vocational training.

So you see, games are more than just childhood pastimes. They have huge social reverberations, as well as being invaluable for actor-training. They also stimulate your emotions in a physical, playful way, and our emotions are the fifth aspect of our acting instrument.

## EMOTIONS

'Can we train our emotions?' you may well ask.

The answer is yes. In fact, it's possible to condition yourself to respond to emotional stimuli, in much the same way that the Russian physiologist Ivan Pavlov (1849–1936) trained his dogs to drool when they heard a dinner bell. You'll find that the training you've done so far on the rest of your 'instrument' – breath, body, voice and imagination – will unavoidably provoke your emotions, because all these aspects of being human are so intricately inter-woven. (We've hinted at this with the voice work, not to mention Overlie's Viewpoints.)

The main tool for directly training your emotions is affective memory, one of the most ubiquitous and useful tools in the acting kit. Affective memory is exactly what it says: the process involves you remembering events from your past that have a big enough affect on your present tense to arouse those emotions here and now.

However, you can't have a storehouse of emotion memories without having some present-tense experiences that may later *become* useful affective memories. So before we tap into the past, let's have a look at the present. In other words, what happens in our bodies and emotions when we have a present-tense experience? After all, there's no point concentrating on what we're trying to remember until we've understood what happened in the first place.

### WHAT ARE EMOTIONS?

Brain activity. Behavioural patterns. Survival instincts. These are all descriptions of our emotions, and as scientific research uncovers more about our brains, it also uncovers more about our emotional processes.

Biologists and psychologists have compiled lists of core emotions, observed in people across the globe regardless of their race or culture. After years of examining facial expressions, in 1972 Paul Ekman listed six basic emotions (anger, disgust, fear, happiness, sadness and surprise). (Remember Descartes' six primary passions in Chapter 1?) By 1999, Ekman had extended the list to 15 (amusement, anger, contempt, contentment, disgust, embarrassment, excitement, fear, guilt, pride in achievement, relief, sadness, satisfaction, sensory pleasure and shame).

Particularly significant for us as actors, I'd suggest, is the research by behavioural psychologist, Orval Hobart Mowrer (1907–82), who divided emotions into just *two* basic responses: pleasure (or satisfaction) and pain (or dissatisfaction). (These are not unlike the seventeenth-century concupiscible and irascible passions that we noted in Chapter 1). Mowrer's premise will become particularly relevant in Chapter 4, when we look at building a character and playing objectives.

So what happens when we experience an emotion?

Basically, our five sense organs (ears, eyes, nose, tongue and skin) are constantly sending messages to our brain. Our brain scans our storehouse of emotional memories, checking whether there's anything in our present situation that cross-references with our past experiences, and alerting our body to whether this situation may be good for us or not. 'Do I like this? Will this hurt me? Am I afraid of this?' If the brain finds something in the present-tense experience which is significantly similar to a past-tense event, it's called a 'match'. The match then helps us evaluate what we should do in this present situation.

Unfortunately, the matching process isn't very precise: it can be a bit like scanning a traffic light and a rainbow, noting that they both contain red, and then figuring that the rainbow is a traffic light. Now suppose you once rear-ended a car at a red traffic light. When you see the present-tense rainbow, your brain alerts you to a potential danger, because it remembers the rear-ended car, and it leads you to believe that the rainbow is a threat. In other words, you can't always rely on your emotional hardwiring: sometimes your brain and your senses simply get it wrong.

Here's another example: suppose you come home one afternoon to find your mother sitting in the kitchen with a face like thunder. You instantly read her emotional state as anger, and you blurt out, 'OK, Mum, what have I done now? Why are you always having a go at me?' To which she quietly replies, 'Your grandfather has died.' In the initial split-second moment of reading the information on your mother's face, your brain scanned the past for other times when you've found her waiting for you to come home – maybe because you were out too late, or you left the oven on, or she tripped over your track shoes at the top of the stairs. But in fact, on this occasion your brain misread the signals and immediately created defensiveness in you, rather than the sadness appropriate to the situation.

Whether it's a match or a mismatch, the important stimuli in your emotional processing are your environment (in the first example, the traffic light) and other people (in the second example, your mother). Both of these *outside stimuli* cause *inner responses* in you. The outer world and our inner world endlessly dialogue and affect us.

### WHY DO WE NEED EMOTIONS?

Emotions are an essential part of our survival strategies, designed to help us *transform* a situation. In fact, they are the ultimate transformers: they transform situations, they transform us, and ultimately they themselves transform.

First of all, how do they transform situations? By inducing us *to action*. In other words, we usually experience an emotion because we want to change a situation: it may be that we want to *survive* that situation, or *control* it, or *gain approval* in a certain situation. We're afraid of the hostage taker, so we try to befriend them, because we want to survive the ordeal. We're sad that our sister is so upset by the death of her rabbit, so we buy her a new one, because we want to try and control the situation by cheering her up. We're excited to meet our favourite movie star, so we tell them how hard we're working on our own acting, because we want to gain their approval. Emotions inspire us to *do* something in order to *affect other people*. They lead us to transform our worlds.

They also transform us. Have you ever noticed how much better you feel after a good cry or a hearty laugh?

And they also themselves transform, because once they've served their purpose of transforming a situation for the better, they're no longer necessary. So, the baby cries until it's fed, but once it receives the succour it sought, it doesn't need to cry any more: its objective has been fulfilled and its circumstances have changed.

So now we understand a little about the raw materials – the present-tense emotions. We've had a brief glimpse at what they are, why we experience them, and their powerful transformative effect. Let's see how affective memory can harness those emotions to strengthen our acting instrument.

### EVERYDAY USE OF AFFECTIVE MEMORY

As we saw in Chapter 1, the term 'affective memory' was coined by the psychologist Ribot. And in fact all human beings use affective memory all the time. Almost every moment of every day our emotions, memories and imaginations work inextricably together to create our moment-by-moment existence.

I walk into Starbucks on Paddington Station. 'Peppermint tea or cappuccino?' I muse. Somewhere in my brain, I recall the last time I had a big chocolatey cappuccino and I was with my boyfriend and we were Christmas shopping and we were having a great time and the caffeine and sugar gave us just the energy we needed to finish our shopping. But then, I remember, 'The taste of peppermint tea is so invigorating – and it's cheaper, so I'll have a few coins left to buy a magazine to complete the pleasure of my journey … ' And so it goes: memory scans the past, imagination conjures up the future, and together they help us create our present-tense decisions and emotional experiences.

### APPLYING AFFECTIVE MEMORY TO ACTING

There are two aspects to affective memory which can be usefully applied to acting: **sense memory** and **emotion memory**. *Sense memory* involves appealing to our five senses (taste, touch, sight, sound and smell) to remember all the details surrounding a particular event. (Don't forget it was the five sense organs that originally sent the messages to the brain when you first experienced the event.) By really allowing your imagination to conjure up all the sensory details, you'll find you start to feel the emotion that you experienced during the original event – and that is the *emotion memory*. In other words, the sense memory provokes the emotion memory: you are *affected* in the present tense by what you're recalling from the past.

As we've already discussed in this chapter, the starting point for all actor-training is relaxation, and it's especially important here. Exercises in affective memory usually entail you sitting calmly in a chair, and they begin with a simple relaxation exercise. You may, for example, imagine warm honey gradually working its way up from your feet through your legs, hips, lower back, upper back, shoulders, arms, fingers, neck and face, etc. When you start off working with affective memory exercises, it's best to have a sensitive teacher guide you through the relaxation and the recollection. (With time and experience, you can do these exercises on your own, but in the early stages, it's advisable to be part of a group or class with a trusted coach.)

Once you've tapped into a remembered event, you then recall the various sensory stimuli. So, let's suppose you won the cross-country race when you were 14. Take a moment to relax, and then put yourself imaginatively back in your body as if you were running the race. Can you *hear* the birds in the trees and the cheering of the crowds? Can you *see* the boy in front of you as you catch up with him and then the red marker tape ahead of you as you overtake him? Can you *taste* the salty sweat on your top lip? Can you *feel* the blisters on your heels from the rubbing of your track shoes? Can you *smell* the freshly cut grass on the school playing field? By tapping into the *sense memory*, you allow yourself to re-experience that immense exhilaration (the *emotion memory*) as you crossed the final line and your dad cheered with pride.

## CONDITIONING OUR EMOTIONS PSYCHO-PHYSICALLY

These kinds of exercises in affective memory can certainly be very useful. And yet the actual process of simply sitting and remembering often overlooks the fact that emotions are physical as well as mental. Let me offer another exercise, which comes from my own

Russian actor-training. It was an exercise we regularly undertook in order to condition our emotions psycho-physically.

We began by sitting in a circle on the floor and, by simply paying attention to each other's faces and demeanours, we would reach a peak of laughter. As each person reached their peak of laughter for that day – and for some it might be a chuckle, for others it might be a rib-splitting, belly laugh – we would each (at our own discretion) turn out of the circle and (independently) focus on whatever might be our depth of despair for that day. For some that might be a vague sense of melancholy, for others it might be overwhelming sobbing. However, once we'd each taken the decision to turn out of the circle, we couldn't carry on laughing and we couldn't come back into the circle. We had to focus our attention on despair. Having tapped into whatever might be the depth of despair for that day, we were to stop the emotional exploration and focus instead on the first five minutes of the day – in terms of what we first touched (e.g. the pillow), heard (e.g. the alarm clock), saw (e.g. the time on the clock), smelt (e.g. the coffee pot) and tasted (e. g. the toothpaste). This simple sensory recollection grounded us and brought our exploration of despair to a definite close.

This exercise was a form of emotional conditioning. It was the actor's equivalent of a pianist practising their scales and arpeggios. The laughter equated to the treble notes, the darker emotions were the bass notes. It was an inner warming-up, as we prepared our creative state.

There's no denying, the exercise was difficult at first. Yet we did it so often that before long our muscles remembered how all the emotions felt, and within moments we could be laughing, crying, and a host of shades of emotions in between. In other words, our affective memories were physical as much as mental. Our bodies retained the memory of the emotions as much as our minds – be it our stomach muscles aching with laughter or our ribcages heaving with sobs.

In fact, we found that all kinds of stimuli could prompt emotional responses. Sometimes the emotions were provoked by pure *observation*. ('Johnny's got a funny face.' Or 'How can anyone graffiti like that on the wall?!') Sometimes the emotions were direct *interactions* with other people. (The energy of twelve people sharing laughter. Or the touch of the tutor's hand on the back of my head which somehow filled me with melancholy.) Sometimes the emotions were provoked by actual *memories*. ('Lucy was hysterical at last Friday's party'. Or the terrible article I read in the newspaper about child soldiers in the Congo.) Sometimes the emotions were provoked by *imagination*. ('I wonder what Bob would look like hanging upside down.' Or 'That dark stain on the floor looks like a pool of blood. Whose is it?') Sometimes the emotions were provoked by *physical sensations*. ('Wow, it's great to have the freedom just to laugh!' Or 'Lying prostrate on the floor feels so overwhelmingly lonely.') Different things appealed to us on different days. And on some days it was far easier to be open to brighter emotions, and on some days, the darker emotions were more accessible.

Why is emotional recall far easier on some days than others?

Regardless of whether we're actors or not, our recollection of emotions is 'mood congruent' – meaning that the 'mood' we're in (or our state of mind) affects how our memory responds. This has nothing to do with whether or not we're good actors. It has everything to do with being a normal human being.

Mood congruence doesn't just refer to how you feel as you recall the emotion, but also how you felt at the time you had the experience in the first place. According to psychologist Dylan Evans, it's easier to remember something happy when we're feeling happy, and we tend to dwell on more distressing memories when we're feeling sad. In fact, educationalists have discovered that students retain far more information if they're in a good mood than they do if they're bored or blue.

That's why affective memory exercises may be easier on some days than on others. If you're trying to focus on positive emotions and you just can't catch them, it could simply be that you're not feeling particularly jolly that day. On the other hand, I'm always rather concerned when I read or hear of acting teachers using affective memory to dwell on darker emotions or neuroses, especially if their tactics become quite heavy-handed when an actor is struggling. There can sometimes be a tendency to focus affective memory exercises on primal, sexual, fearful and raging emotions, with the argument being that these are the ones that we're most likely to repress in our 'civilised' society, so they're harder to access and, therefore, need more practice. However, it may simply be that you're in a good mood on that particular day and you can't tap into the anger very easily. Maybe tomorrow – when you suddenly get a parking ticket – your bad mood will make you far more accessible to the darker colours in your palette. A particular 'mood congruence' on a particular day doesn't necessarily mean you're emotionally repressed.

## THE POINT OF EMOTIONAL CONDITIONING

Ultimately our challenge as actors is to be so emotionally accessible that we can launch into a musical comedy even if we've just had a bust up with our boyfriend. Or shake with Macbeth's murderous cries even if we've just come from a delightful birthday tea. The point of our emotional conditioning is to help us eliminate the gap between our state of mind (or mood) on a particular day and our ability to tap into the emotions relevant to the play. And personally, I think it's just as difficult to be ecstatic on demand as it is to be erotic or primal. And it's even harder to be calm and contented, when first-night nerves are coursing through our veins.

Hopefully by now you can see that the *process* of emotional training involves all aspects of your instrument (breath, body, voice and imagination), all of which need to be equally flexible and sensitive. And as we've seen, training your emotional responsiveness involves observation, interaction with others, past experience, imagination, and physical sensations. It's not just about remembering the day your dog died.

The *result* of 'being in condition' psycho-physically is that you gradually need less and less time to prepare yourself to be emotionally accessible. In fact, Strasberg said that in the end you may only need as little as a minute to tap into an emotional memory, because you've already trained your instrument.

And there's one more aspect of that instrument to consider, before we head out into the professional world.

## SPIRIT

Perhaps one of the most significant parts of your acting instrument – one that becomes strengthened through all the tools and processes we've listed so far – is your 'spirit'. By 'spirit', I mean nothing more than the unconscious communication – or

**communion** – between human beings when they're engaged wholeheartedly in dynamic, all-consuming actions. Stanislavsky writes a good deal about the spirituality of acting, as indeed do many leading American practitioners, including Stephen Wangh (New York University) and Robert Benedetti (CalArts and University of Southern California). The spiritual aspect of acting incorporates all the elements we've already mentioned, including intuition, imagination and body. (In Chapter 6, we'll see that it also includes your 'presence', as Barba and Lecoq encourage.)

There have been times in theatre history when talking about the soul or spirit of an artist was vital, just one example being the French symbolist writers in the early part of the twentieth century. And of course, as we've already mentioned, acting has its roots in ritual and sacred spaces. Certainly for composer Nachmanovitch, tuning your instrument is the same as tuning your spirit.

Creativity – especially acting – is an incredibly mysterious and strange process. The entertainment industry, as it exists in the twenty-first century, often seems to work against that mystery, but as creative artists, we need to resist the mundane. Dynamic listening involves perceiving subtle shifts in a person's body, psyche and energy, as much as hearing the actual words that they're saying. Stanislavsky calls it 'grasp' – if you can get each other in each other's grasp, the audience will be magnetised towards you. (As we've already suggested, Meisner's whole training through repetitions works towards this quality of listening.) Actor-training accesses the unseen, intangible parts of our humanness, as much as it involves breathing, movement training, articulation, voice production and improvisation.

## THE PAY-OFFS OF TRAINING

There's a notable difference between actors in the UK and actors in the USA. Although many actors in the UK have passed through RADA, Central School of Speech and Drama, the Bristol Old Vic, the Royal Scottish Academy for Music and Drama (et al), I've also worked with several actors, who never trained and yet enjoy extremely successful and lucrative careers in both theatre and television. In the USA, and particularly in Hollywood, actors are constantly encouraged to take classes and to train, just like athletes or musicians or dancers. Acting tutors are taken very seriously, to the extent that you list the individuals with whom you've studied on your CV, and it's almost expected that when you're not in work – and even when you are – you're attending workshops with the host of coaches available on the circuit.

There's no question that training can give you confidence: the security that comes with knowing you have some kind of personal toolkit or technique can bolster your creativity. The essential paradox of training is that you consciously set about learning various tools so that you can trust yourself enough to forget them in performance and simply be alive to whatever's going on. By being in control of this extraordinarily complex instrument at your disposal – your self – you can allow yourself moments of being 'out-of-control' and vulnerable to the playfulness of each moment. As Mamet puts it, technique gives you the confidence to get out of your own way and to be comfortable being uncomfortable, as you hurl yourself into the 'terrifying unforeseen' of the live acting encounter. (See Chapter 6.)

The important thing is to find the kind of training that serves you – to contact your 'authenticity', free your natural voice, access your emotional repertoire, activate your imagination, create physical versatility, and connect with your onstage partners. Once you've done your training, it's time to head out into the real world and start auditioning for the roles.

## SUMMARY

In this chapter, we've looked at:

- why training is useful
- breath and relaxation
- approaches to the body and movement, including the Feldenkrais and Alexander Techniques, Laban's Efforts, and Overlie's Viewpoints
- voice
- developing imagination through games and improvisation
- enhancing your emotional accessibility, through both aspects of affective memory (sense memory and emotion memory)
- tuning the 'spirit'.

## SELECTED READING

For various kinds of psycho-physical training: Stephen Wangh's *An Acrobat of the Heart* (Vintage Original, 2000) is a truly inspiring take on Grotowski's work. David Zinder's evolution of Michael Chekhov's work in *Body Voice Imagination* (Routledge, 2002) includes excellent exercises and insights. Phillip B. Zarrilli's *Psycho-Physical Acting* (Routledge, 2008) is a dense and exciting investigation of his unique, Eastern-influenced, training system. My own *Beyond Stanislavsky* (Nick Hern Books, 2001) draws on contemporary Stanislavsky-orientated training in Russia. *Training of the American Actor* (Theatre Communications Group, 2006) (edited by Arthur Barstow) is incredibly useful – and this is where you'll find Mary Overlie's own writings on Viewpoints.

With regard to Movement Training: there are rich pickings in Lorna Marshall's *The Body Speaks* (Methuen, 2001) and Anne Dennis's *The Articulate Body* (Nick Hern Books, 2002). For a fun and terrifically illustrated insight into the psycho-physicality of the body, Stanley Keleman's *Emotional Anatomy* (Center Press, 1985) is a great reference book.

For Voice work: Kristin Linklater's *Freeing the Natural Voice* (Nick Hern Books, 2006), Patsy Rodenburg's *The Actor Speaks* (Methuen, 1998) and Cicely Berry's *The Actor and the Text* (Virgin Books, 2000) are simply invaluable for exercises and insights.

Despite the wide range of books on games and play, the pioneers of this work are still the best: Spolin's *Improvisation for the Theatre* (Northwestern University 1990, first published in 1963); Barker's *Theatre Games* (Methuen, 1982); Johnstone's *Impro* (Eyre Methuen, 1979); and Boal's *Games for Actors and Non-Actors* (Routledge, 1992) are terrific. Stephen Nachmanovitch's *Free Play* (Tarcher/Penguin, 1990) is deeply inspiring and wholly applicable to the kind of 'constant state of improvisation' that Stanislavsky encouraged in his actors.

## USEFUL WEBSITES

www.rada.org – for an insight into a British training ground.
www.tisch.nyu.ed – for an insight into an American training ground.
www.gitis.net – for an insight into a Russian training ground.

www.ecole-jacqueslecoq.com – for an insight into a European training ground.

www.sixviewpoints.com – Overlie's own site.

www.feldenkrais.com – for some good articles, etc.

www.alexandertechnique.com – for some useful insights.

# 3

# 'YOU GOT THE PART!': AUDITIONS

Auditions are unlike any other acting environment in which you'll find yourself. From the moment you hear about the casting, you develop a strange inner feeling, like building up to a blind date. You desperately want this to be 'The One' and that they'll like you as much as you like them, but you don't want to invest too much in it, in case you're disappointed.

In this chapter, we'll look at the conditions surrounding auditions, their purpose and the expectations involved. There are several excellent books detailing how you prepare yourself, so this chapter examines more broadly the extraordinary nature of performing in auditions, and some strategies for handling the uniqueness of the experience.

## THE PSYCHOLOGICAL CHALLENGES

### EXISTENTIAL ABSURDITY

There's no question: auditioning has a certain existential absurdity about it. You usually have very little time to prepare, as you may only get the script a couple of days, or even a couple of hours, beforehand. Acting under these circumstances is a skill in its own right, quite different from the process in which you engage once you've got the part and have a definite purpose to your work. You may well find that you expend a mass of nervous energy for no longer a lifespan than the five minutes or half-hour spent in the casting room. Added to which, your objective is not to create a role (which is art), but to get the job (which is marketing). In other words, you wear your Business Head in an audition, as much as your Creative Head. Which is tricky, as not all great actors are great sales people.

## LACK OF ATMOSPHERE

The second challenge is that the casting room can be a creative void – no props, set or other actors. So, you have to discover what you personally need in order to prepare yourself fully for that creatively cold atmosphere – especially as there's no preparatory 'sacred' space of a rehearsal room, dressing room, Winnebago or Green Room. You're called on to prepare publicly, surrounded by other actors who are also preparing publicly and, like prize fighters, they're in competition with you. Do you sit quietly and hold on to the inner sense of the character? Do you distract yourself by reading a book or doing the crossword? Do you wait in Costa Coffee until five minutes beforehand? Do you go through your lines in the loo? Do you engage the other actors in conversation? Preparing for an audition is unlike preparing for any other kind of performance because, in the moments just before you perform, you're extremely exposed. Added to which, the people who are auditioning you often have no idea about acting processes and they may engage you in all kinds of welcome chit-chat as you enter the room, instantly dispelling whatever 'inner creative state' you've managed to prepare. (As we'll see in Chapter 6, 'preparation' is a key part of Meisner's technique.)

## LACK OF CONTROL

The third challenge is that you have no control. An actor's whole life is a constant battle with disempowerment. Unless you create your own company, you're dependent on whichever jobs your agent puts you up for, which depends on the casting breakdowns that come your agent's way, not to mention how they perceive you as a client on their books. Are you the tall, romantic lead? The exotic Asian? The fat funny one? Or the quirky character type? Once you do secure an audition, your lack of control is even more evident, as most casting selections have less to do with your talent and more to do with the opinion of the people casting you. And opinion is not only unbelievably diverse, it's also highly unreliable. The reality is that, regardless of your talent, you'll be rejected for more jobs than you win. While that shouldn't put you off, it's important to understand that it's as much a part of the profession as actually doing the job.

### ONGOING REJECTION

The fourth challenge is that the rejection is ongoing – not even Brad Pitt gets every part he's up for. Auditioning is a lottery. For every role available, maybe a hundred or more actors are being considered at some point along the line. Every Acting Hopeful is warned: 'Can you deal with the rejection?' It's a question few of us can genuinely answer until we've been in the acting business for some time – maybe decades. Yet the crucial thing is not to take it personally: it just comes with the lifestyle. In no other profession is more time spent in seeking work and going for interviews than in actually doing the job we've trained for. Not succeeding in auditions is part of an actor's life, and learning to love them is an invaluable step towards maintaining self-belief.

## WHAT'S THE POINT OF AN AUDITION?

While the answer to this question might seem obvious, it's worth considering in some detail, as a little insight can enhance your sense of self-worth in what can otherwise be an overwhelming situation. British actor Margo Annett suggests in *Actor's Guide to Auditions and Interviews* (2004) that there are three key reasons for auditions: (1) to show your talents as an actor; (2) to demonstrate your suitability for a role; and (3) to indicate your understanding of the character and your empathy for the part. These are good starting points for discussion, so let's look at each of them in turn.

## TO SHOW YOUR TALENTS AS AN ACTOR

Your talents include your ability to take direction, which indicates both your versatility as an actor and your rapport with this particular director. You might be asked in the audition to do something completely contradictory to your own interpretation of the character, but your objective at this point is to get the job. If the director wants to assess whether or not they can work with you, it's important to demonstrate your flexibility, however consummate you feel your original interpretation to be.

## TO DEMONSTRATE YOUR SUITABILITY FOR THE ROLE

Your suitability for the role can have much to do with your ability to work well, say, under the high pressure of television and film, as your height, weight, look and temperament regarding the character for which you're auditioning. If you clearly find castings stressful, a television director might feel nervous about working with you in the fast turn-around of a TV series. Your professionalism impacts on your auditors from the moment you walk into the room until the moment the door closes behind you. In other words, your audition lasts for as long as you're in their company, and not just for the duration of your reading.

## TO INDICATE YOUR UNDERSTANDING OF THE CHARACTER

Your understanding of the character is largely connected to your ability to make bold, artistic choices and to go with those choices. If you make a brave choice and it's completely wrong, it won't necessarily indicate that you don't understand the part; it'll reveal your desire to interpret and to be a creative resource for your director. If your choices are way off beam, it shouldn't be a problem for an intelligent director, as long as you're able to adjust to his or her suggestions. We have to have courage in auditions. As Michael Shurtleff (a Broadway casting director and acting coach) writes, you have to go for broke: 'Don't do the scene like an exploratory operation: It is life-and-death surgery' (Shurtleff, 1978:177).

Those are three potential reasons why you audition. Now let's meet the auditors who determine our careers.

# THE *DRAMATIS PERSONAE*

The casting director, the director, the producer, the writer, the advertising agency, the clients. One of those, some of those or all of those may be present, depending on whether it's television, theatre, commercial or film. The most crucial thing to remember is that they're not demons and monsters; they're human beings who are just as nervous as you are. Unlike any other audience for whom you perform, this audience desperately wants you to do the job well, as their own professional careers are on the line as much as yours.

### THE CASTING DIRECTOR

The situations are rather different in the UK and the USA. In the UK, it's quite likely that in television and high profile theatre you'll meet both the casting director and the director and, in the case of TV and film, your audition will be videotaped. In the USA, the casting director arguably has more weight than in the UK, and they may be the only person at your interview, often actually giving you direction. They then look at the videotapes, make a shortlist for the director and call you back. It's at this point that the casting director's nerves increase: if you don't step up to the mark at the callback, they've potentially wasted Very Important People's very important time. Life in Hollywood works at a much faster rate than, say, London: they need the result and they need it now, and if the casting director doesn't bring in good talent, they might not work for that director again. At the same time, an audition is a curiously human environment, and the casting director genuinely wants you to be good and to succeed. So if they like you, it could be their opinion that tips the scales in your favour.

### THE DIRECTOR

The director is equally nervous. If jobs are hard to come by for actors, consider the director's situation: for every 25 people in a Shakespeare play, there's only one director; for every 200 people in a movie, there's only one director. Ultimately, you're the one on the screen or stage, honouring their direction; so, their professional careers are absolutely dependent on you. In which case, they need to know that they can work with you. The auditions and callbacks are their opportunity to understand how well you'll take direction.

In all honesty, many directors don't really understand acting processes – and it's not their fault. Unlike Russian director-training (which involves a five-year programme, the first four of which comprise the same actor-training as the actors), training for directors in the West is rather more ad hoc. As a result, they don't necessarily share your vocabulary, and sometimes you have to interpret directors' instructions in a way that makes sense both to them and to you. 'Sit forward on that line' may have to be translated into something like 'urge your partner' or 'confront your partner' or 'enlighten your partner'.

Auditions are based on personality or temperament, as well as talent. If it's a TV or film casting, the directors want to be sure you can be relied on to work efficiently and effectively. In the theatre, they want to know they can work in rehearsal with you, day in, day out, as well as connect with you socially and publicly. All these interpersonal communications have to be intuited in a very short period of acquaintance within the very unnatural situation of the audition.

## THE PRODUCER AND THE WRITER

The producer – in charge of making sure the financial backers are happy – also has to be wooed. After all, they're persuading people to invest big money in you, so they have to be convinced that you can absolutely sustain that kind of investment.

Sometimes, the producer – or the director, for that matter – might also be the writer of the project. General advice differs in the UK and the USA regarding how to treat a script in a casting. Usually if you've learnt the part for a UK audition, the casting people will forgive a few ad libs if you're not quite word perfect. Advice from the USA tends to be that this is an out-and-out 'NO-NO!' Director-producer Sam Weisman says that nothing offends a writer more. You sometimes need to be especially cautious, as so many writer-producers now run television, and if you change their scripts you could well lose out on the job.

Weisman's advice is particularly applicable to comedy, where the rhythm of the comic pay-offs are absolutely dependent on your honouring every punctuation mark, let alone every word. Once again, the success of the casting people's work is dependent on your talent.

## WHAT DO THE AUDITORS WANT FROM YOU?

Here are some examples of what the auditors might be looking for: intelligence, emotional honesty, diversity, simplicity, analytical awareness, a sense of humour, courage, energy, talent, co-operation, flexibility, directability and that you're appropriate for the part.

This list is gleaned from a diversity of sources, from Heads of Acting programmes at drama schools to casting directors and producers. Don't panic: no one can be expected to possess all these qualities. The list is there just to give you an idea of some useful traits. Above all, the auditors need to know that you can respond to them, and vice versa. As we've noted, their reputations are at stake here, so they want to be sure they've got somebody in every role who is talented, interesting and brings something unique to the part. In terms of the specifics of what that 'unique' quality might be, they themselves might not know exactly until they see it. So there's no need to expend energy trying to second-guess them. The very fact that they've seen your CV and photograph, and they called you for audition, is an indication that you might just be perfect.

Since there's no way of knowing for certain what they want, you should trust yourself, and be yourself.

### BEING YOURSELF

'Being yourself' doesn't mean 'playing yourself'. Your job as an actor is to enter the soul of the character. That said, there are four key words which come up time and again in acting books with regard to auditions: 'relaxed', 'confident', 'warm' and 'open'. The audition is an unnatural situation, and in many ways the auditors rely on you to make it seem natural. They want to know that you're in control – of your nerves, your talent and the situation. If they can see that you're comfortable in the audition environment, then you free them up to be comfortable too.

'Being yourself' also pinpoints another huge challenge of the acting profession, which the audition process particularly highlights. We have to acknowledge what our attributes are, in terms of our body, face and temperament. Unlike any other profession, actors are employed for their looks. It's tricky, but we have to be absolutely honest about what Nature has given us so that we can start to identify our 'type' and understand what kind of parts will best serve us and which we can best serve.

Some acting coaches advise against auditioning for a role for which you know you're not the right type. Others say that, if the auditors have seen your CV and photo and they still want to audition you, then don't worry about whether or not you're right. Go to the audition anyway, and see if you can change their perception of the part. When *The Graduate* (1967) was being cast, they were looking for a tall, blond athlete; then they saw Dustin Hoffman, and the rest is history.

## RESEARCH

One way in which we increase our sense of being relaxed and confident is to be sure we've done the research on the role. That research covers all sorts of areas, including: the facts of the play; the director; any historical background that might be relevant for the part; watching episodes from the TV series; perhaps investigating the play's previous production history, since knowing who has played the part before may give you some insights into its essence.

Research also covers the character's relationships – to others in the script and to the key events. If it's a TV or film script, you may not have much information. Again, there's a difference between the UK and the USA. In the USA, agents are frequently given far more information about a part than they are in the UK. Also the actors' unions are stronger and there are ways in which an actor can access the whole script of the piece they're up for, rather than just the **sides** (i.e. the few pages of the relevant scenes). With UK television, you may not have any sides given to you in advance, in which case you show up half an hour early and work like crazy to turn those black-and-white pages into something resembling a flesh-and-blood person.

If you are only given a few sides, you can work out where the scene comes in the narrative simply by noting the page numbers. This is minimal research, but it can provide you with important information about rhythm, atmospheres and how high the stakes are at this point in the narrative. Look for the clues, wherever they might be.

Hollywood coach Margie Haber believes that auditions are 40 per cent psychology (who you are and whether they like you, etc.) and 60 per cent preparation. Yet some actors are curiously reluctant to spend too much time preparing for an audition. It's often a deeply unconscious defence mechanism, so that if they don't get the part, they can believe it was down to lack of preparation rather than because they weren't good enough or simply not right for the role. It's a self-protective belief that 'I would have got an A for that exam if I'd done the revision'. While it's perfectly understandable, it's not necessarily the best strategy for getting the part.

## COSTUME

And preparation needn't be arduous. Sometimes it's as simple as wearing the right clothes. A casual look is usually fine for theatre, but something suggestive of the role is better for television and film, as long as it doesn't distract from your audition. When it comes to commercials, the sky's the limit. I've done commercial castings where I had to dress as a witch, a tramp and a mobile phone.

For non-commercial auditions, it's wise to avoid black. So many actors have a passion for black that, if the auditors spend the whole day watching a bunch of black-clad people parade through their doors, their memories are likely to linger on the girl in the red dress or the boy in the green shirt. Your objective is to get the job, not to be sartorially chic. Similarly, for recalls, you should wear what you wore for the initial casting, as the auditors may be using clothing as prompts to remind them who you are. Anything to make their lives' easier and your performance more memorable.

When it comes to the big movies and the clinching screen test, full hair and make-up are expected; now you're in the realm of near-performance, so the stakes are even higher and you really have to embody the part.

## READINGS

The chances are you'll probably be asked to do one of four things at an audition: just chat, maybe improvise a scene, read a script, or present a monologue. There's limited preparation you can do for the first two apart from being yourself and being open to the environment. There are various strands of advice about the third. Most casting directors, who write about readings, repeat the advice that you *do not need to memorise the script*. Indeed, the suggestion is that, if you do know the lines, you'll lead the directors to believe that that's the full extent of your interpretation, and they'll judge your audition as a performance rather than a reading. Even if you're very comfortable with the text, they encourage you to refer to the page every so often, to remind the auditors that there's room for improvement once you get the job. After all, they want to know you can act, not that you can learn lines fast (though, of course, that in itself is a necessary skill, as often in television and film, lines are changed split seconds before the filming begins).

Personally, I disagree with the general advice, as I find having a piece of paper in my hand prevents me from really engaging with the given circumstances of the script. I tend to find that the more I can 'own' the part, the more relaxed I feel in the casting. While I'm still very open to changing the choices I've made if the director makes suggestions, I want to inhabit the role as much as possible. Ultimately, you have to do whatever helps you to get the most out of yourself in the situation, though experience proves that you won't necessarily be penalised because you do know the lines.

When it comes to callbacks and screen tests, the auditors will expect you to give a much fuller interpretation.

## MONOLOGUES

Presenting a monologue operates along different lines from readings, and again there seem to be varying practices in the USA and the UK. Since the demise of the repertory theatre in Britain, it's rare for you to be asked for audition speeches, beyond entrance into drama schools or summer intensives. In the USA, where open auditions are common and where it's far more accepted that actors will take classes whether or not they're in work, there's a greater expectation that you'll have half a dozen speeches up your sleeve that you can whip out on request.

There are some great books on how to prepare monologues for auditions (see the selected bibliography), so although I won't go into detail, here are some useful tips to consider and some invaluable lists of questions (which can act as a checklist for any actor presenting a monologue, regardless of experience).

## CHOOSING A MONOLOGUE

First of all, choose speeches that are suitable for your age, gender, physique, etc. Be realistic, and give yourself a chance. Ask yourself honestly: 'Would I be cast in this role?' It's generally not advisable to cross-gender or cross-age cast yourself in audition speeches: you've got enough to contend with as it is.

Second, choose speeches you like. It may sound obvious, but many of us have been guilty of hastily picking a speech that seems 'okay', rather than finding the perfect fit.

Having chosen a monologue, pay special attention to where it comes in the play, as this gives you invaluable insight into the function of the character at this point in the narrative, and therefore what kind of energy drives the speech.

Within the speech itself, there needs to be an exciting progression and journey, so that we get a sense of how the character is altered by saying these words. What do they feel at the end of the speech that's different from what they felt at the beginning? What's their attitude to the person they're addressing by the end of the speech, compared to their attitude towards them at the beginning? Is the speech *preparing* your character for something? Putting something *into action*? Or *reacting* to something? The greater the journey, the more delight you'll have in delivering the speech. That said, it's best to avoid speeches from the climax of a play as, in the audition, you simply don't have the build-up of the story to bring you to the relevant state for that climactic moment. You can then run the risk of manufacturing generalised emotions to microwave the moment and falling into the worst traps of forced acting. You don't have to prove to the auditors you can be emotional; you just have to take them on a journey.

## ASKING QUESTIONS

Once you've found a speech that excites you, there's a myriad of questions that you should ask yourself before you even start to commit the words to memory. Annett's *Actor's Guide to Auditions and Interviews* is a good reference, asking questions such as these.

What has happened before the speech begins?
What are you doing?
Who are you talking to?
What do you need from the person you're talking to? (Annett, 2005:38)

These questions are very straightforward and instantly usable, referring to the past context, the present action, and the future intention, and having at the heart of your questions the other person onstage with you. These points of focus are crucial for audition monologues; it's dangerously easy for us to become so focused on ourselves and our own anxieties about getting through the speech that we forget the basic principle of acting: that we're speaking solely to have an effect on our listener. As Shurtleff says in his wonderful book *Audition*, 'Most actors don't need enough from their partners. Need the most. Need the most love, the most response, the most belief, the most of whatever it is you want. Only the most will give you a reading of dimension' (Shurtleff, 1978:179).

### FIND THE PASSION: ROMANCE, DREAMS AND INCONSISTENCIES

Shurtleff offers some terrific pieces of advice in *Audition*, one of which is to consider every scene a love scene. Almost every scene has love at its heart – be it the presence of it, the loss of it or the deprivation of it. Once you start reading plays in this light, you'll see how canny Shurtleff is in his observation. He incites us to bring back romance, as romance is often the secret life which motivates a speech.

Along with the romance, Shurtleff also suggests you celebrate the character's dreams. In life, it's our dreams that keep us going; they're our way of dealing with the problems created by reality. Shurtleff urges you not to settle for anything less than the biggest dreams your character has for the future, and to fight hard to make those dreams come true. As he knowingly states, half the time we follow our dreams to prove to the people who doubt us that we really can 'make it'. There's no denying that dreams and competition are extremely powerful forces in the acting industry, and we shouldn't be coy about our own endeavours. Instead, we should celebrate the energy and fierce passion that fuel us to actualise ourselves, and feed that energy into our auditions.

Another passionate piece of Shurtleff advice is to find the inconsistencies in your character. If there are two considerations in a scene that cancel each other out, 'Do both!' For Shurtleff, consistency is the death of good acting – and I agree. Human beings are eternally adaptable, and we often act 'out of character' when situations push us there. Ironing out inconsistencies can easily take the edge off your characterisation, as well as curbing the pleasure you can take in playing it.

### LEARNING THE MONOLOGUE

Armed with all these insights, you should find learning your monologue quite easy. It's important that you learn the text through your body and muscles, and not just your head – and that means engaging your imagination. As you look at the other (imaginary) characters around you, picture them as people you know: let the Duke of Buckingham be your cousin, the Duke of York – your physics teacher, the Duke of Warwick – your dad. Picture them: see them. Then your experience in the audition room will be much easier. (All the work we look at in Chapter 4 regarding building a character is completely relevant here, too.)

### FEELING THE SILENT INTERRUPTIONS

As you learn your monologue and picture the invisible partners, it's worth remembering that a speech is not really a speech. It's rare in everyday life that we set out to speak uninterruptedly for two and a half minutes. So it's helpful to look for the moments in a monologue where the other character might actually be trying to interrupt you, but the energy and drive of your own thoughts – your need to express your argument in a torrent of words – prevents them from getting a word in edgeways. In other words, feel their imaginary energy and impulses.

Even with a soliloquy, there's a dialogue going on. In Hamlet's 'To be or not to be', his *head* is arguing with his *body* about whether or not he should kill himself. As the conflict unfurls, his *emotions* are drafted in to the conversation, as the terror of perpetual nightmares puts him off the whole idea.

With all this preparatory work behind you, you're ready to enter the audition room.

### THE OPENING BEAT

Before you start your monologue, take a moment to consider the 'opening beat'. The opening beat is a vital mini-pause before you begin speaking, filled with all the psycho-physical information that your character brings into the scene. What has just happened? What's the physical energy behind this opening beat fuelling the monologue? Having a real imaginative sense of, and connection to, the opening beat can help you find the appropriate rhythm and pace of the scene, and prevent you beginning the speech hesitantly slowly or nervously fast. This isn't a thirty-second public preparation; it's an instant prompt to your imagination of your character's impulse to say these words.

An important consideration with the opening beat is 'place'. Place becomes doubly important in an audition situation, as the location in which the scene or monologue takes place is probably a million miles away from the cramped, little, casting director's office, in which you actually find yourself. The opening beat allows you to conjure up in a moment (as long as you've done the preparation) the atmosphere of a Dickensian workhouse or Mamet's realtors' office or Macbeth's castle.

As you establish that vital opening beat, it's wise not to eyeball your auditors; they want to be able to listen to your monologue objectively, and if you look them in the eye, they may feel obliged to give you some kind of reaction and then they'll struggle to enjoy your storytelling freely.

### THE FINAL MOMENT

When you get to the end of your speech, hold the final moment as if you're observing how your last words have landed in your imaginary, onstage partner's ear, and whether you've achieved the effect you intended in order to fulfil your need. Allow the monologue to resonate with the sense of a complete performance in its own right. And then go and have lunch with a friend or buy a DVD. Reward yourself for your intensive work.

## COMMERCIAL CASTINGS

One of the most absurd acting scenarios in which you'll ever find yourself is the commercial casting. Of the half-dozen commercials in which I've been cast – from chocolate bars, to Chicken McNuggets, to pizzas, to a child protection charity promo – I've never been entirely sure how I got any of them. The truth is that appearance and personality are everything in commercials. Sometimes they just want you to improvise. Sometimes they want you to handle simple props. Sometimes they want you to enact a storyboard that you've studied in the waiting area. Sometimes they want you to deliver a script that you've just had five minutes to learn. Once I had to place my head in a cardboard box with a rectangular hole cut out of it, as if I was a broadcaster in a television set. Another time I had to don a swimsuit and make up a synchronised swimming routine. (Synchronised? On my own?) Another time I had to be a fish. Sometimes you just have to smile. The vital qualities you need are spontaneity, openness, humility, imagination – and humour. After all, five minutes in a commercial casting can earn you several thousands, sometimes tens of thousands, to tide you through the leaner times. And they make your agent love you!

## STRATEGIES FOR REMAINING SANE

Auditioning is ultimately about practice. It's a fact of an actor's life that you won't secure most of the castings for which you audition, so you might as well enjoy each one for the opportunity it gives you to flex your creative muscles. You can only practise auditions by doing them; mock-up auditions never really work, as the risk factor just isn't there. Over half your professional life is spent trying to 'get the job', so there are diminishing returns in being afraid of them. That said, of course we do get nervous ...

## WORKING WITH ADRENALIN

Olympic sports psychologist Don Greene has studied audition anxiety and says that fear is normal and should be accepted as such. The racing heart, the perspiration, butterflies and clammy hands are your body's way of acknowledging that the adrenalin has kicked in – because something important is about to happen. With an audition, something very important is about to happen: you're about to spread your creative wings and fly. It may only be for a matter of minutes, but you're giving your artistic muscles a chance for a wonderful, exhilarating workout.

Of course, you can make matters easier by trying to justify why your *character* might be feeling nervous. (They've just murdered the king. They're about to propose to their girlfriend. They were just caught speeding. Whatever.) You can then legitimise your own feelings by converting them into something relevant for the role. And if you can do this, you very usefully and creatively reduce the fracture between what you're actually feeling and what you need for the part. As Stanislavsky would say, whatever you have here, today, now – use it! And this applies to mistakes!

## EMBRACING THE MISTAKES

Not being afraid of making mistakes is another great way of wrestling with your nerves. Mistakes are gifts: they put you on your toes and bring you right into the present tense. Through that moment of vulnerability, you open yourself up to all sorts of stimuli that you might never have imagined before. After all, what's the worst case scenario? The sky won't fall on your head. Your boyfriend won't drop down dead. There's an outside chance you won't get the casting, but most auditors are experienced or intelligent enough to see beyond the odd stumble or stutter, and you'll learn a huge amount about your creative processes by living through the experience.

## LETTING GO

The existential absurdity of auditions can linger once they're over. If by any chance you don't get the job, knowing when to relinquish your hope is another art in its own right. Some casters know within moments of meeting you whether or not the job is yours; others take weeks to assemble the perfect ensemble. And should the role not have your name on it this time round, you have to 'let go' psychologically. However punishing it may feel at the time, it really isn't personal: you're not a bad person simply for not 'passing' an audition.

Of course, the opposite of 'letting go' is 'holding on' – in the right way.

HOLDING ON

On my first day at UK drama school, our acting tutor said, 'There are two types of people in this room – stickers and quitters.' Twenty years on and I still ain't quittin'. In many respects, it's all a lottery anyway, so as long as you keep playing, eventually you'll win. After all, somebody has to get the job, and there are very few moments in life more exciting for an actor than hearing those words 'You got the part!' And then – unless it's a one-day commercial, when you've just got to go out there and be that talking chicken – you can start the real, exciting work of plunging into a text and building a three-dimensional character in the fascinating realm of rehearsal.

## SUMMARY

In this chapter, we've looked at:

- the psychological challenges of auditions
- the point of auditions
- the people who cast you
- the qualities they look for
- the research you can do
- readings and the expectations attached
- monologues
- commercial castings
- strategies for remaining sane.

## SELECTED READING

There are some great books on auditions, particularly by American authors.

Michael Shurtleff's *Audition* (Walker and Company, 1978) is terrific. Although it's thirty years old, it's written in an immediate, pithy, no-nonsense way and full of wisdom gained from Shurtleff's years as a New York casting director and acting coach.

Margie Haber's *How to Get the Part without Falling Apart* (Lone Eagle, 1999) has its finger on the Hollywood pulse. She has some useful tips on reading in auditions, now patented as The Haber™ Technique.

For the UK-based actor, there's Margo Annett's *Actor's Guide to Auditions and Interviews* (A & C Black, 2005). This is a gentler look at the cut-and-thrust of the industry, with specific British reference points.

Many acting books contain chapters on audition technique, and there are many others specifically devoted to auditions, not to mention the wealth of compilations of suggested speeches. There's a lot for you to choose from.

## USEFUL WEBSITES

www.actors.centre.co.uk – for classes offering audition technique, once you've been in the profession for a couple of years.

www.musicaltheatreaudition.com – a fun site, offering all kinds of tips and ideas.

There are also numerous websites featuring various castings and auditions.

# 4

# 'BUILDING A CHARACTER': REHEARSAL PROCESSES

The celebrated British director Max Stafford Clark (1941–), once described the rehearsal room as either a magical world like a second childhood or a prison camp. It's true; the rehearsal process can be a journey of creative ecstasy or a voyage to the centre of your darkest soul, where you lose any faith that you could ever act at all.

But what exactly is the purpose of rehearsal – when, in radio, you barely get a read-through and, in television and film, you often get more information at your interview than you do on the set?

I'd suggest there are three main purposes: (1) to collectively map out the territory of the fictional world; (2) to tell the writer's story as clearly as possible; and (3) to create characters who seem plausible within the dramatic style of the piece. Since Chapter 5 looks in detail at screen acting, we'll mainly focus here on building a character for theatre, though of course there are cross-over points.

## THE POWER OF REPETITION

A theatre rehearsal – *répétition* in French – involves just that: repetition. As you have probably realised by now, acting takes courage, and many actors – including very experienced ones – confess that, when they first encounter a role, they have absolutely no idea what they're doing. The terrain can look terrifying and the journey may be daunting. It's only by constantly revisiting the text that the play begins to reveal itself, and each repetition deepens your understanding.

In reality, there's actually very little repetition. Even if the words are the same every time you rehearse a scene, each revisiting is a new phase of exploration. It's like a flautist endlessly re-working small phrases of the flute concerto: the more they understand the intricacies of the composer's work, the freer they are to find their own interpretation in performance. (As we'll see in Chapter 6, Meisner's whole actor-training is based on repetition and the nuances of each repeat.)

## THE DIRECTOR IN REHEARSAL

The person at the helm, guiding the actors through the uncharted waters of rehearsal, is the director, and (as we touched on in Chapter 3) that relationship is one of the most influential and personal you can have. A large part of your creative experience is based on your connection with the director – their working process, their vision of the play, their view of the character you're playing, and their general understanding of how actors work.

Directors deserve our empathy, as their role can be very isolating. Throughout the rehearsals they have to be the perfect audience of one, laughing in the funny places, weeping in the poignant places, sharpening each moment, unlocking problematic texts, focusing on the whole production, as well as understanding how to bring out the best in everyone. It's a challenging task, and the actor–director relationship depends on the mutual nurturing of each other's talents.

### CREATING A PRODUCTIVE REHEARSAL SPACE

To make sure this mutual nurturing can happen, a good director takes responsibility for establishing an openly creative rehearsal room. To be genuinely exploratory as actors, we thrive in an atmosphere where we feel safe enough to take big, imaginative risks. Far too often if we're not careful, we can spend rehearsals trying to suss out what the director really wants. As we saw in Chapter 2, we're afraid of following our intuition and taking chancy choices, just in case the director doesn't like them and we end up looking stupid. Instead, we lay low and try to fathom out what's going on in their head. And yet (as we saw in Chapter 3), directors often don't know what they want until they see what we give them. Therefore, it's basically our job as actors to offer up as many choices as possible, and the director's responsibility to create a working environment in which our acts of creative vulnerability are encouraged and celebrated.

## THE MONSTER OF EXPEDIENCY

When it comes to taking risks, one of our biggest enemies in the rehearsal room is what the American theatre-maker Charles Marowitz calls the Monster of Expediency. The usual short time-scales demand very efficient rehearsals and, as an actor, you sometimes find yourself leaping to rapid decisions because you're afraid there's no time for exploration. The trouble is that if you make choices *too* early, you can clip your creative wings. Yet it takes a confident director to defy the growling of the Monster of Expediency and invite you to take the time to find more unexpected choices.

It's a confidence worth finding, because if you can't be bold in rehearsal you'll find it doubly hard to be bold in performance. Inhibited rehearsals equals tame performances equals dead theatre – which is why, in Chapter 2, we talked about taking risks. And that bravery applies to directors, too. I confess: the worst kind of director, in my opinion, is the one who cowers beneath the Monster of Expediency and 'blocks' the play, telling the actors where to go on which lines and fixing the stage pictures as early as possible. I personally find 'blocking' (as far as theatre is concerned) a fairly ghastly practice, as it does is exactly what it says – it *blocks* any kind of creative flow *within* the actors or *between* the actors. (NB In filmed work, the fixing – or 'blocking' – of positions is absolutely vital because of cameras, lights, microphones, etc., and you have to work hard to keep really listening to each other.) In my experience of theatre, the good directors are the ones who rarely impose a pre-formed idea of the play in rehearsals; they uncover the organic life of a production by listening to what the cast are giving them. (Be warned: you'll come across the term and practice of 'blocking' time and time again. If you share my discomfort with the term, you'll have to tolerate it and, when necessary, silently 'translate' it into something that works for you.)

## THE ART OF DYNAMIC LISTENING

Throughout this book, we've talked about dynamic listening. Dynamic listening really lies at the heart of a creative rehearsal atmosphere. The directors listen to the actors, and the actors listen to the characters. And that means listening with your whole body, and not just your ears. Dynamic listening involves an open heart, a relaxed mind and a receptive spirit, all of which are hopefully tools that have been nurtured in your actor-training.

In fact, dynamic listening is the absolute key to building a character: it's the secret of brilliant acting (as we'll review in Chapter 5). Stanislavsky insisted upon it; MAT actress Maria Ouspenskaya (1876–1949) imported it from Russia to America in the 1920s; consequently, Strasberg and Meisner repeatedly impart the necessity of listening in their writings. Yet it's arguably the most difficult thing for actors to do. And we can largely blame the Monster of Expediency. Just as some directors are anxious to put the 'blocking' in place as quickly as possible, we're very anxious as actors to learn our lines as fast as possible, with the result that we don't actually hear either what we ourselves are saying or what the other characters are saying to us. Real listening takes time – to absorb, process and then respond to what has been said. With the added complexity, of course, that the way in which the *characters* listen to each other may be very different from the way in which the *actors* must listen to each other. The communication between the characters might be lousy, but the actors have to be fully tuned in.

### ACTION-REACTION-DECISION

True dynamic listening requires a sequence of Action-Reaction-Decision. This sequence dominates all human interaction, and impacts hugely on how we get inside a text and build a character. It goes like this: (1) I do something to you (Action); (2) you instinctively respond to my Action (Reaction); and (3) you then consciously decide how you're going to respond to me (Decision). Based on that Decision, you then (1) execute a new Action on me:

(2) I have an instinctive Reaction to what you've done, and (3) I then take a Decision about how I'm going to respond to you ... And so it goes, ad infinitum. Take any scene from any script and you'll see this is the sequence underlying everything that's going on between the characters: Romeo and Juliet, Will and Grace, Batman and Robin.

The time lapse between the beats of this sequence will depend on what the Actions are and the temperaments of the people involved. For example, I may kiss you (my Action): you may be repelled by my kiss (your Reaction), and then instantly push me away with a speed that almost fuses into one beat your Decision and your new Action. This may be because your temperament is very impulsive, or because our relationship is particularly fraught.

If, however, you're a sensitive type and you don't want to offend me, your Reaction to my kiss may still be one of repulsion, but there might be a longer moment of Decision in which you opt not to push me away. Instead, you distract my attention to the beautiful sunset over the sea (your new Action).

The important thing is that you've taken the time to really *listen* to what I'm saying or doing to you. You've heard your inner reaction; you've assessed both the current situation and the potential consequences of whatever you decide to do in response; and then you've executed a new Action. How you decide to respond also depends on how high the stakes are: if I'm not that important to you, then hurting my feelings won't cause you much grief. Of course, it's important to remember that your moments of decision are a response to listening to your partner. In other words, you can't really unlock the rhythm of the Action-Reaction-Decision sequence until you encounter the other actors and hear how they're delivering their responses to you. That said, just being aware of the process can prime you for good listening right from the early stages of rehearsal.

If you ignore the moments of decision, it can lead to dead acting, and the real problem often lies in the nuts and bolts of the way a play is rehearsed. Before you can know which actions to take and which stage pictures to make, you really need to know your character's *thought processes*: this is what underpins the Action-Reaction-Decision sequence. A character's thought processes determine how they behave. But you may well find that the characters' thought processes are rarely a consideration in the way rehearsals are conducted. Let's take a look at why.

## THE STRUCTURE OF REHEARSALS

The usual rehearsal process (certainly in the UK) is that we stage a play by wandering around the rehearsal room with our scripts in our hands, trying to find some appropriate moves (or 'blocking'). These moves are determined fairly early on, before any of us – actors or director – have had the chance to understand the real dynamics between the characters, let alone any possible thought processes. If we're honest, most of us would agree that these early rehearsals can be rather superficial, and we end up ditching much of the work once we're all more familiar with the play.

But why is it so superficial?

The answer is easy.

The brain activity involved in reading lines off a page is completely different from the brain activity involved in communicating living thoughts and responding to our impulses. The reason why we end up ditching so many of our early staging choices is because the rehearsal process short-circuits any genuine communication. There's little opportunity for real eye contact because you're reading the script, and since the eyes are 'the windows to the soul', there's little chance of really understanding what's going on between you and your partner. In fact, it's a pretty topsy-turvy way of staging a play and building a character, like putting on your overcoat before your pants and shirt. And yet it tends to be the usual way in which a play is rehearsed.

Before we take a look at a liberating alternative – Stanislavsky's Active Analysis – let's use another of Stanislavsky's tool as a means of assisting our process and helping us build a character: the **inner psychological drives**.

## INNER PSYCHOLOGICAL DRIVES

Stanislavsky's *An Actor Prepares* includes a chapter devoted to what he calls the 'inner motive forces'; these are the three centres of thinking, feeling and doing. There are no other human activities: we're either thinking something, or feeling something, or doing something, and usually an intricately synchronous matrix of all three. In Jean Benedetti's 2008 translation of Stanislavsky's writings entitled *An Actor's Work* (see Chapter 6), these three centres of thought, emotion and action have been translated as the inner psychological drives. I find the term more user-friendly and so I've adopted it here.

As we discussed in Chapter 2, it's hard to make absolute distinctions between thoughts, feelings and actions when, as human beings, we're so innately psycho-physical and all three centres intercommunicate very rapidly and spontaneously. If we want to resist Descartes' distinction between body and mind, then perhaps we shouldn't even separate thinking, feeling and doing at all. And yet, in terms of rehearsal processes, it can be very useful to do so, as each one taps into slightly different aspects of building a role.

We'll start with the head, i.e. the thought-centre.

## THE THOUGHT-CENTRE

### YOUR FIRST READING

Your first encounter with a script is usually on your own, and this can be wonderfully fruitful, revealing intuitive discoveries that won't necessarily come from any future reading. To make sure you capture the flavour of these fruitful first impressions, Stanislavsky suggests that you create a sense of ritual for this encounter with your character's world, beginning by reading the whole play in one sitting. If you try to read a few pages on the train, in the bath, by the bus stop, you may miss these irresistible impressions. You'll certainly miss the flow and rhythm of the unfolding drama and, instead, you'll be left with a piecemeal sense of fragmented storytelling.

### READING SCREEN SCRIPTS

With film and television scripts, you need to pay special attention to the screen directions. Whereas in a playscript we might be tempted to cast a cursory glance over the stage directions – in fact, some actors cross out all the directions to do with personal feelings or attitudes straight away – in the visual media of film in particular, they're as much a part of the storytelling as the dialogue. The public consumption of a movie is going to be on thirty-foot screens; that's a big picture, so images are naturally the main concern. And that's how you have to read the script. There will be long screen directions, with some scenes consisting of nothing *but* screen directions (also called 'Actions'). And it's important not to skim over them to try to find your lines. These descriptions provide vital clues for building your character, as well as giving you insights into the genre of the film, the rhythm, the potential atmosphere, and the way in which the director and the director of photography (DOP) may choose to film you. You have to picture that high-rise block of flats, cut to the puddle of dirty rain-water on the sidewalk, then cross to the lone face staring from the fifth floor window out across the city at dusk. Note particularly the close-ups and the POV (points of view, where the camera is showing the scene through the eyes of a particular character). It takes time to read a screen script properly and for the printed page to convert itself into living images for you. Within each image there's a cumulative atmosphere and rhythm, which demand an imaginative commitment from you, even as you read them for the first time.

## THE FIRST PUBLIC READ-THROUGH

Your next crucial encounter with the role is your first public read-through. Most theatre rehearsal schedules (and some TV and film) include the opportunity for the whole cast to gather together to read the script out loud.

There are all kinds of ways of doing a read-through: you'll find that some actors hold back as they delicately find their way forward; others give a great deal of energy, injecting the reading with a sense of vitality (even if this isn't the characterisation they end up giving in their final interpretation). The important factor is that everyone hears the melody of *this* script with *these* voices, and how the lines live in the ensemble of the people cast. Personally, I veer on the side of taking risks in the initial read-through: if you can overcome any timidity at the very first step, you set yourself on the path for taking risks all along. Even if you're not giving the director your ultimate performance, you're allowing them an insight into your working process, and that in itself can enable them to understand how they might help you access your best work.

After the first read-through, 'round-the-table' work might last anything from half a day to three weeks, depending on the script, the length of the rehearsal period, the medium and the director. Table work can involve all kinds of explorations. If you're rehearsing a Shakespeare play, it might feature in-depth discussion of each reference, image and pun. If you're rehearsing a new play, there might be some analysis of the scene structure, the storytelling devices, and how the individual voices have been articulated.

Let's look at some specific tools for thought-centred work on a script, all of which you can use either independently or collectively.

## GIVEN CIRCUMSTANCES

The given circumstances are your springboard into the text. They include all the basic pieces of information that the writer has given you about where and when the action takes place, the social and economic milieu of the characters, the style and the genre.

There are then the given circumstances brought about by the medium and the director. An outdoor production of *Romeo and Juliet* presents you with different given circumstances from a schools' tour of *Peter Pan*. A screen adaptation of *Wuthering Heights* makes different circumstantial demands from a West End musical, not least of which is that you may be called to location at 6am rather than being onstage at 8pm. This in turn affects the rhythm of your working day and the schedule of your creative energy. Enacting an intimate love scene while a camera man, dolly grip, focus puller and boom operator stand three feet away from you is another set of given circumstances altogether. All these given circumstances impact on the choices you make as you apply yourself to the task of creating a role.

There are lots of books featuring the given circumstances (not least Stella Adler's own book highlighted in Chapter 6). So rather than provide an exhaustive study here, I want to look at Stanislavsky's Six Fundamental Questions of 'Who?', 'Where?', 'When?', 'Why?', 'For what reason?' and 'How?' These six questions cover a range of informational bases, as well as gradually moving your focus from the playwright's text to your own imagination, and then into your interaction with your live scene partner.

## THE SIX FUNDAMENTAL QUESTIONS

### 'WHO?'

'Who am I?' refers to age, gender, occupation, religion, social status, etc., and most of the answers can be found in the text. These details form the springboard from which you can start to make your interpretative leaps. If you were playing Juliet in Shakespeare's *Romeo and Juliet*, your 'Who?' would include: 'I'm a girl, I'm Italian, I'm fifteen, I'm a wealthy Capulet.'

### 'WHERE?'

'Where am I?' is also very straightforward, but can have a number of concentric circles. In Act III of Chekhov's *Three Sisters* (1901), the action takes place in Russia, in a small town many miles away from Moscow, in a house belonging to three sisters and a brother, in a bedroom occupied by two of the sisters. As the focus becomes intensified throughout the act – and more and more characters make various confessions – the real hotspot of the scene is slap-bang centre-stage, with other areas of the onstage bedroom obscured by screens. 'Where am I?' is very important in this scene: 'Am I centre-stage making a confession? Am I obscured behind a screen avoiding a confession? Am I hiding in the wardrobe as a bit of a prank? Am I crossing the stage silently with a candle? Or am I poking my head through the bedroom door looking for my wife?' The broad brushstrokes and the moment-by-moment specifics are equally important. In fact, 'Where?' is almost one of your most important given circumstances. Just take a moment to notice how differently you behave according to whether you're in a classroom, down the pub with some mates, at your girlfriend's parents' house, or in a church. 'Where?' can highlight for you just how many social masks you wear and when each one comes to the fore. Two possible 'Where?'s for Juliet are: 'I'm in Verona, and I'm in a sepulchre' – that's a broad brushstroke and a specific detail, each of which will stimulate your imagination differently. (We'll note in Chapter 6 how important 'Where?' is for Adler.)

'When am I there?' is also more textured then may at first appear. Wherever you are right now as you read this book, just make a note of the time. Other than by looking at your watch, how do you know what time it is? Is the warm sun streaming through the window? Is the late-night music pounding from the local pub? Can you see the strange light from the snow lying thick outside? Is the smell of the morning coffee dancing its way up from the kitchen? 'When?' is dictated by all sorts of elements other than the hands on a clock face. All five senses are drawn into our appreciation of time. How are you feeling as you read this book? Is it the day before you're due to hand in an assignment on acting processes, so you're begrudgingly trudging through as many books as you can? Is it Christmas morning and you received this as a gift? Are you browsing through it in a bookshop as you wait to meet your best friend for lunch in half an hour? Intriguingly (as we've seen with affective memory), the present tense is constantly influenced by the past and the future, be it consciously or unconsciously. Some people prefer clocks with hands and faces as opposed to LED displays: they visually want to experience the present moment in relation to what lies before and after, whereas the LED display only gives them that moment. For Juliet: 'Is it two days before I'm supposed to marry Paris or a moment after I wake to find a dead Romeo?'

Most of the answers to the first three questions – Who? Where? When? – are provided by the writer. As you delve into the script to find the answers, your creative juices will begin to stir, as your senses are drawn into the full implications of the imaginative answers.

The fourth question, 'Why?' takes us into the realm of objectives (detailed below). For the moment, let's consider this question from two perspectives: (1) 'What does your character want?' and (2) 'Why has the playwright written this scene?' The answers to these two questions stimulate two different but complementary avenues of inquiry. (1) Discovering what your character wants begins to ignite the rhythm and drive of your personal narrative. (Your answer is *subjective*.) (2) Discovering why the playwright has written this scene unlocks more information about your character's 'function' in the dramatic structure. (Your answer is *objective*.) Unless it's a one-person play, you're just one piece in a more complex puzzle. So, understanding your character's function helps you to give it the most appropriate weight: playing the Apothecary as if he's Lord Montague would pull *Romeo and Juliet* completely out of shape.

The function also influences the choices you make in understanding how your character contributes to the play's meaning. By 'the play's meaning', I'm referring to the writer's **superobjective**: 'Why did they write the play? What was the driving force stirring them to commit to paper these characters and this story? Is this a play exposing the corruption of the legal system? Is this a docudrama celebrating the abolition of slavery? Is this a farce revealing the absurdity of sexual antics, or a tragedy exploring the fighting between two neighbouring houses?' If I'm a guest artist in a television hospital drama, then my relationship to the regular medics probably forms the heart of my character's journey. In and of itself, my part may not be that significant, beyond providing a story which highlights the personality of the regular character.

Making decisions about 'Why?' our character is in the scene begins to take us into the realm of our imaginations. While some of the answers are provided by the writer, we start to bring in our own interpretative skills.

### 'FOR WHAT REASON?'

'For what reason?' takes us even further into the realm of imagination. In English, the questions 'Why?' and 'For what reason?' can seem very similar. However, the words are quite different in Russian, and it was only through one of my own Russian acting masters, Vladimir Ananyev (1955–), that I really understood the difference between the two questions. I was playing Pimple the maid in Goldsmith's (c.1728–74) *She Stoops to Conquer* (1771) at the National Theatre, London, and one of my scenes involved the very simple task of bringing in a tray of ingredients for Mr Hardcastle (the master of the house). After seeing my performance, Ananyev provoked me with a series of questions to open up my character's 'For what reason?'

'Why does Pimple bring in the tray?' he asked.

'To help Mr Hardcastle prepare a punch for his guests,' I replied, 'that's my objective.'

'For what reason does she want to help Mr Hardcastle prepare for his guests?' Ananyev provoked. After I'd stuttered some uncertain answers, he came up with a scenario along the following lines: Pimple wants to help Mr Hardcastle as best she can because, if he thinks she's doing a good job, he might reward her with a pay rise. Then, the next time she's at the market, she can afford that lovely shawl she saw, and if she's wearing that shawl, she might catch the eye of the Lord of the adjacent manor, who has been paying her some attention. If she can secure that attention, he might actually fall for her, and he might even propose to her, and thus she might raise her status from Pimple the Maid to Lady Pimple.

All these answers to a series of 'For what reason?' questions were pure imagination. There was nothing in the text to suggest they might be there. The audience didn't know about them. The director certainly never knew about them. But suddenly I had a whole series of imaginary provocations, which injected my simple scene with a dimension that made it increasingly pleasurable to play. I had an entire secret scenario, which boosted the objectives behind my behaviour and gave me what Stanislavsky calls 'a second plan', which is like the part of the iceberg hidden under the water. I really 'owned' my performance of this very simple role, with an individuality that until that moment I hadn't really thought was possible.

'For what reason?' helps you to individualise your part in whatever way makes it imaginatively fulsome for you. I repeat: these answers needn't be shared with anyone; they needn't take up rehearsal time; and they certainly shouldn't distract from the clear storytelling. But the imagination is a vital tool for actors. Directors may not want to spend hours discussing what your character had for breakfast, but if you feel more creatively excited by imagining that your character is wealthy enough to have smoked haddock rather than a bowl of cornflakes, or they're too busy on Wall Street to have anything other than a cup of coffee, or they're too concerned about their cholesterol to have anything other than porridge with hot water, then who's to stop you? If these imaginings fuel you and give your interpretations colour, resonance and texture, and – I repeat – *as long as they don't make your acting self-indulgent* or *obscure the story* or *take up valuable rehearsal time*, then exploring this kind of imaginary territory can be invaluable.

### 'HOW?'

The final question, 'How?', is one which really can't be answered. If you know the answers to all the other questions, then your 'How?' will change in every performance or every take, according to your genuine dynamic listening and responding to the other actors. 'How?' is really your 'being in the moment', and you won't know the answer until you get there. (The nuances of 'How?' are at the heart of Meisner's Repetition exercises: you don't know *how* you're going to say something until you get out on stage with your partner to listen and respond. Without your partner, you can't predict *how* you're going to behave.)

So you see, the Six Fundamental Questions are answered through a combination of cerebral detective work on a script, imaginative work on your own, and interactive work with your scene partners.

There are other elements of thought-centred detective work which also require close analysis of the text, though curiously, text analysis brings with it a controversy of responses. American actor-trainer Harold Guskin believes that it can weaken an actor's instinctive responses and over-neaten their performance edges. Robert de Niro, on the other hand, is reputed to do as much research as possible, so that no other actor could conceivably be playing the part but him. Mamet eschews text analysis, saying that the writer has done that work for you already, so just get on with playing the lines. That's probably because Mamet is a genius writer. I'd suggest that the less layered the writing, the more preparation is required of us, so it's worth getting into the habit. And as long as your textual analysis is charged by creative curiosity rather than detached intellectualism, then it can only do good.

OBJECTIVES

At some point in rehearsals, most actors want to work out their objectives. An objective is basically a want, desire, need, drive, goal, task, intention: all these words are used by different practitioners on different occasions. Most would probably concur that your objective is a goal which could actually be *achieved* if all the actions you used to pursue that objective were successful. In other words, it should be realisable and not abstract.

When you're approaching a scene, there are various, simple questions you can ask yourself to connect you with the power of objectives.

1  What do I, as my character, want or need in this scene? (As Juliet, maybe: 'I want to woo Romeo.' Just be aware, though, that we don't always *want* what we *need*. I need to pay my rent, but I don't necessarily want to go out tonight and do my twelve-hour taxi shift. But I do *want* a juicy steak, rather than a take-out hamburger – though all I really *need* is food in my belly.)

2  What am I going to do to get what I want or need? (The actions you choose to pursue your objective can be very simple physical tasks. As Juliet: 'I'm going to hang out on the balcony, even though I should be in bed.' Say my objective is: 'I want/need you to lend me £2000.' To make sure I successfully achieve my objective, I want to be sure you're in the most propitious mood when I ask you. So I prepare your favourite burrito supper, take off your coat when you come in, settle you down on the sofa, open a bottle of wine, pour you a glass, and ask you about your day. Little by little, I execute a series of simple physical tasks to prepare the ground for achieving my ultimate objective. At the same time, I undertake a series of inner actions: I comfort you, relax you, nurture you, basically knead you like clay until you're soft enough to mold.)

3  What obstacles arise to prevent me from achieving my objective? (As Juliet: 'My mother, my father, and the eternal feud with the Montagues are getting in my way.' As far as the £2000 is concerned, maybe you arrive home late, so the supper is burnt. You're in a bad mood because your business partner

screwed up a deal. You don't want any wine because the stress has given you a headache.)

4   What adjustments do I have to make to get what I want? (As Juliet: 'I make out that I will marry Paris, so that my parents don't rumble my real plan.' As for the £2000 scenario, I bin the burnt burritos and I rustle up a little snack from whatever's in the fridge. I stuff a cork back in the bottle and I work harder through the tone of my voice and my body language to overcome the unexpected hurdle of you being in a bad mood. In other words, I empathise more with the state you're already in. Whatever happens, I mustn't create any undue antagonism to put you in a more tense, less accepting state of mind – or I'll never get the 2K.)

The crucial aspect of objectives is that they're entirely based on your onstage partners. As we'll see with the emotion-centre below, the most important thing in your environment is your fellow people and how, through your actions, you can change them and transform the situation – for better or worse, depending on your character. Therefore, it's impossible to set any objectives in stone without taking into account the choices made by your other actors. ('Romeo chooses to make love to me.' Yippee! 'Paris chooses to ask my father for my hand in marriage.' Shucks!)

You'll only know whether or not you're successful in achieving your goal by observing your other actors and seeing what effect you have on them. ('Does Romeo come back to the balcony when I call him? Yes!') If you're not successful in achieving your objectives, you'll have to change your actions – in other words, your objective *defines* your actions. ('Does my father accept the fact that I don't want to marry Paris? No! Therefore, I'll have to make out that I will marry him.')

## BITS OF ACTION

One of the soundest ways of unlocking a script is to break it into its **bits of action**. These are sometimes called 'units' or 'beats'. 'Bits' is a literal translation of Stanislavsky's original Russian term *kusok*: 'bit' is a straightforward word and implies any size or shape, whereas 'unit' can seem overly regular. Apparently 'beat' comes from the émigrés of the MAT (including Boleslavsky and Ouspenskaya) in the 1920s saying 'bit' to their American students with very strong Russian accents. Whatever the origins, 'beat' is also a good word, as it implies rhythm and musicality – both of which are very useful concepts for text analysis. I'd suggest you use 'bit' or 'beat' or even 'unit' according to whatever excites you most creatively. Again, there are many good books illustrating how to break down a piece of text into its bits of action. (In fact, I detail the process both in *Konstantin Stanislavsky* [2003] and *The Complete Stanislavsky Toolkit* [2007]). So here's just a brief outline.

A bit of action may last from about two lines to half a page depending on the nature of the scene and the playing of the tactics, though in the early stages of working on a script, it's advisable not to break the scene down into too many small chunks or you'll lose sight of the bigger picture. As Stanislavsky put it, look for where the river completely changes its course, rather than noting all the kinks in the banks.

There are often 'bleeds' between one bit and another, where one character has clearly changed tactic, but another is still hooked on the previous energy. British director Katie Mitchell suggests that you determine the beginning of a new bit when the maximum number of people is affected by the change in the river's course. To some extent, this strategy accommodates the 'bleeds'.

You can often spot where a new bit has started because a character enters or exits the scene; a character changes the subject matter; or a character clearly adopts a new tactic (for example, one minute they were soothing you, now they're berating you).

Some practitioners like to label the bits, so that they can get a sense of the dynamic flow. I have no hard and fast rules about how to name bits of action: I firmly believe that whatever works collectively for those playing the scene is fine. Labels for a bit can be as specific or as broad as is useful. Broad labels might include: The Meeting; The Seduction; The Rejection; The Closure. More imagistic labels might include: Casing the Joint; Sussing the Options; Giving him the Cold Shoulder; Quitting the Joint. You might want to attach certain characters to the different bits: Romeo and Rosaline meet; Romeo seduces Rosaline; Rosaline rejects Romeo; Romeo and Rosaline mutually conclude the encounter. It's simply a question of whatever fuels the director and the actors working on the scene.

All you're really doing when you break a scene down into bits is marking the streets along which you're walking as you get to know the town. If your objective is in effect your destination, the bits of action are the A–Z of roads to get you there – unless, of course, you get lost, and then your objective is thwarted.

## ACTIONING

For some practitioners, the round-the-table preparatory work also includes working out some possible line-by-line inner actions for the play. This process is often called **actioning** a text, and is most extensively used in the UK by director Max Stafford-Clark in an evolution of a process introduced by Stella Adler (see Chapter 6). Actioning involves labelling each line of your script with a transitive verb, indicating what you're trying to do to your onstage partner: e.g. 'I educate you', 'I threaten you', 'I delight you', 'I undermine you', 'I correct you', 'I entreat you'. (These are all inner actions directed towards your scene partners.) This kind of preparatory work can be wonderfully precise, encouraging you to dissect each line of a speech, so that you soon realise how, in every moment, you're using subtly different strategies to affect your partners and achieve your objective. Of course, you can only name your actions *in relation to what your fellow actor is doing*, as your actions will always be reactions (with moments of decision) to what your fellow actor is doing to you. This is why Stafford-Clark involves everyone who is in a scene in the process of actioning. It's another way of creating a 'score' to guide your building of a character.

As with objectives and bits of action, the labels you initially choose with actioning may well change as you get to know the terrain better. However, they give you a rock-solid starting point, ensuring that everyone in the scene has a common vocabulary and a shared view of the foundations upon which the scene might build. (The best book on 'actioning' is Stafford-Clark's *Letters to George* [1997)].) In some ways, your objective is your destination, the bits of action are the main roads, and the line-by-line actions are the little streets linking the main roads.

By now, you've: (1) looked at the given circumstances (which, for some directors, also includes making lists of all the things your character says about themselves and all the things other characters say about you); (2) sussed out some juicy objectives to activate your needs or desires; (3) broken the scenes down into some building blocks or 'bits of action'; and (4) pinpointed some potential line-by-line inner actions (in collaboration with your fellow actors, using insights gained from the choices they're making).

You should also look at the language, imagery and punctuation your character uses. Are the sentences long and complex? Or is the language streetwise slang? Do they ask lots of questions? Do they express themselves directly or obliquely? The text is a series of clues and codes for you to decipher.

If you've done all this thought-centred work, you're well on your way to understanding the text and your character's thought processes.

The second of Stanislavsky's inner psychological drives – the emotion-centre – is our next focus in building a character. I repeat: all three centres – thought, emotion and action – are absolutely interconnected, and separating them is always going to be some-what artificial. Yet, given the unavoidably linear structure of a book, you can still extract some useful things by looking at them separately.

## THE EMOTION-CENTRE

The emotion-centre is probably the most controversial of Stanislavsky's inner psychological drives, not least because of the tricksy nature of our emotions as we saw in Chapter 2. However, if you've done the work on training your emotions through affective memory or other psycho-physical exercises – becoming more emotionally accessible both to all sorts of imaginative stimuli and to your onstage partners – then using your emotion-centre for building a character should be quite straightforward.

I'd suggest that there are three ways to do this. (1) Find a parti-cular lure or hook that propels you into the character's narrative. That lure is a point of connection which ignites your own sense of empathy and your creative desire to 'get inside' the character. (Finding this lure is your own, private work.) (2) Ensure that you then remain emotionally accessible in rehearsal to everything your partners are doing and to the given circumstances of the play. That way, you're really building your character in relation *to other people* and *to the environment* and, as we saw in Chapter 2, it's those very interactions with other people and the environment that provoke our emotions. (3) Respond to the actions that your emotions prompt; don't forget that emotions are calls to action, and actions are the very basis of acting. We've already seen how spontaneous, real-life emotions involve *actions* directed towards *other people* to achieve an *objective* in order to *change a situation*. As we already know, emotions are *physical* and *interactive*.

Your own lure. Your objectives aimed at your partners within the given circumstances. Your actions. These are three major inroads to your emotion-centre. Before we look at these three inroads in more detail, let's just clarify a few general things about 'living the part', so that we keep on the inroads and don't send ourselves up the garden path.

### LIVING THE PART

We tend to think that when Stanislavsky – and then Strasberg, following in the footsteps of Boleslavsky and Ouspenskaya – said we must *live the part*, that we have to feel the anger, shed the tears, laugh from the belly just like the character does. (See 'Where life and acting differ' later in this chapter.) Actually, characters don't 'feel' anything – they're just lines on a page. Characters are nothing more than a series of clues in black ink, which we – through our inner psychological drives and our imaginations – turn into 'believable', three-dimensional beings. *We* do whatever feeling might be necessary. And that's why our actor-training is so necessary: to condition our emotion-centre so that by the time we get to rehearsals and performances, we know we've done all the inner preparatory work to be open and accessible to the details of the play. Indeed, a director will usually assume you've done all that preparatory work on yourself, so there may be little specific emotion-orientated work in rehearsals.

So, let's look at the first major inroad into our emotion-centre: the lures. The starting question here is: 'How do we find the lures?'

There are two invaluable tools in your toolkit which will help you: imagination and objectives. We'll take each one in turn, beginning with *imagination*.

## IMAGINATION AND THE MAGIC 'IF'

As we saw with affective memory, one of the huge contributors to your emotional experience is your imagination, and your imagination will help you find your own personal lure into the character.

To do this, start by looking at the given circumstances of your character and then ask yourself: 'What would *I* do *if I* were in this situation … ?' This simple question is what Stanislavsky calls the Magic 'If'. The 'if' part is important because it appeals to all the possibilities that lie in your imagination, and it's 'magic' because it catapults you headlong into the world of the play. 'What if … ' lies at the heart of all children's games: 'What if I were a pirate? What if this broom were a pony? What if I had a genie in this bottle? What if this potion could make me appear dead?' The magic allows for anything to happen or exist, restricted only by the boundaries of your imagination. You could almost say it's the bedrock of Stanislavsky's 'system', because it combines so wonderfully relaxation and imagination.

## AS IF

The Magic 'If' has been adapted in various schools of acting to 'as if'. 'As if' is different, but connected. On the one hand, the Magic 'If' invites you to take the imaginative leap directly into the given circumstances of the play: 'What would I do *if* I were married to a Scottish laird called Macbeth, and I knew he had the potential to be the King of Scotland?' On the other hand, 'as if' invites you to find circumstances from your own life, which are comparable and easy to connect with. So, you might approach the role of Lady Macbeth: '*as if* I were trying to convince my boyfriend that he shouldn't have been picked as the reserve for the football team – he should be the goddamn captain!'

## ADJUSTMENT, JUSTIFICATION, SUBSTITUTION, TRANSFERENCE, PARTICULARISATION

You may encounter the idea of 'as if' through a number of other terms. It's similar to Evgeny Vakhtangov's (1883–1922) idea of 'adjustment' or 'justification', where you draw upon situations or motivations which have nothing to do with the play itself, but which galvanise a direct, organic connection between something that means something to you and the circumstances of the character. 'As if' is also associated sometimes with 'substitution' (a term from Uta Hagen, which she later changed to 'transference') – for example, you imagine that the actor lying dead as Romeo is your real-life boyfriend. It's also connected with Meisner's 'particularisation', where you adjust the text in your head to connect with something that has a particular resonance for you. So, if you're playing Konstantin in Chekhov's *The Seagull*, and your mother, Arkadina, calls you a 'Decadent', you might 'translate' that in your imagination to whatever you most dread your own mother calling you: a 'drop-out', a 'waster', an 'elitist prick', or whatever *particularly* goads you.

Whichever of these versions you adopt, just be sure that your 'as if' doesn't become too pedestrian or you'll divert yourself too far away from the realm and dimensions of the script. Ultimately, though, I'd suggest you use whatever tool works for you – as long as you're telling the story for the audience's benefit. The Magic 'If' and its various evolutions are simply means of luring you into the world of the play, finding the umbilical cord that connects you directly and pulsingly with the act of building the character. To some extent – as long your acting doesn't become self-absorbed – it's nobody's business what helps you to access the appropriate 'thin skin'. And once you've found a trigger into the role, your creative journey is so much easier – though there are some cautions.

### CAUTIONS ABOUT USING YOUR OWN LIFE FOR LURES

While finding the lure into your character is usually very intuitive, some actors consciously trawl through their own emotional memory-bank to find a direct link between the lines on the page and their personal experience.

'And why shouldn't they?' you may well ask. 'After all, what's the difference between using a substitution or an "as if" and trawling your emotional storehouse?'

There is a difference, but it's subtle. Suppose the scene involves your character visiting their dying mother. You could either go into the scene substituting (in your imagination) the actress in front of you with your own mother and talking to her *as if* you were talking to your own mother. Or, as your private homework before rehearsals, you could recall the time you went to visit your dying uncle, tapping into all the sense memories surrounding that experience to awaken your affective memory.

Sometimes this second process can be very immediate and effective. However, I'd suggest there are a few more details you should know about emotion memory and how it works in everyday life to give you a better understanding of why affective memory may not be very reliable when applied directly to a play (apart from the fact that the writer didn't necessarily know you or your mother or your uncle when they wrote the play, so all the script details – language, objectives, subtext, etc. – are likely to be completely different from how you would behave with your own family).

### BROKEN SHARDS, NOT MOVIES

As we touched on in Chapter 2, the hardwiring involved in our brain's interpretation of an emotional experience *even as it happens* is fairly unreliable. That process becomes even more unreliable when you're dealing with memories of past experiences – because memory *changes* events. There's no doubt that affective memory in actor-training can be very useful as an awakening tool, but if you're hoping to hunt out a specific memory from your own past to apply to a specific event in the play's narrative, you could find the process rather more slippery.

That's because your brain can only store a certain number of key impressions and words, particularly when you've had a traumatic experience. And it doesn't matter whether it happened seven years ago or seven minutes ago: shock can zone out the unnecessary details, so that when you recall the event, the imagination has to fill in the blanks with some educated guesswork. As psychologist Dylan Evans puts it, it's more like 'reconstructing an old antique pot from a few broken shards than replaying an old movie'. Although it may seem as though some of your memories are re-living the event exactly as it happened, it's just 'an illusion caused by the power of our imaginative reconstruction' (Evans, 2001:80). The simple alert is: don't expect that recalling your grandfather's death will necessarily help you play Hamlet.

The second (potentially more reliable) tool for helping you find a lure is your *objective*, a tool which links very directly with the thought-centre (as we saw earlier in this chapter). It also merges us into the second major inroad to your emotion-centre: your *given circumstances* and your *onstage partners*.

## EMOTIONS AND OBJECTIVES

Do you remember Mowrer's belief in Chapter 2 that our emotions ultimately boil down to two aspects – pleasure (satisfaction) and pain (dissatisfaction)? This is actually a very useful principle to apply when building a character. If we pursue an objective and we're successful (i.e. we affect the other person, we change the situation and we get what we want), then we experience pleasurable emotions: we're amused, contented, excited, proud, relieved or satisfied. (The baby gets its milk, so it stops crying and it's satisfied.) If we're unsuccessful (i.e. we don't affect the other person, we don't change the situation, so we don't get what we want), we experience painful emotions: we're angry, disgusted, embarrassed, afraid, guilty, sad, ashamed or dissatisfied. (So if the baby doesn't get its milk, it carries on crying, afraid that it's been abandoned.)

Take a moment to look at the character you're building. Suppose it's Shakespeare's Richard III. Notice how often he does achieve his objectives and gets what he wants. You could say that the texture of his emotional state is one of satisfaction and pleasure. Take Willy Loman in Miller's *Death of a Salesman*. Notice how rarely he achieves his objective: he loses his job, he falls out with his family, he tumbles into despair. You could say that the texture of his emotional state is one of dissatisfaction and pain. You don't have to indicate those emotional states to the audience, but just by taking an overview of whether a character tends to achieve their objectives or not, you'll begin to get a flavour of their emotional temperature and terrain. Then you can start to find the specifics of how they pursue their objectives and manifest their emotions.

I propose that if you play your objectives precisely scene by scene by scene, while really attending to your partner and noticing whether or not they're genuinely affected by what you're doing (through their faces, their reactions, their words, their silences and subtexts), you'll find that you can't help but have an emotional connection to the dialogue. Which brings us onto the third major inroad into the emotion-centre: *action*.

In fact, the action-centre is a whole inner psychological drive in its own right, which we'll come onto shortly. Before we do, however, there are a few final cautions about the emotion-centre, which are worth your while noting, because the way our emotions operate in everyday life is quite different from the way they operate when we're involved in playing a character. Let's take a moment to look at those differences.

## WHERE LIFE AND ACTING DIFFER

For all his brilliant pioneering into acting, Stanislavsky got some things wrong. As a young, rather head-bound actor looking for emotional liberation, he was extremely impressed by the words of the great Italian tragedian Tommaso Salvini (1829–1915):

> If you do not weep in the agony of grief, if you do not blush with shame, if you do not glow with love, if you do not tremble with terror, if your eyes do not become bloodshot with rage, if, in short, you yourself do not intimately experience whatever befits the diverse characters and passions you present, you can never thoroughly transfuse into the hearts of your audience the sentiment of the situation.
>
> (cited in Archer, 1957:112)

The idea that you 'intimately experience whatever befits the diverse characters' is highly dubious as an acting strategy, because the way we use our emotions for our professional work is quite different from the way our emotions operate in everyday life. Whatever our forefathers in previous centuries may have maintained, there's no point beating ourselves up because we don't feel Juliet's fear or Othello's jealousy, because that's not actually the way our human natures operate.

As we all know, emotions in life can arise quite unexpectedly. They may last just a few moments or linger for several hours. In absolute contrast, emotions onstage or in front of a camera have to be expressed at a certain time in a certain place and last for a certain length of time. This fact alone suggests that the kind of emotions we experience in our acting work must be very different from those we experience in everyday life.

Not least, there's the crucial addition of adrenaline. Whether we're waiting for the shout 'Action!' or we're about to do a first run-through or a fiftieth performance, there's a level of excitement involved that inevitably colours the nature of our emotional experience. What the *character* is supposed to be feeling (bearing in mind that lines on a page don't 'feel' *anything*) and what *you're* actually feeling could be absolutely polar: Lear may be over-whelmed with despair at Cordelia's death, but you come off stage feeling totally exhilarated.

## KONIJN'S TASK-EMOTIONS

Dutch psychologist Elly A. Konijn has monitored actors in all kinds of acting situations, including monologues. She discovered that, whatever the emotional content of the character's speech, the actors' heart rates reached extremes of 180 beats per minute. Compare this to the average person's resting pulse (60 beats per minute), and a parachutist's pulse just before jumping (which can reach 140 beats). So the adrenaline rush of a monologue can be greater than a parachute jump! And this was regardless of the content of the speech, which might be very calm or totally laid back.

Konijn calls the emotions used by actors 'task-emotions'. These are emotional states that essentially enable you to do your job, i.e. tell a story and take an audience on an appropriate journey. Through extensive interviews, scientific experiments and questionnaires for her study *Acting Emotions* (1997), she came to the conclusion that your task-emotions as an actor are 're-designed' versions of your real emotions: they have the relevant external form and details, so that they look like real emotions, but ultimately they gear your focus towards crafting the play (getting on with your professional 'task') regardless of what your actual emotional state might be (e.g. excitable, fatigued, terrified, wired, etc.). Basically,

Konijn has given new terminology to something that we do automatically as actors. We balance our actual inner state with the processes demanded by the play's narrative. In other words, we integrate our understanding of the character's emotional journey with the actual fact of being on a stage or in front of a camera plying our professional trade.

## HORNBY'S IMAGINARY EMOTIONS

Another term given to the kinds of emotions used by actors in performance is 'imaginary emotions'. This phrase comes from American actor-trainer Richard Hornby and in his provocative book, *The End of Acting* (1992), he compares and contrasts the basic qualities of real emotions with those of imaginary emotions. The qualities of real emotions are as follows: they can be aroused quickly; they can subside slowly; they're often painful; and they're difficult to control. Imaginary emotions, on the other hand: can be aroused slowly; they subside quickly; they're always pleasurable to experience; and they're easily controlled. They have to be: speed is of the essence. My character might be very angry in Scene ii and very jolly in Scene iii: clearly I can't use real emotions, as that's not how real emotions operate and I wouldn't be able to do my job.

## TEARS AND TECHNIQUE

The real thorny issue of acting and emotion can be boiled down to crying, or, as the eighteenth-century philosophers would have put it, 'irresistible weeping'. Although all mammals have tear ducts, it seems that only human beings weep – monkeys don't – which indicates that the whole process of crying has come late in evolution. Why this evolutionary process happened at all, who knows? But as actors, it shines the spotlight on 'Do I feel it?' or 'Do I fake it?' And weeping bothers us because all that water and snot are very hard to fake: which is why tear sticks exist. A tear stick is a small stick, very much like a lipsalve. When the light grease is gently smeared under your eyes, it quickly causes your tears to flow and your nose to run. It's used a good deal in film and television, where numerous takes and close-ups might otherwise literally dry you out.

(You might like to know that the chemical content of distress tears and crocodile tears are apparently different. So don't worry that, if you're using a tear-stick, you're not being truthful. A quick swab in a science lab would probably prove that, even if you've generated the tears yourself, they're still not *emotionally* 'true' – unless you're genuinely in distress. And I'd say that anyone genuinely distressed by the experience of performing shouldn't be an actor in the first place.)

Despite popular belief, being emotional does not equate to good acting. Otherwise, as Group Theatre founding-member Robert Lewis (1909–97) once said, his Aunt Fanny would be winning Oscars. Of course, good acting can certainly *lead* to emotions being stirred. Actors as diverse as Judi Dench (1934–) and Kevin Bacon (1958–) are wonderfully 'thin-skinned'. They also have great technique. As Chapter 2 illustrated, technique is not a dirty word, it's the springboard into emotional accessibility. Charles Marowitz cites a conversation with the director of the Moscow Art Theatre, Viktor Stanitsyn (1897–1976), in the early 1960s:

'Are the tears real?' I asked Stanitsyn, referring to the innumerable lachrymose outbursts one found in the [MAT's] Chekhov performances. 'In almost all cases they are,' he explained. 'And if the actor has got to reach a high emotional climax and just does not feel it, what does he do?' I asked. 'He relies on technique,' Stanitsyn answered, 'but the technique of our performers is so good that when a performer reaches such a climax, he is *really* there and he doesn't have to fall back on indications.'

(Marowitz, 1978:24)

If your training and technique are founded on relaxation, concentration of attention, observation, imagination and emotional accessibility, you won't go far wrong.

The key issues to remember when you're unearthing the emotional nature of your character are: (1) play your objectives with utter commitment and the highest possible stakes within the given circumstances of the scene; (2) listen to yourself and your partner; and (3) give your imagination free rein. If you allow yourself to believe in your character's situation and the actions you take in that situation, you'll usually find you can tap into the right emotional seam.

Action plus Involvement-in-that-Action leads to the appropriate Emotional Experience.

So now let's find those Actions.

## THE ACTION-CENTRE

If you've done the textual work with your thought-centre and harnessed your imagination to your emotion-centre, then your body (your action-centre) will be bursting to make some discoveries of its own. We know acting is psycho-physical: the body is one of the most important and immediate ways of accessing the life-blood of a script, and yet, as we've seen, rehearsal processes all too often short-circuit its true input. There's one rehearsal process, however, that goes straight to the body's 'intelligence': Stanislavsky's Active Analysis.

### ACTIVE ANALYSIS

Stanislavsky was exploring this approach to rehearsal at the very end of his life and it was recorded by one of his assistant directors, Maria Knebel (1898–1985), in her book *On the Active Analysis of Plays and Roles* (published in Russian in 1982. In 2002, I commissioned friend and Russian scholar Mike Pushkin to translate the book orally and I then transcribed his recordings. I emailed the transcription to a couple of contacts in UK and USA, and it has subsequently found its way into the international arena, so you may find you can access it yourself.)

The joy of Active Analysis is that you never take the paper-and-glue script out onto the rehearsal room floor. Through a simple sequence, repeated over and over, you work towards a dead-letter-perfect performance. The sequence is: (1) read the scene; (2) discuss the scene; (3) improvise the scene; (4) discuss the improvisation; and (5) re-read the scene, noting where your improvisation was very close to the playwright's script and where something was completely forgotten and why.

There's an increasing number of books available detailing Active Analysis, including Sharon M. Carnicke's *Stanislavsky in Focus* (2009) and my own *Beyond Stanislavsky* (2001). Here and now, I'll focus on the benefits of Active Analysis in terms of working your body into building a character.

## FINDING THE PICTURES

The reason why the process is called Active Analysis is that, from Day One of rehearsals, you analyse the scene actively, i.e. *through your body*. The sequence of the necessary actions and the relevant stage pictures (i.e. the *mise-en-scène* or 'the putting on the stage') emerge organically through your improvisations, as you discover intuitively what you need to do and where you need to go in relation to the other actors and the set. It's hard to make the 'wrong move', as you only move according to what feels natural, impulsive and appropriate in the imaginative circumstances so that you can achieve your objective. You're utterly dependent on your fellow actors and their intuitive choices, so a very intensive ensemble is built right from the start.

The director simply observes what's going on and begins to shape what occurs naturally. At some point, they may need to fix the stage pictures, so that the production has an aesthetic coherence, and sometimes they may even have to impose a move. With psycho-physically open actors, it's not a problem: after all, it has to happen in film and television (as we'll see in Chapter 5). As Hornby suggests, a director can either say, 'Cross downstage left' or 'Humiliate the bastard', and you understand that these are simply different ways of dealing with the same issue. You should know your instrument well enough by now to mentally adapt the instruction to whatever you need in order to breathe the appropriate, imaginative impulse into the move.

## OWNING THE TEXT

Having directed several full-length plays using Active Analysis (including American realism, German Expressionism and Russian melodrama), I know it's always exciting, invariably challenging and ultimately wildly liberating for the actors. There's no 'block the play in three days, then learn the lines'; rather, lines seem to learn themselves by a wonderful osmosis through the constant re-reading, improvising and discussing. As a result, the actors are very calm in performance because they've learned their lines through a process of 'ownership', where valid thought processes, credible stage pictures and dynamic listening are almost unavoidable.

### TESTING THE BOUNDARIES

With Active Analysis, your imagination has to be like a child's: instant, unfettered by your inner policeman, inventive and bold. Rehearsing is about bravery and the irreverent risks we talked about in Chapter 2: often by going too far, by giving too much, you uncover the boundaries of what might work. In fact, Stanislavsky used melodrama a great deal in his laboratories, because he felt that melodrama's extremes of emotion were invaluable learning models. The actors had to find the heights of passion while keeping their sense of truth firmly rooted.

Having found the extremes to which they dared to go, Stanislavsky then encouraged his actors to take away **the little plus**. The 'little plus' is the one tool that we should consciously try to avoid – though most of us have fallen victim to using it at some point. It's when you don't just drink a cup of tea; you *show* the audience you're drinking a cup of tea. You don't just lean against the wall; you *show* the audience you're being casual. Some call it 'telegraphing', some call it 'indicating'; it's that sense of using a little more energy to do or say something than you really need, just to be sure the audience 'gets it'.

In short, Active Analysis binds body, heart and mind in a deliciously creative way, as well as building a rock-solid ensemble.

Ultimately the task of all rehearsal processes – be they traditional or experimental – is to develop an intimate relationship with a writer's work.

## WRITERS

As an actor, you need a performable text. That needn't be a script; it could be a movement or mime score. But for most of us in theatre, film and television, we work with the written word. It may be that you devise this script yourself or you draw your words from real encounters, such as the verbatim dramas which have had a serious resurgence in Britain in the new millennium. Usually it comes from a writer.

If you're lucky enough to be working with a living writer, their contribution to rehearsals is a rich treasure trove. A good writer will

thrive on seeing their imaginative world becoming three-dimen-
sionally manifested, allowing you freedom of interpretation and yet
filling in the blanks when you're simply flummoxed. That said,
legend has it that Ralph Richardson (1902–83) turned down
*Waiting for Godot* (1953) because, when he asked Samuel Beckett
(1906–89) what the play was all about, Beckett uttered words to
the effect of, 'I don't feckin' know!'

## SPEAKING SHAKESPEARE

Shakespeare is probably the actor's 'ultimate' writer. The rehearsal
processes involved in getting inside a Shakespeare text are both the
hardest and the easiest. The 'hardest' because the audience knows
the words you're going to speak almost as well as you do. The
'easiest' because Shakespeare gives you more clues and insights into
human behaviour than any other writer in the world. Again, there
are wonderful books from real experts on acting Shakespeare, so
here are just a few words of advice if you're rehearsing something
from his canon.

### LINGUISTIC ENERGY

Many of the experts – including Cicely Berry, Oliver Ford Davies,
John Barton and Patsy Rodenburg – remind you that the energy
required to speak a Shakespeare text is not a naturalistic energy: it
ain't telly! Berry refers to the fierceness behind the words as burning at a hotter temperature than naturalism, because the poetry
compresses the images, making the language extremely charged.
So, as you prepare yourself for each rehearsal, you need to be
sure that you're in an appropriate 'inner creative state' to be ener-
getically bold. For actor Ford Davies, having the courage to find
that energy in rehearsal involves *needing* the extreme language to
express yourself – finding a necessary extravagance – as if nothing less would accommodate the richness of your character's
experience. For Berry, that energy has to carry you right through
the whole play to the final full-stop: word leads to word; line
leads to line; thought leads to thought; speech leads to speech;
scene leads to scene; act leads to act – until the very last sentence.
Full stop.

You have no choice but to 'enter the size' of Shakespeare's language, because the imagery is key. For Berry, the characters live in their images, and you have to *feel* the language. And each linguistic structure will make you feel different. *Antithesis* (the juxtaposing of two opposite ideas) has the power of a pendulum swing, so you can allow yourself to enter the boldness of extreme images. *Metaphors* appeal to the listener's imagination in their playful collage of images, so you can allow yourself to enjoy the weaving of ideas in your audience's imagination. *Puns* are mischievous and light, and they give us a sense of 'being in the gang' and knowing what we're all talking about, so you can allow yourself an inner gurgle of pleasure with the language. And *monosyllables* often have a weighty, emphatic or portentous tone, so you can allow yourself to let that weight affect you psycho-physically, like the beating of an inner drum. If you can feel the inner quality of each linguistic device, you can catch a flavour of the speaker's personality.

## IAMBIC PENTAMETER

Most of Shakespeare's dramatic verse is written in the living, pulsing force of the **iambic pentameter**. An iamb is a 'foot' of two beats with the stress on the second beat: di-dum. Put five of them together and you get the iambic pentameter. The iamb sounds like a beating heart, which is why the pulse of Shakespeare's language feels so natural. As far as director and scholar John Barton is concerned, you shouldn't get too hung up on the verse or follow it too slavishly; do whatever feels right for you and simply use the rhythm to unlock the natural thought processes.

## SUBTEXT AND PSYCHOLOGY

Pinpointing what the character is thinking is vitally important with any play: all the more so with Shakespeare, when the language and the references can seem strange to us at first. If you have a sense of what the character is *thinking*, then you'll understand what the character is *doing*. Some scholars argue that there's no subtext in Shakespeare: what a character says is what they think. I disagree: Iago may confide to the audience exactly what he's going to do to Othello, but then when we actually see them talking, we have a real sense of the distance between what Iago is saying and what he's thinking. And that distance creates subtext.

Other scholars argue that there's no 'psychology' in Shakespeare, since his plays were written before the science of psychology was formalised. Again, I disagree: just because something didn't have a label in the sixteenth century doesn't mean it didn't exist. For me as an actor, psychology is the study of the spirit, the behaviour, the essence of the person and how that essence is revealed through interactions with other people. And that's been going on since the fish crawled out of the water, whether Shakespeare's audience had a name for it or not.

Ford Davis backs this up, pointing out that the multitude of disguises, role-playings and theatrical illusions in Shakespeare's plays indicate the fervour with which he used drama as a laboratory for exploring human identities. (And if that doesn't have some psychological resonance, I'm not sure what does.) It's very useful to understand the conflicts *within* the characters – which are often (though not exclusively) bound up with their disguises and social identities. It might be Viola wrestling with her disguise as Orsino's page, or Othello wrestling with his dignity and jealousy. These inner wranglings about who we are become even clearer (as Ford Davies suggests) if you think of the characters' speeches as living, unfurling, thought processes, rather than set patterns: they flit and change and counterpoint from one moment to the next moment. With any play – classical or modern – I'd suggest you don't need to worry too much about finding an arc or a through-line for your character (a superobjective), as you don't want to obliterate the contradictions. Shakespeare wrote about fleshy, inconsistent people, just as Anton Chekhov and Arthur Miller did; as we've seen in Chapter 3, it's a character's inconsistency that makes them seem real.

## THE POWER OF PUNCTUATION

The punctuation itself can help you unlock a character's inner life. As Rodenburg points out, full-stops, question marks and exclamation marks tell you that the thought is complete, while commas, colons and semi-colons reveal how a thought is twisting, turning, diverting and re-shaping. So just by looking at the black dots on the page, you can start to morph the text into indications of living, dancing, inner and outer actions. (On a similar but different tangent, the importance of punctuation is made wonderfully clear in Scott Sedita's *The Eight Characters of Comedy* [2006]. Check out his chapter 'Finding the Funny' for real insight into how to use punctuation to best comic effect.)

All you have to do is look for the clues in a Shakespeare text, and the language gives you exactly what you need to build a character.

## RUN-THROUGHS

You now have a heap of tools in your kit, and your experience of creating a role should be gaining in texture. As the rehearsal period unfolds, you'll start to do run-throughs – of scenes, of acts, and eventually of the whole play. Different directors have different strategies with run-throughs. Some like to do them as soon as possible once they've found the stage pictures, so that they can get a sense of the play's flow. Others, including Stafford-Clark, leave run-throughs as late as possible, in the knowledge that the one guarantee you have once the play opens is that you'll be running it every night, so it's better to use the rehearsal time to fill in the details that compose the living pictures.

One of the crucial aspects of a run-through is tempo-rhythm: at last you begin to see the montage of scenes, the peaks and troughs of its emotional energy and dramatic climaxes, and you feel the inner pulse of the play.

Whether or not you have any actual props or costumes, you do have the chance to experience the play in its entirety, feeling your character's function in the storytelling, understanding the musicality of the images and the narrative, and appreciating your fellow actors' work. After all, this is the main opportunity you have to watch the scenes in which you don't appear.

## TECHNICAL REHEARSAL

In most theatres, a technical rehearsal is a complete run-through of the play on the stage with costumes, props, lighting, set and sound. Occasionally a tech rehearsal may involve simply hopping from one technical cue to the next in a 'cue-to-cue' run, but this usually only happens if you're touring a play that has already had a full-blown tech.

Technical rehearsals are great, because they give you the chance to walk the set in your full costume, pick up the real props, sit on the real chairs, open the real doors, and acclimatise yourself to the world in which you're going to be living for the next few weeks, without the full pressure being on you. The director, by this stage, is focused on the lighting design, the sound levels, and whether the costumes and set look right under the lights. Because, for once, you're not under the beady attention of their rigorous eye, you have the opportunity to check out all sorts of details – from the auditorium acoustic to the actual staircase (rather than the mock-up lines on the rehearsal room floor). Technical rehearsals can produce a mine of fantastic information for building a character, and those actors who find them either a long, tedious struggle or a half-hearted performance potentially rob themselves of some invaluable last-minute epiphanies.

## DRESS REHEARSALS

There's both a magic and a terror to dress rehearsals. The magic lies in the fact that suddenly the pieces of the jigsaw galvanise: the soundscape, the lighting effects, the darkened auditorium, the projections.

The terror lies in suddenly discovering the performance challenges: your costume change can't be completed in thirty seconds and the intimacy of the rehearsal room seems terrifyingly lost in the vast, black auditorium. However, your vocal energy soon shifts up a gear, the adrenalin has a delicious kick, and the reality of the exciting storytelling begins to dawn upon you.

There's still time to make discoveries about character, as the transformative effect of full costumes, make-up, lights, sound and set can open all sorts of nuances that weren't there in the linoleum-floored, fluorescent-lit, under-sized rehearsal room.

If there's an opportunity to sit in the auditorium during the scenes you're not in, it's a perfect time to see what effects the lighting designer is creating. A good lighting design takes the audience on a very subtle, but profound emotional journey, intelligently complementing the other aspects of the storytelling. Often when you're in the centre of the onstage action, you have no idea of the lighting narrative being painted.

You can also sharpen your understanding of the performance energy needed to tell this story in this space, by sitting in the auditorium and learning from the choices made by your fellow actors.

Technical and dress rehearsals can provide creative gold-dust for alert and curious actors.

## REHEARSING FOR THE CAMERA

In the realm of film and television, where rehearsal time may be extremely limited, you may have to make many of the discoveries about character (described throughout this chapter) on your own or with an acting coach. Your interpretation has to be three-dimensional before the first day's shooting, so that all your action and reaction shots are second-nature to you. The director has their eye on so many other components that you need to have your character and emotions ready at a moment's notice: efficiency and effectiveness are the order of the day.

That said, you may be called for a rehearsal a few days before shooting. Usually the room is nothing like the space in which you'll be filming, so you need a certain flexibility with any decisions made. The 'blocking' is crucial (and here I do use the word 'blocking', as it has to be as fixed as you might fix a block of wood). The director is mentally planning the camera positions as much as focusing on your interpretation. You may find that trying to discuss the 'blocking' may not be very fruitful, as so many considerations (beyond your character's motivations) dictate where and when a move has to occur. It's wise to accept the moves you're given and then quietly justify them to yourself so that you feel you 'own' them.

With major movies and leading roles, it may well be you have several weeks' rehearsal – much as you would in theatre. In which case, all your anxieties about turning up on the day and just doing it are allayed.

### ON-SET REHEARSALS

Once you're on set, it's advisable to seize the opportunity wherever you can to run the lines with your fellow actors. It's also good to walk the set (particularly if it's a kitchen or an office where your character lives or works): you want to feel at home in the space and to be very easy with any props you have to handle. That's unless, of course, the set is 'hot'. 'Hot' means that the shooting has been temporarily suspended and, for continuity's sake, everything must be left exactly as you see it.

## HITTING YOUR MARK

The director rehearses you, first of all for the lines (with the script supervisor, who notes any deliberate or inadvertent script alterations) and then for the moves, so that the camera people know where to go and the appropriate lighting can be rigged. Part of this rehearsal process involves fixing where you come to a standstill, to ensure that you're lit and focused at that specific point. A mark is made on the floor with tape, usually in a T-shape, with your feet either side of the downward stroke. It's vital you hit this mark, as the composition of the frame depends on your position. The mark is determined pretty much according to what feels natural and right for you, so if it feels horrendously wrong, voice your concerns straightaway.

Once it's fixed, then it's up to you to rehearse hitting the mark. One way is to start at the mark, turn round and walk back to your starting place, counting the number of strides. (Walking backwards from the mark will give you an inaccurate reading, as backward steps are usually shorter.) Also find visual markers, such as the corner of a table meeting the edge of a rug, as the last thing you want to do is look down at the floor to find your mark. Sometimes a small sandbag is used so that your foot can feel where to stop. Your psycho-physical co-ordination can also help you, so that the rhythm of the number of steps or the height of the visual marker can be remembered by your body as much as by your brain. Whatever happens, try not to worry about hitting your mark: the camera reads everything, so you don't want it picking up on anxieties that have nothing to do with your character. If you walk it a few times, your body quickly builds a certain muscle memory and you'll know what feels right. As long as you don't get in anyone's way as they light the space, no one should begrudge you practising your journey.

TAKING RISKS

Given all the pressure of Time Equals Money, the danger as a young film actor can be to play it safe. Action picture director Isaac Florentine (*Ninja*, 2009) once told me how wonderful it is when an actor takes him by surprise; for Florentine, that was the mark of a star. So, use the rehearsals to be bold. If the director doesn't like your choice, they'll quickly tell you. But if you can take the risk and fly with a sense of fearlessness, you'll start to carve your unique performance style.

Of course, your choices have to be appropriate to the character, the given circumstances and the genre, and your sense of spontaneity must come from the *character* rather than from yourself. If you've prepared the part thoroughly, then you should find your choices are steeped in the character's thought processes and, therefore, entirely appropriate.

Some acting coaches encourage you to take yourself by surprise in an actual take. In fact, movie star, Glenn Close (1947–) considers filming to be 'one big rehearsal': 'You can loosen up. You can breathe. You can try things. There's such a huge flexibility in film. That to me is what's fun about movies' (cited in Guskin, 2003:120). Film director Alan J. Pakula (1928–98) backs this up: 'Think of [filming] as rehearsing, and trust the moment in rehearsal. When it really happens, that's the take I'm going to use' (cited in Guskin, 2003:120).

Some directors actually shoot the rehearsals, as the actors' adrenalin can sometimes access a level of spontaneity which isn't always repeatable in a take. So just be aware that even an early rehearsal could end up being your big screen performance.

## WHO SAID IT WAS EASY?

Building a character, telling a story, portraying a role, forging an ensemble, embracing a director's vision: these are all complex processes. Yet at the same time they can be so simple, depending on how well the glove fits the hand in terms of the play, director or medium. One thing's for sure: it's *your* body, imagination, spirit, intellect and emotional landscape, which are going to be offered up for public consumption. And that can be both exhilarating and terrifying, as you head into the performance arena.

## SUMMARY

In this chapter, we've looked at:

- repetition
- the actor–director relationship
- dynamic listening and the Action–Reaction–Decision sequence
- the inner psychological drives of Thought, Feeling and Action
- the significance of thought-centre work
- the intricacies of the emotion–centre
- the action-centred use of the body in rehearsal, looking at Stanislavsky's Active Analysis
- the impact of writers, with particular reference to Shakespeare
- the significance of different rehearsals (including run-throughs, technical rehearsals, and dress rehearsals)
- rehearsing for the camera.

## SELECTED READING

There are endless books on acting, adopting a vast range of approaches to building a character, and it's very much horses for courses. The following are just a tiny sample.

A great starting place would be *An Actor's Work*, Jean Benedetti's translations of Stanislavsky's *An Actor Prepares* and *Building a Character* (Routledge, 2008). With some juicy new terminology and some provocative re-appraisals of familiar terrain, it's an important and impressive work.

For a quick view of what goes on in our inner lives, Dylan Evans' *Emotion: A Very Short Introduction* (OUP, 2001) is a wonderful eye-opener. There are other excellent books for non-scientists on the biology of the brain listed in the Bibliography.

Oliver Ford Davies' *Performing Shakespeare* (Nick Hern Books, 2007) is a warm and insightful contribution from an experienced actor, full of ideas which may have by-passed the voice coaches.

My own *The Complete Stanislavsky Toolkit* (Nick Hern Books, 2007) is designed as an accessible manual and it fills in some of the gaps unavoidably left in this book.

## USEFUL WEBSITES

www.theatrefutures.org.uk/stanislavskicentre – for some great photos of Stanislavsky's work and some interesting articles.

www.stagework.org.uk – for various rehearsal diaries including Simon Russell Beale as Galileo at the National Theatre and Peter Reynolds on *The Crucible* at the Birmingham Rep.

www.steppenwolf.org – for some interesting backstage articles and photos, with contributions from Chicago-based, Steppenwolf's playwrights and directors.

www.rsc.org.uk – for the Royal Shakespeare Company's home site with various rehearsal diaries including *Romeo and Juliet* and *King Lear* from the 2004 season.

Various theatres have online rehearsal diaries including Northern Stage's *Son of Man* (2009) at www.northernstage.co.uk and Bolton Octagon's *The Caretaker* (2009) at http://octagonbolton.blogspot.com/2009, both of which are fun to check out.

5

# 'ANOTHER OPENING, ANOTHER SHOW': PERFORMANCE PRACTICES

You can see by now that compelling acting involves the balance of technique and spontaneity, and it's in the realm of performance – both on stage and screen – that that balance is really tested.

Before we step in front of the camera, we'll visit the live theatre – described by British scholar Baz Kershaw as the 'last bastion of the truly human'.

## THE AUDIENCE

Let's face it: without an audience, we wouldn't have a job. It's the spectators who give our work meaning. Their responses are the final stage of the creative process, as they take over the role of director and we listen to where they gasp, laugh, rustle wrappers, or engage so entirely that you can hear a pin drop.

### 'SPIRITUAL RESONANCE'

The relationship between an actor and an audience can be utterly transformative. When you fully commit to the storytelling, an unseen connection is made between you and the spectator. It's what Charles Marowitz calls a 'spiritual resonance', and he even suggests that the inherent magnetism can have the power of hypnosis, where the audience become 'one half of the psychic bargain'. When it's really buzzing, live theatre can be as transformative as the ancient rituals and the seventeenth-century affectivity we touched on in Chapter 1. If you allow yourself to plunge into the moment of existence, the magic of the theatre is a combination of the alchemy you create with your audience and their complicity in completing the performance.

## STYLE AND FORM

That complicity isn't just mystical and spiritual, it's also incredibly practical. Through an audience, you can discover a play's entire genre and form.

'Form' is essentially your contract with the audience: if you tell me the play is a thriller, I'll respond to it differently from if you tell me it's a farce. Through the process of performance, you discover the rhythm of the piece: where you need to pause to allow for the spectators' gasps; where a walk down a staircase can be slowed right down because your audience can see the ghost in the study before your character does; where you can sustain a moment of absurdity far longer than in rehearsals as the spectators' laughter magnificently snowballs. From Restoration comedies, to Victorian melodramas, to farces, to musicals, to a brand new play – for all your work in the rehearsal room, it's only in the presence of a human mass that you can really unlock the codes of the play's dramatic form. And that's one of the reasons that live performance can be so exciting.

## DUAL CONSCIOUSNESS

Being able to walk the tightrope of rehearsed performance while spontaneously adapting to the audience's nightly responses requires you to have an acute sense of dual consciousness. That means you need the ability to embrace what's happening both on the stage and in the auditorium at one and the same time. You can make passionate avowals of love to your onstage partner, while projecting your voice just a little bit more to top the woman having a coughing fit on the fifth row. We looked at this split focus in Chapter 1 with Coquelin's division of the actor into Number One and Number Two. Number One is an impassive observer who analyses what's going on inside you, even if it's a very emotional moment. Meanwhile, Number Two is the part of you doing all the loving, hating, weeping and laughing.

In terms of style and form, certain plays ask you to be more conscious of your Numbers One and Two. Brecht's *Threepenny Opera*, for example, draws attention to you as an actor far more deliberately than Chekhov's *Three Sisters*. And when it comes to screen work, One and Two have to be completely indistinguishable so that you can hit the mark and accommodate any last-minute script changes without the camera revealing that you're anything but the character.

### CROSSING THE THRESHOLD

If there's one place in the theatre where your awareness of dual consciousness becomes heightened, it's in the 'wings'. The wings are one of the most magical parts of the theatre in terms of channelling performance energy. This backstage area, usually lit by blue light, is an almost womb-like, liminal, transitional space between the safety of your dressing room and the exposure of the auditorium – between the single-mindedness of preparing for the task in hand and the dual consciousness of performing that task. Anyone who has ever walked on stage knows that the energy of the wings is unique: it's excitable and concentrated, and that moment when you step from one reality to another can have an immensely powerful resonance. Once you've crossed the threshold from the wings to the stage, you have to tune your creative antennae and use your dual consciousness to sense the energy you need to connect your story to every listener.

## FILLING THE SPACE IMAGINATIVELY

Both the Mystical and the Workmanlike blend here, too. There are some very practical ways of connecting with each member of the audience, both physically and vocally, and they both involve you *expanding* your performance to a certain degree. The first thing to do is to make sure the audience can see you, and this requires something as obvious as turning your body out physically. To stop yourself from simply giving them your right or left profile (however noble that profile may be), you have to break the invisible fourth wall between you and the audience and let them see your full face from time to time. This is so direct, but so necessary, and it can feel unnervingly unnatural at first. Consequently, many of us fall victim to dropping our eye-line down to the stage floor, rather than daring to face out front.

You can overcome your coyness by reminding yourself that, in the two hours of the play's drama, most of the characters are probably going through some pretty big experiences – and that warrants them playing their objectives with the highest possible stakes. You need to expand your performance not just physically, but metaphorically, so that you can dare to 'think big'. If you open up mentally, you'll start to feel how the back wall of the auditorium is actually a far more enjoyable perimeter to play to than just the orchestra pit. What you're doing is heating up the emotional temperature to the appropriate degree and expanding your performance *imaginatively* as much as *technically*. And in this way, you won't sacrifice any sense of 'truth': in fact, just the opposite – you'll increase it. The big space will no longer feel uncomfortable, but absolutely necessary to accommodate the size of your character's experience.

Another good reason for making sure the audience can see your face is that 'being seen' relates directly to 'being heard'. Rodenburg suggests that audiences convince themselves that, if they can't see your face, they can't hear your voice. That's not to say you shouldn't turn your back at certain points, but allowing the audience to see your mouth can subconsciously reassure them that they can hear you.

## FILLING THE SPACE VOCALLY

Of course, being seen doesn't automatically mean being heard, so here are four very simple techniques for expanding your performance vocally:

First of all, Rodenburg points out that a big space requires you to speak at a slightly slower pace, as it takes fractionally longer for your words to touch your listeners.

Secondly, Cicely Berry adds that a bigger space needs more muscular articulation. It's a matter of giving your voice more energy and your diction greater 'consonant value'. After all (as we saw in

Chapter 2), it's the consonants that shape your words, so that they're not generalised, open sounds that then become lost in the auditorium.

Thirdly, slowing down and giving 'consonant value' both require greater breath support, and of course bigger spaces require more volume. Just as importantly, they demand sustained thought processes. If you drop the thought before the end of the line, you drop your energy, and then your verbal actions don't reach the audience; instead, they flop straight onto the floor. As Rodenburg reminds us, not everyone in the auditorium knows the play, so they need to hear every word. If you hold on to the story by sustaining your thought processes, you can hold on to your audience, and then you have the opportunity to create that 'spiritual resonance', to which Marowitz alludes.

Fourthly, Maria Ouspenskaya suggests that the beginning of a play needs a very special energy, with you using extra voice and articulation to 'win' the audience. Once you've captured their attention and they've settled into the story, you can adjust that vocal energy to whatever is required for the play.

You can see how transformative journeys involve – in equal measure – intangible, magical complicity and clear, effective technique. Acting is mystical and practical at one and the same time.

## PERFORMING SHAKESPEARE'S SOLILOQUIES

Staying with speaking texts for a moment, let's return to Shakespeare. Although in Chapter 4 we discussed rehearsing Shakespeare, there are a couple of additions to make in the actual performing of the bard – particularly when it comes to soliloquies. While there are many wonderful soliloquies in the classical canon, you'll find that Shakespeare's are amongst the most exciting and rewarding, not to mention the most frequently quoted.

The soliloquy is a wonderful opportunity for you to have a very fluid and accessible connection with your audience. You're taking them into your confidence. You're telling them things that you might not tell anyone else in the play. You're endowing them with a certain dramatic power that none of the other characters may have, weaving them further into that sense of complicity for which we ultimately strive.

To ensure you're really making your soliloquies *dependent* on the audience's silent complicity, there are two questions to ask yourself: (1) 'Why does my character need to share their thoughts at this moment?'; and (2) 'What does my character find out about themselves through the very process of sharing these thoughts?'

The first question invites you to sharpen your objective: 'What do you want from the audience here and now? Do you want their assurance, their consolation, their wisdom, their confidence? If they were to interrupt you, what kind of suggestions would you want them to make?' (Remember the silent interruptions we talked about in Chapter 3?)

The second question invites you to consider the soliloquy as a kind of one-way dialogue with a wise counsellor. Someone who doesn't actually interrupt you, but simply gives you the opportunity to put into words all those thoughts milling round your head. Often it's only by having the chance to articulate what's going on in our brains that we can actually formulate a plan of action. And having a listener can be just the catalyst we need.

With both questions, the role of the audience is vital. The more you believe it's only through this (albeit one-way) dialogue that you'll know what to do next, the more you can use a soliloquy as a unique and complicit, live interaction – and not just a talking head.


For all the buzz of the adrenalin and the thrill of the applause, we all know that live performance can also be strangely angst-inducing (particularly with soliloquies, as we saw with Konijn's noting of the highly raised heart-beat). In certain circumstances, that angst can quickly become stage fright.

## STAGE FRIGHT

### WHO EXPERIENCES STAGE FRIGHT?

Given the strange and multi-textured nature of live performance, it's not surprising that many actors suffer from stage fright. I've experienced it twice, and both times were totally unexpected and utterly terrifying. The curious thing is that it afflicts both the inexperienced and the very experienced alike, and it can hit you either on the first night or the hundredth performance without any rhyme or reason.

It's rare for actors to talk openly about stage fright, but two highly acclaimed British actors – Laurence Olivier and Anthony Sher (1949–) – write eloquently about it, so I include them here.

In his description of the first night of Ibsen's *The Master Builder* (1892), Laurence Olivier refers to 'a merciless attack of stage-fright with all its usual shattering symptoms' (Olivier, 1987:27). As his courage failed him, he went on stage feeling certain that within a matter of minutes, he'd forget his lines and would have to leave. His voice faded, his throat closed and the audience began to spin giddily. He managed to get through the play, but with his teeth clenched so tightly, that he could hardly be heard. For five long years, Olivier's stage fright tormented him.

Anthony Sher had a similar experience during his first night playing Iago in *Othello* at the Royal Shakespeare Company in 2004. At first he felt good, as if he'd fly through the performance, but gradually – despite having gone over his lines again and again – they began to slip from his grasp. He then felt 'The Fear settle in – dry mouth, gabbling inner voices' and his performance became 'a question of survival rather than achievement … ' (Sher, 2005:56).

Just like Olivier, Sher found that the Fear wouldn't go away. Five months later, his battle was still raging, and – as if to give himself a justification for not having to go on stage – he began to develop all kinds of psychosomatic illnesses. When *Othello* went to Japan, Sher experienced such alarming losses of balance that he nearly fell off the stage. In fact, the first time it happened, he thought it was an earthquake! In a vague attempt to beat it, he 'drew an image of The Fear as a nightmarish hyena, and showed it slinking away. (In performance when The Fear visits, one of my inner voices shouts at it: Fuck off!)' (Sher, 2005:59).

## SO, WHAT IS STAGE FRIGHT?

There's been very little scientific study of stage fright in actors, though some investigations have been undertaken with musicians. Stephen Aaron's *Stage Fright: Its Role in Acting* (1986) is a very useful resource, in which he describes stage fright as having two kinds of manifestation – physiological and psychological – and unfortunately the first can often prompt the second.

## PHYSIOLOGICAL STAGE FRIGHT

Basically, a surge of energy is sent into our autonomic nervous system, which (in the words of British sports psychologist Craig Sharp) is responsible for 'frolic, fright, flight or fight'. The point of this adrenalin kick is to send more oxygen into our body and more blood to our muscles, and generally prepare us for action.

With stage fright, the natural excitement of performance seems to morph from frolic to fright, and the audience turns from friend to fiend. Under normal circumstances when we're in distress, we have all kinds of physical and mental strategies to calm ourselves down, like sitting calmly for ten minutes or having a cup of sweet tea. With stage fright, none of these are possible, because we can't flee or fight – as our job is to stay on the stage and tell the story. So we have to contort our natural instinct to run or riot into Staying Power. And this is one of the challenges we face: when we're caught like a rabbit in the headlights of stage fright, we have to hide from the audience the very thing that's roaring inside us like a dragon.

The physiological symptoms of stage fright include dizziness, sweating, trembling, palpitations, nausea, dryness of the mouth, diarrhoea, frequent peeing, physical tension and shallow breathing. My own experience certainly involved dizziness, rapid heartbeat and an overwhelming sickness. It also involved another common symptom: a sense of unreality. Many of us as actors have had terrible nightmares in which we suddenly find we're on stage in the wrong costume or in the wrong play, or we can't find our shoes or we don't know the lines. Stage fright to me had exactly that dreamlike sense of 'this can't really be happening'. And because it didn't feel real, I couldn't guarantee that I wouldn't suddenly do or say something completely inappropriate – like shout at the audience or walk off the stage! It's that fear of losing control which underpins many experiences of stage fright.

Both of my encounters with The Fear happened totally unexpectedly in the middle of a scene, and during performances when I hadn't even been nervous. Of course, on subsequent nights, I suffered overwhelming anxiety, even before I'd set foot on the stage. And this tends to be the more common experience of stage fright: the psychological angst.

## PSYCHOLOGICAL STAGE FRIGHT

Psychological stage fright often occurs when there's a sudden fracture between your 'functioning self' (i.e. the part of you that's 'in character' telling the story – your Number Two) and your 'observing self' (i.e. the technician juggling the various occupational demands – your Number One). As we've seen, both 'selves' are necessary parts of your dual consciousness. However, if the gap between Actor-as-Person and Actor-as-Character becomes too self-conscious, you're in danger of falling into the abyss between the two.

Stage fright manifests itself most frequently as a fear that we're going to forget our lines – or indeed we do actually forget them. Memory plays a huge part in stage fright. The one expectation the audience will have of us is that we know the script, and if we can't even remember our lines, then what sort of an actor are we? In other words, our concern for the audience's approval suddenly seizes more of our attention than our simple task of telling them a story. Added to this, we suddenly feel immensely responsible. 'I mustn't let the director down, I mustn't let the cast down, I mustn't let the playwright down, and (perhaps most crucially) I mustn't let myself down.' Everything focuses on fear: fear of the consequences that might arise if we forget our lines – not least of which is the consequence that we might look foolish.

## THE FEAR OF LOOKING FOOLISH

Nachmanovitch suggests that the fear of looking foolish has two aspects: fear of being *thought* a fool (the loss of your reputation) and the fear of actually *being* a fool (the loss of your senses, i.e. 'Have I gone mad?'). These fears incarnate a huge monster in our heads, which Nachmanovitch refers to as 'the judging spectre': 'We feel like victims of circumstances beyond our control, a malevolent fate, a rival, or petty tyrant who has entered our lives' (Nachmanovitch, 1990:138).

And possibly the scariest thing about stage fright is that it's *ourselves* incarnating it! The fact that we become our own worst enemies, our own *saboteurs*, can bring the moment of stage fright closest to the sense of utter madness and loss of control. Our inner judge makes us doubt we're any good, and with that comes a self-censorship which prevents us from having any genuine moment-by-moment interactions. All that work we've done on dynamic listening and communion vanishes. Stage fright blocks us like nothing else.

## HOW CAN YOU OVERCOME IT?

The mysterious thing about stage fright, as Aaron points out, is that sometimes it's there, sometimes it's not. It can be very intense some nights and negligible at other times, depending partly on how you might be feeling that day, what variables have made up your day, and what processes you've gone through to prepare yourself for performance. Sometimes doing nothing but have a cup of tea and a chat can be just what's needed: endless stretching, vocal exercises and running through your lines can sometimes overcharge the batteries.

How you overcome stage fright will depend on who you are, the part you're playing and the rest of the cast. A good policy is to 'befriend' the auditorium, by standing on the empty stage before the show and sending out very welcoming energy to each empty seat, reminding yourself that the audience have come to hear a story. They're our collaborators, not our enemies. They want to be there, they want to enjoy themselves, and they haven't come in judgement.

Other useful pre-show tips include making sure you're not dehydrated. According to Patsy Rodenburg, nerves can dry you out far more than you know. She also suggests taking ten minutes in silence just to reflect on your character and the journey they make, as well as the whole journey of the play.

In the actual performance, simply focusing on your objective – what you want and how you go about getting it – keeps your circle of attention on your onstage partner and activity. If your objective excites and engages you, then the chances of you straying off it are radically reduced.

Since nerves can cause you to speak faster than usual, Rodenburg recommends that if you find yourself feeling nervous, hold on to the very physical nature of the words themselves, the actual make-up of each syllable and thought, and how your body and mouth shape them. That way you can 'cling onto the rock-face, not fall off, climbing up and over your fear' (Rodenburg, 1998:349).

Your backstage behaviour during the show can also be influential. Some actors adopt an aggressive, ballsy kind of backstage manner, with phrases like 'Knock 'em dead' or 'Get out there and maim 'em'. Olivier was known to stand behind the curtains whispering to the audience, 'You bastards!' In one company with whom I was performing, we'd meet in the interval and ask, 'What's the score? Are we winning?' Others prefer calm focus or easy nonchalance.

Whatever strategy works for you, acknowledging and accepting the adrenalin kick can be half the battle: those sweaty palms and trembling knees are simply signs that our body knows something important is about to happen. As Mamet says:

> The actor before the curtain, the soldier going into combat, the fighter into the arena, the athlete before the event, may have feelings of self-doubt, fear, or panic. These feelings will or will not appear, and no amount of 'work on the self' can eradicate them. The rational individual will, when the bell rings, go out there anyway to do the job she said she was going to do. This is called courage.

(Mamet, 1998:59)

## FILM ACTING

It may seem that the one thing the film actor doesn't have to worry about is forgetting their lines; after all, the director can shout 'Cut!' and the shot can be re-taken. That said, there are a whole host of other performative issues that arise for the film actor, making your job equally challenging and exciting.

### THE CHALLENGES OF FILM ACTING

Camera acting is the ultimate in combining technique and art. Experienced film coach Mel Churcher lists some of the skills you need, including: knowing what the frame is; knowing where to look; knowing how much you can move; understanding the importance of continuity; knowing how to hit your mark; understanding sound levels; and knowing how to use props intelligently. The art of film acting involves you transforming into the character (which you've researched and prepared entirely on your own) within an instant and without any build-up of playing a narrative in sequence. The demands on your imagination and emotional technique are huge – and exciting.

First of all, the rhythm of a day's filming is very strange. There may be long stretches where nothing seems to be happening (though technically there's a lot going on) and then very intense activity, where all your powers of concentration are put to the test as you repeat the same lines over and over and over – from different angles and with different intensities. Yet each time, those words and actions must be freshly minted.

And the subtlety of your performance is absolute, demanding dynamic listening of the highest order. You don't need to play to the camera: *it* observes *you*. As its attention is wholly on you, you need do little more than let it read your mind and pick up on all your thoughts.

Movie star Joan Crawford (1905–77) described film acting as painting with the tiniest brush. It's certainly the most precise of all arts – more so than television, as we'll see – because it really is what it says: moving pictures. And every picture is a composition of lights, set, main actors and extras. A skilled film director works intensively with his director of photography (DOP) to ensure that every frame could be captured as a still.

For this level of aestheticism to exist, each image has to be split into the smallest details. You might think you've just given your best performance, but an 'extra' playing a body guard was a bit too far to the left. Or there was the merest hint of a boom shadow across the top of the screen. Or a bulb blew and it has to be changed. Or a plane flies over or a car alarm goes off. At any moment, your intensely emotional and imaginative work can be interrupted because of technical difficulties, and it's as much your job to remain relaxed and patient, as it is to focus on your acting.

Added to which, the constant tension between Time and Excellence means that you want every contribution you make to be timely and excellent. Not to forget that you're walking a personal tightrope of your careful preparation and your in-the-moment availability to those moments of spontaneous discovery that the camera loves. You can see why acting for the camera has been described as distilled, exposed and demanding.

## DIFFERENCES BETWEEN STAGE AND SCREEN ACTING

In terms of building a character, the strategies you adopt for stage and screen are exactly the same, so most of the information contained thus far is entirely applicable. The inner psychological drives of your character and their objectives are the same, whatever the medium.

The differences lie in the technical modes of delivery. If theatre acting is about finding a kind of artificial truth – one that will affect the person in the Gods as much as in the front row – screen acting is about absolute sincerity. You need no more energy to communicate to your partner on-screen than you would in real life. To all intents and purposes, what you do on screen *is* real life, and the camera is simply an observing bystander.

Then there's the technicality of space. Theatre is often about being further away from someone than you might normally be, as the audience takes in the whole proscenium picture. Screen acting, on the other hand, is often about being closer to someone than you might normally be, as you both have to be fitted into the frame.

Another main difference is that you have no control over your final performance – it's all in the hands of the director, producer and editor. And of course you have no direct interaction with your audience: when they're viewing your performance in the cinema or the living room, you're sunning yourself in the Bahamas. (Hopefully … )

Perhaps the most daunting difference between theatre and screen is that, unless you're a leading role in a major movie (which might involve as much rehearsal time as theatre), you usually have to do all the preparation on your own. In the theatre, the relationship between actors and director is collaborative, intimate, often social as well as professional, and very interactive. The director is your mirror in rehearsals, reflecting back to you what they see and hear, and helping you shape your performance. In film and television, you're often entirely on your own on the day, and it's rare to get much feedback from your director, because they're so busy multitasking (as we'll see later). This factor may well explain why Hollywood is so full of acting coaches, and it's perfectly normal for even the most experienced star to prepare their role in collaboration with a tutor.

## THE QUALITIES OF A GOOD FILM ACTOR

Given the delicate balance between technique and art – added to the fact that Time Equals Money in an overwhelming way – there are certain qualities worth developing as a film actor, most of which are fairly straight forward. Reliability, professionalism, competence, availability and relaxation are just a handful:

*Reliability* in terms of being there – physically, mentally, emotionally and imaginatively – at exactly the moment you're needed.

*Professionalism* in terms of having done all the necessary preparation that you would have covered with a director if this were theatre. You also need a knowledge of the whole script: if suddenly the weather means that Scene 28 can be shot now, rather than next Friday when it was originally scheduled, the director can rely on you to know the scene back to front. At the same time, you're not so fixed in your learning of the lines that you can't take on board all the tiny (or significant) changes that often happen at the very last moment.

*Competence* in the sense that you can do the job well: this might sound obvious, but there's so much more responsibility on you as an individual creative artist in film and television. They also need to be sure that, when you say you can ride a motorbike, they know you really can.

*Availability* in the sense that, although you have to do so much preparation on your own, building a character truthfully and authentically can only really come from your interaction with your fellow actors. In the brief moments of rehearsal that film and television usually allow, you have to be able to adjust all your prepared work to be in genuine communication with your onscreen partner. And it's possible they've come up with a completely different interpretation of their character from the one that you'd imagined.

*Relaxation* in terms of being able to deal with all these factors, and yet remain totally unfazed by the myriad technical activities going on around you while you're giving your creative all.

Perhaps two of the most useful qualities for film and television acting are *confidence* and *sociability*. Unless you're the star of a movie or TV series, the chances are that much of your career will involve arriving on sets where the activity has been going for several days or weeks. Everyone will be going about their business and many of them will be very familiar with each other. You have to parachute into this situation and be socially open and confident enough to join the 'family' at the drop of a hat, and to have no problem finding out who the first assistant director is or where the canteen wagon is or where your fellow actors might be lurking to do a quick line-run. This part of the job is potentially the most challenging in screen acting, because you have no character to hide behind.

Despite all the vulnerability, you can prepare yourself in advance for your filming, by following a few simple guidelines. These include: learning your character's thought processes; learning the lines (of course); and charting the emotional journey. All these are applicable whether you're a major movie star and you've had ten weeks' rehearsal, or you've just got a few days' shooting and you're doing the prep on your own.

## LEARNING THE THOUGHT PROCESSES

The dialogue of a screen script is much sparser than that of a play, because the characters' thought processes are as important as their words – even in an action movie. Close-ups are the fruits of film, and they reveal the characters' inner thoughts and feelings in a way that theatre just can't, because the audience is simply too far away.

In theatre, learning a character's thought processes is useful for remembering great swathes of text. In film, learning the thought processes is vital, as these thoughts are exactly what the director captures in the close-ups. In many ways, film is the ultimate medium for subtext and inner monologues. Since reactions are so crucial, you may want to consider that you're not so much learning your *lines*, as learning your *responses*. 'What are the inner stimuli that prompt you to say your next line?' (Actually, as we've seen all along, this is actually just as relevant for theatre as film. After all, the other characters are the reason why you're behaving as you do here and now.)

As with a play, the Northern Star guiding you in this work will be your character's objective. As you pursue that objective, don't forget the power of inconsistency. Moments where the character seems to contradict their objective may be exactly the moments in which we see into their soul, and you reveal to the audience the authenticity of your portrayal.

Bits of action can also be very useful to anchor you, especially as this is how the director and the DOP usually break down the script to understand how best to shoot it. Where the bit changes could well be where the shot changes from a two-shot to a close-up. So you might find your textual detective work could put you well ahead of the shooting game.

LEARNING THE LINES

Whatever the medium, learning thought processes always makes learning lines easier. There are two – diametrically-opposed – attitudes to learning a film script. British movie star Michael Caine (1933–) suggests that you should learn the lines so thoroughly that saying them is a predictable reflex, which can safeguard you from any unnecessary anxiety on the day of the shoot. The trouble is that some scripts change right up until the final moment. So some actors choose not to bed the lines in until they're on the set, simply because they want the flexibility to adapt at the very last minute.

To some extent it depends on the calibre of the script. If it's as rhythmically structured as Mamet's *Glengarry Glen Ross* (1992), there won't be much need for change. In an action movie, where the dialogue is a gateway to big, physical sequences, then there may be lots of last-minute tweaks, as the script is less character-driven than action-led.

With experience, you'll discover your own relationship to text, memory, stress and preparation. Then you can find that happy medium between feeling as confident as possible on the day, and not being so fixed in the learned script that you can't accommodate quick-fire adjustments.

## CHARTING THE EMOTIONS

It also helps to have an understanding of the emotional temperature of each scene. Screen scripts are shot out of sequence for budgetary reasons: if all the street scenes can be shot at once, followed by all the scenes inside the bank, then it saves immense time in rigging lights and moving cameras. In order to have a complete handle on where each scene fits into the arc of your character's emotional journey, you may want to chart your way through your script. Here are a couple of suggestions for how to do that:

Some coaches suggest making a card for each scene, on which you write the key given circumstances plus whatever happened in the preceding scene. If you carry these cards with you to the set, you can use them as prompts to help you tap into the required emotional temperature. Others suggest finding a song or a piece of music that somehow encapsulates specific scenes, so that you have an *aide memoire* of the atmosphere, tempo and emotional pitch that differentiate one dialogue from another.

How you emotionally prepare yourself on the day will again depend on how you function as a psycho-physical instrument: you'll know what you have to do to get to the point where you feel appropriately 'thin-skinned'.

## THE TEAM

A final way in which you can prepare yourself for your film performance is to really understand what each member of the team does. As Caine points out, film is such a technical medium that the real stars make it their job to acquire a thorough knowledge of the science. Not only does it boost your confidence, it also informs your understanding of how collaborative film is. There are some excellent books (recommended at the end of this chapter) which give all the details of the crew, so here are just the main players.

## THE DIRECTOR

The director's job is overwhelmingly responsible – and they are the Ultimate Big Cheese. Whatever happens, only they call 'Cut!' – unless the sound mixer hears a glitch on the headphones, or the camera operator sees a problem through the lens. Actors don't call 'Cut!', unless they're about to injure themselves or someone else.

Some film directors love working with actors and know exactly how to bring out the best in them. They're the kind who will probably include some serious rehearsal time (maybe several weeks), and will engage in full debate with you about the development of your character. Some of them are actors themselves – Clint Eastwood (1930–) and Robert Redford (1936–), for example. Others have worked extensively in theatre and know the way that actors work – such as the Brits Sam Mendes (1965–), Richard Eyre (1943–), Stephen Daldry (1961–) and Nicholas Hytner (1956–).

It's worth remembering that a film director has a multitude of technical considerations, some of which – such as the weather – will be out of their control. In many situations, they have little involvement in the building of your character: they've hired you for your competence, which for them includes creating a role independently. As Caine suggests, get on with your own contribution and leave everything else to the director: they may be looking for angles of which you'd never thought, or they're going to edit the film in a way you can't imagine.

The reality is that directors in both film and television regularly come up through Script Development departments, or assistant directing or editing. Therefore (like theatre directors), they may know very little about acting processes. Often there isn't time for them to understand how you've come to a choice; just give them the choice and if they don't like it, they'll tell you. At the end of the day, they want to bring out the best possible performance in you, because of course they want the movie to be a hit.

## FIRST AND SECOND ASSISTANT DIRECTORS

The first assistant (first AD) keeps the movie together. They're the director's right-hand person. They herd the rabble just before a take, they make sure everything runs to time, and they chivvy the director if they're going over schedule. They basically run the set.

The second assistant (second AD) looks after you: checking you've arrived and you know where to go for wardrobe and make-up; alerting you to any script changes; letting you know when you're officially 'broken' (finished for the day); and arranging your transport home. You shouldn't go anywhere without telling the second AD.

## DIRECTOR OF PHOTOGRAPHY

The director of photography (DOP) is sometimes called the cine-matographer, and they work in conjunction with the director to create the look for the film. They choose the film stock and the lighting, while the electricians then set up the lights to create the required effect.

## CAMERA OPERATOR

The camera operator is the one looking through the lens and seeing the image that will be recorded. You need to show them what you intend to do in a shot, so that they can keep the camera on you. To help them when you're sitting down or standing up, move frac-tionally slower than normal, so that the camera can hold you in frame.

## FOCUS PULLER

The focus puller keeps you in focus by measuring the distance from your head to the camera, which is why 'hitting your mark' (see Chapter 4) is so important – or you'll be blurred. The focus puller can tell you which lens is being used, so that you know whether the take is a master shot, a two-shot, an over-the-shoulder or a close-up (though in most cases, it'll be fairly evident).

While there are many other important people to negotiate – including the script supervisor (who keeps a note of any changes you inadvertently make to the script) and the continuity team (who ensure that you've got your handkerchief in the same pocket each take) – the books detailed at the end of this chapter and in the selected bibliography will alert you fully to these.

## THE SHOTS

To make the most of your filming experience, it's good to understand the psychological aspect of each shot, as well as the aesthetic composition, so that you have a sense of being a creative collaborator, rather than a photographed object.

As Richard Brestoff describes in *The Camera Smart Actor* (1994), most movies are filmed according to the 'Classic Hollywood Style'. This means the story follows the line of Exposition, Complication, Development, Climax and Dénouement. And the way in which that story is told is by breaking each scene down into the following shots: master, two-shot (sometimes call mid-shot); over-the-shoulder; and close-up. This sequence (which moves from the big picture of the master into the intimacy of the close-up) mirrors the way in which we tell a story, by drawing the listener deeper and deeper into the action, and closer and closer to what's going on in our minds. Each shot has a different rhythm and a different intensity, as the spectators hone in on the intimacies of the characters' interactions.

Just be aware that whatever you do in the master has to be repeatable in all the other shots – where it might not be so comfortable or appropriate. So if you're given a prop – maybe a walking stick or a cigarette holder – be sure that you make simple choices with it.

## CLOSE-UPS

Although we won't look at every shot in detail, the close-up is worth some attention. We've seen how close-ups reveal your character's thought processes and, although dynamic listening is vital in all acting, it's especially important here. Close-ups often focus on the character who's *not* speaking, and you can really take the time in your reaction shots to hear what the other character says to you and to allow yourself to be touched by it. If the pace isn't right, the director and the editor can always change it in the final edit. It's far easier for them to speed the pace up by snipping out the pauses, than it is for them to expand a shot to make it look as though you genuinely absorbed what you just heard.

Often the key to film acting is simplicity and stillness. Stillness of mind, body and eye can be extremely captivating on the screen, as you'll see just by watching a few close-ups of the greatest – from Jack Nicholson (1937–) to Sean Penn (1960–) to Julianne Moore (1960–) to Denzil Washington (1954–) and beyond. As we all know from everyday life, finding the impulse to turn our thoughts into spoken text – especially when we know the enormity of what we're about to say – can often take immense energy. Film acting (more than stage or even television) is often about keeping the emotional kettle at simmering point, rather than letting the whistle blow. The repeated mantra from many film practitioners is: less is more, and for that reason, close-ups are among the most exciting forms of acting we can do.

## TAKES

Film acting is really about 'repeating spontaneity' over a multitude of takes, and there are various ways you can help yourself. Before the first take of a scene, it's worth re-reading the scene preceding it, to remind you of the necessary emotional pitch and rhythm. (Or consult your aforementioned card.) It may be that this shot is the continuation of a walk from the street to the inside of a building, for which you filmed the outside part three weeks ago. What had happened on the street outside? At what speed did you walk off the street and into the bank? With which hand did you grasp the handle? What was your intention as you walked through the door? (Meisner's 'preparation' is particularly useful here – see Chapter 6.)

The challenge to the film actor is: 'How do I keep my intensity and commitment going through take after take after take?' The answer is: 'Don't worry about it', because you can't repeat exactly what you did anyway. If you did, it would be dead – and the camera would pick up on that deadness. Each take is really 'the first take of that take' and there will inevitably be some variation. With some directors, you may have the opportunity to change your choices quite radically each time, so that you can offer a range of options for the final cut. As movie star Morgan Freeman (1937–)

puts it: a talent for acting is really a talent for listening (as indeed we've been saying all along). So the key to repeated takes is simply to listen hard and just keep the pot simmering.

That said, don't feel you've got to keep making new choices for the sake of it: *your* objective is the *character's* objective – no more, no less.

By the way, if you fluff the lines in a take (and the sky won't fall on your head if you do), take a pause, then pick up and keep going, as there might be part of the scene that can still be used. Besides, you don't want to screw up the other actors' performances, as this shot may be going scorchingly for them. And you never know, if the fluff is tiny, the director may choose to keep it because it sounds so natural. The quick whizz of adrenalin caused by the fluff thrusts you into present-tense reality with such a force, it can sometimes produce something really wonderful in your performance that you could never have pre-planned. So – as we said in Chapter 3 ('Auditions') – celebrate the mistake and move on.

## CONTINUITY

Although each take has a new inner life, there are some things that have to stay the same – like the hand in which you held your cup.

A certain amount of continuity involves muscle memory, allowing the weight of the coffee cup to register in your left hand as much as in your brain. This is where screen acting is truly psychophysical: the more in-tune you are with your acting instrument and its intuitive wisdom, the more you can save yourself from being too head-led.

Continuity doesn't just relate to which hand the coffee was in (or was it tea?) but also to sustaining your inner life *between takes*. As we saw in reference to composition, every detail in film is crucial, as it's going to appear in vast magnification on the big screen. So wardrobe and make-up play a vital role. While it might seem unnecessary to you to be primped and powdered for every take, moving pictures are moving paintings: aesthetics and beauty are a significant part of the audience's final experience – be it the breathtaking landscapes in *Australia* (2008) or the sleekness cut-and-thrust action in *Quantum of Solace* (2008) or the impressive physical exertion in *The Wrestler* (2008). Part of your professionalism is to allow the tweak to your hair or the straightening of your tie to be important to those focused on that detail. Meanwhile, you have to remain connected to the inner life you created in the over-the-shoulder shot, and which must now be repeated in the close-up.

## VOICE AND FILM

Although you have a microphone (so you don't need any more volume than you would in real life), you want to be sure that you don't under-pitch, or you could end up having to add your voice afterwards in ADR (automated dialogue replacement). While this is technically quite straightforward, ADR is usually recorded several months after filming. So it can be imaginatively challenging having to propel yourself from a sound studio wearing a pair of head phones and gazing at yourself on a screen, back into the given circumstances and the intensity of working opposite a living, breathing actor on a snowfield in Alaska.

## THE FINAL CUT

At the end of the day, the construction of your final performance is completely out of your hands. However brilliant you are, if the movie is twenty minutes too long and your storyline takes up twenty minutes, then sadly you'll end up on the proverbial cutting room floor. Of course this is hugely disappointing. Although your bank account may be healthier as a result of the job, your CV can't boast it and there's no credit at the end of the film. But you have to try not to take it personally. Sometimes it's the producer, not the director, who has the final say, which means the money may be talking louder than the art.

You may also find the script you were given at the start of filming and the movie that's finally cut together are worlds apart. Legend has it that, instead of creating an arc to a character throughout an entire film, Robert de Niro plays each scene very openly moment-by-moment. This openness means that any of his scenes could be used at the beginning, the middle or the end of the movie, depending on how the editing team choose to construct the final cut. This way, de Niro guarantees that more of his performance stays in the film. Whether this tale is true or not, the strategy is canny!

## TELEVISION ACTING

When it comes to television, there's far less chance of your performance being edited out. Because TV filming is so fast, there's usually very little difference (certainly in the UK) between the script that you receive through the post and the episode you see on the box.

Much of what applies to film acting applies to television, too, with one big difference: there's far less time. A movie generally films one or two minutes per day. In comparison, a UK police soap opera shoots as many as six or seven scenes a day. The chances are the regulars are filming more than one episode at a time, so they're juggling scripts and storylines in a vigorous mental gymnastics, not to mention leaping in and out of cars to get from one location to another.

Most young actors cut their teeth in television, and the main advice is to be extremely prepared and highly flexible. I know of an actor who received his script for *The Bill* at seven o'clock in the evening to shoot at seven o'clock the following morning. He had seven long scenes, and when he arrived on set in the wee small hours, he discovered that they were all going to be filmed in one long stretch, like a piece of theatre. No time, then, between scenes to rapidly absorb the next one. Television requires mental agility and relaxation, and it's best to leave your nerves at home.

### TELEVISION SCRIPTS

Unlike the sparse writing of film, most TV scripts are rather more wordy. Viewers are often doing something else while the television is on: ironing, doing their homework, having a pint in the pub with the box in the background, so they're not necessarily glued to the screen. The dialogue is, therefore, needed to feed the ear, as much as the images are needed to feed the eye: there's very little time for subtext.

### FAST, BUT FUN – AND PRECISE

Since most television filming is such a frenzy, it's unlikely you'll have much discussion with the director about your character beyond whatever they told you at the interview. If they're approachable, you may catch a few moments in the canteen, but generally you're expected to look after yourself. That in itself can be fun, as to some extent, you have more control over your characterisation than you do in film. Since you can be fairly sure you won't be edited out, you can create some really interesting roles. Bear in mind, though, that you're generally cast to type in TV. In other words, your look and physique will have gone a long way towards securing you the job in the first place, and that's what the director will (to some extent) be expecting in your performance. So any big choices you make should probably still reside somewhere within your natural physical type. And don't dye your hair or shave your beard; keep to what you looked like in the casting.

If a drama series is being recorded with multi-cameras, you need to be very precise in hitting your mark, as more than one camera will be relying on you to be in exactly that spot. Although the composition of each shot may not have as much finesse as film, television still has high ideals, and good directors are keen to create powerful visuals.

## AND FINALLY ...

Acting is a drug: a wonderful, challenging, intoxicating drug. That said, I'm sure by now you've realised that it's also hard work. Be it theatre, film or television, your job is to combine the technical demands of the different media with your own creative ingenuity (as we said at the top of the chapter). You walk a tightrope of exposed vulnerability and utter creative elation. Who ever said that anyone can act?

## SUMMARY

In this chapter, we looked first of all at theatre performance, in terms of:

- the role of the audience
- dual consciousness
- expanding your performance physically, imaginatively and vocally

- soliloquies
- stage fright (Who suffers it? What is it? And how do you overcome it?).

Then we turned to the camera, in terms of:

- film acting and how it differs from stage acting
- television acting (the scripts and the speeds).

## FURTHER READING

Most of the books mentioned in Chapter 4 on building a character are just as relevant here. In addition, here are some suggested books for screen acting.

Richard Brestoff's *The Camera Smart Actor* (Smith and Kraus, 1994) is very accessible, as the bulk of the book takes the form of a fictional narrative, featuring Newcomer, a novice movie actor arriving for his first day of filming.

Both Tony Barr's *Acting for the Camera* (HarperCollins, 1997) and Mel Churcher's *Acting for Film* (Virgin, 2003) can be divided into two sections: the first focuses on building a character (as relevant to theatre as film), and the second addresses the specific technicalities of film acting. Barr's chapter 'Day One on the Set' is another very useful look at the do's and don'ts. Churcher's 'Make-up of the crew' is great, too. See the Bibliography for other useful film books.

Finally, Stephen Aaron's book *Stage Fright* (University of Chicago, 1986) is a cracking insight into what causes some of our angst: the more you can look the demon in the eye, the more you realise it's not a monster, but a mouse.

## USEFUL WEBSITES

www.theatrevoice.com – for some audio interviews with leading British actors, directors, playwrights and producers, as well as Arts Council debates and other contributions.

www.imdb.com – for all the details of films, directors and stars.

www.filmsite.org – a great place for looking up favourite actors or directors whose work you admire.

# 6

# 'PASSING THE BATON': ELEVEN EXECUTORS OF ACTING

There's no question that acting processes in the last one hundred years have evolved faster than any other century. The title of this chapter has resonances with Frank Wedekind's cabaret group *The Eleven Executioners*, who scythed through conventional art, hacking away the old and inflaming the new. In this chapter, I've selected just eleven of the most influential acting practitioners, who are not so much executioners as 'executors', highly responsible for the trends and legacies of acting as we currently practise it.

There were many who could have featured here, not least Artaud, Boal, Bogart, Brecht, Brook and Littlewood (all of whom have made a huge impact on theatre practice, especially in directing and playwriting), not to mention Vakhtangov (who is considered by many as a vital bridge between the Russian 'system' and the American 'Method'). I've chosen to focus on practitioners who have directly addressed the actual mechanics of acting in their own writings. The lack of women is noticeable, but a future over-view of twentieth into twenty-first-century influences may well change that.

The geographical areas we visit are Russia, America and Europe, with a swift trip to Japan. (The absence of Brits, I'd suggest, is down to the heritage of *institutions* such as RADA, LAMDA, Central, Drama Studio, etc., rather than the *individuals* who teach in those institutions, perhaps with exceptions such as Christopher Fettes, Yat Malmgrem [1916–2002] and Doreen Cannon [1930–95].)

I don't include very much biography or context for each, as a quick whiz on the Internet will give you that information. Instead, I've homed in on one particular book for each practitioner, providing some suggestions on how you might adopt the wisdom within. Some of these books are now considered primers, and we'll see how some tools are instantly useable, while some ideas need to be treated with caution.

I'm certainly not advocating that all you have to do is read each executor's book and suddenly you'll be an expert in their training process. Far from it. Indeed, for many of them, it would anathema. The trouble is that once a person publishes their words, the information is out there. Anyone can pick it up and read it, and make of it what they will. So, while I completely endorse that you can't possibly absorb a training through a book, I want to access for you certain principles or philosophies that you *can* apply to your own acting ethos. Based on what you discover here, you can then make informed decisions about what kind of training or classes you may want to explore more fully in the future.

And I warmly encourage you to read all the books, as you'll get a real sense – through the way each executor expresses themselves – of their different cultures and styles, as well as their shared philosophies. In fact, there are myriad cross-over points, basically because – as I said in the Introduction – all roads lead to Rome, 'Rome' being the quality of listening and reacting to which we've referred all along.

Let's start with Stanislavsky, as he was incontrovertibly the first modern practitioner to try and put into a system the issues that challenge us as actors.

## THE RUSSIAN CONTINGENT: KONSTANTIN STANISLAVSKY (1863–1938)

You won't get very far in the English-speaking acting world without encountering the influence of Stanislavsky. He devoted his life to analysing, practising and writing about the intricacies of acting, and those writings have spread across the globe. A combination of his own uncertainties as an actor, his belief in the power of theatre, his curiosity for psychology, philosophy, anatomy, music and world performance, led to a wealth of investigations through what we'd now consider 'Practice as Research'. Part of that research involved him setting up a number of satellite studios as 'laboratories' outside the main Moscow Art Theatre. The short-lived Theatre-Studio of 1905 allowed Meyerhold to flex his experimental muscles. And the First Studio of 1912 involved Vakhtangov and Michael Chekhov in some extremely successful productions, sometimes directed by Boleslavsky.

In 1906, Stanislavsky lost confidence in his acting, and began his first tentative steps towards formalising a 'system', which was to evolve throughout the course of his life. He applied himself to directing, acting and teaching, constantly questioning how we can harness all our normal activities (emotional, intellectual, physical, spiritual and imaginative) to the artifice of the stage. He claimed that he invented nothing: he simply dissected and re-constructed natural, human behaviour to create a system by which actors need never again be victims of their elusive inspiration.

There's no denying that what Stanislavsky did was revolutionary and yet I have a suspicion that, in the fullness of time and given the ways in which art and science were developing, somebody else would have done it eventually if Stanislavsky hadn't. That's not to diminish his genius, but rather to demystify the 'system' for those who are afraid it's something complicated and untouchable. It's actually very easy and full of common sense. And I'd suggest it's more of a toolkit than a system. He doesn't say 'Do A, then B, then C, then D – and then you'll be a great actor.' He basically investigated – in the studio and on stage – what it is we do as actors and how we can make our seemingly random processes more transparent and reliable. The most mystifying question is: 'Why – after more than 80 years since *An Actor Prepares* was first published – are there still so many misinterpretations and so much bad actor-training out there?'

Part of the answer is that Stanislavsky's ideas evolved in relation to his experiences, and some people don't see the whole picture. In the early part of his experimentation, he fought against the false, declamatory style of acting which swamped the international stage. Instead, he encouraged actors to connect as fully as possible with the 'truth' of a character's situation, drawing on rather more *inward-looking* tools (including affective memory) to find some kind of umbilical, creative cord between the actor and their role. By the end of his life, he was probing actions aimed *outwards* at an onstage partner. The Method of Physical Actions and Active Analysis (his two rehearsal legacies) have, at their centre, actions (physical, verbal and inner) and communication – with both your onstage partner and the audience.

The important thing to remember – as we saw in Chapters 2 and 4 – is that it's your actions and your onstage partners that inevitably provoke your emotions. It's all too easy to split Stanislavsky's work into two sections – early emotional work and later action-driven work. But he never abandoned affective memory. Why would he? As we've seen throughout this book, it's an inherent part of being human. Likewise, he recognised the importance of action right from his very first attempts at directing at the MAT. We won't necessarily advance our own practice if we split Stanislavsky in two: action and emotion were *always* important for him. But he was an experimenter: how he worked on activating and exploring these two components shifted during his life according to his 'research questions'.

Many people have picked away at Stanislavsky's legacy over the years, claiming some tools and rejecting others. As I hope we'll see, as we start to look in particular at the American 'executors', that all of them have simply highlighted one part of the whole (and holistic) system that Stanislavsky started to put into place. No one school of acting is necessarily any better or worse than another (though, be alert: certain teachers you encounter may well be better or worse than others). You need aspects of all these schools to get a sense of the holistic, psycho-physical nature of acting, or your whole process will be askew.

And it's not only practitioners who have differing views of Stanislavsky. Academics and scholars also wrangle over issues of translation and terminology. Two of the leading scholars in the field – British Jean Benedetti (author of many books on Stanislavsky) and American Sharon M. Carnicke (author of the exciting *Stanislavsky in Focus*) – have both done some wonderful, pioneering work, and yet neither necessarily agrees with everything the other is saying. These debates are healthy and exciting.

Personally, I'm an unholy mix of actor and scholar. Having trained in Moscow, but acted in the UK and the USA – where I've also worked in universities and drama schools – I'm keen to get the Russian terminology right, but I'm also being sensitive to the fact that some terms work better in the studio than others. Stanislavsky himself declared that he hadn't written a gospel. So I'd suggest that he intended us to evolve it according to what's useful to each generation and medium, not to mention each individual.

In the light of all this discussion and debate, let's turn to one of the most exciting publications to have come out in recent years.

## AN ACTOR'S WORK (2008)

In 2008, a new translation of Stanislavsky's original writings, familiar to us as *An Actor Prepares* (1936) and *Building a Character* (1949), appeared in one volume entitled *An Actor's Work*, translated by Benedetti. This is truly significant.

The crux of Stanislavsky's 'system' is the constant dialogue between our physical (seeable) bodies and our inner (unseeable) psychologies. As we've discussed throughout this book, we're all psycho–physical beings: our bodies give huge amounts of information to our imaginations, and our feelings and thoughts are transmitted through our bodies. Inner and outer are utterly interdependent. This is why Stanislavsky's 'system' was so revolutionary: it addressed your body and your inner life simultaneously.

Although he never really wanted to commit his ideas to paper, Stanislavsky was eventually persuaded to write his 'system' down, resulting in a volume so huge that no publisher would consider it. So the first (let's say *inner*) part, *An Actor Prepares* was published in a heavily edited (and not always well translated) version in America in 1936. It wasn't until thirteen years later that the equally important second (let's say *physical*) part, *Building a Character* appeared, and even today, most actors take the first book far more seriously than the second. The titles themselves are misleading, as one implies that you're working on your own instrument and once you've done that work, you're ready for the second book when you can start building characters. The reality is that both books are intrinsic parts of an ongoing training.

## BENEFITS

With its all-embracing title, *An Actor's Work* brings the two sides of the coin back together. It's a hefty tome, but while it may look daunting, it's an invaluable read, and there are many pearls of wisdom that you won't find in the other two (highly edited) books. It's great to be reminded that, while Stanislavsky's actors were working on imagination, communication and emotion memory, they also undertook exacting classes in speech and diction, as well as physical training in ballet, fencing, acrobatics, Swedish gymnastics, eurhythmics, and 'flexibility of movement' (which could well be the yoga lessons led by Stanislavsky's invaluable colleague, Leopold Sulerzhitsky [1872–1916]).

The semi-fictional style of the original *An Actor Prepares* has been known to put actors off, often because the heavy editing makes it seem rather clunky and fractured. While the story-telling device is still Stanislavsky's vital way of setting out his ideas in *An Actor's Work*, it's much fuller, richer and generally more engaging. The characters of the other young actors are more rounded and you get a much brighter sense of a whole class of students.

One way in which *An Actor's Work* will instantly engage you, both in debate and in practice, is the actual naming of the tools. The newly translated terminology is very provocative: **tasks** instead of 'objectives'; 'inner psychological drives' instead of 'inner motive forces'; 'bits' instead of 'units'; and 'communication' instead of 'communion'. I've no doubt some terms will become currency far faster than others; yet, it's exciting that you (as a young acting student) can become part of that debate. What works best for you? Which terms excite you creatively? Which terms engage your imagination most powerfully?

## CAUTIONS

To be honest, there are certain terms with which I struggle. As you'll see from this book, I find myself as an actor and trainer using 'objectives' more than 'tasks'. That's simply because 'What's my task here? What problem am I trying to solve?' tends to put me into more of an intellectual space, whereas 'What's my objective? What do I want / desire / need?' grabs me viscerally and full-bloodedly – but that's just my predilection.

I also grapple with 'concentration and attention': perhaps 'focus' might be a more useful rehearsal-room term. And I prefer 'communion' to 'communication', partly because we're in such a technologically, communication-orientated world, that I take 'communion' to be as much about energy exchanges, body-language and silences, as the exchange of words conjured up by 'communication'. Perhaps 'communion' was thought to have too religious an overtone?

And this connects to my own biggest bone of contention: I've always celebrated the number of references in the original *An Actor Prepares* to 'spirit' and 'soul'. Personally, I find 'spirit' is a very significant aspect of acting, one that I've found is readily talked about in both Europe and the Americas. However, these references have been translated to 'mind' in *An Actor's Work*, I gather because 'spirit' sounds too specifically religious. This raises interesting issues of what we accept as 'spiritual' in our turbulent twenty-first century. My own feeling is that we've done Stanislavsky something of a disservice to fight shy of spirit and soul, when the intangible connection between living human beings (implicit in the idea of spirit) is not only a vital part of our everyday interactions, but its absence is often what makes some acting seem pretty dead.

Basically, you'll yield to whichever terms work for you, and it's wonderful that this timely new translation heats up the debates. Certainly, Benedetti has made sure that really important material (previously edited out of the shorter translations) now has a place in our understanding of Stanislavsky's 'system'. And the appendices are absolute treasure troves of exercises and insights into how Stanislavsky sought the right images and scenarios to boost his own actors' imaginations. They're a real 'must-have'.

Although Stanislavsky was obviously a pioneer of immeasurable proportions, other members of the MAT have proved equally important in developing our acting practice, as we shall see.

## VSEVELOD MEYERHOLD (1874–1940)

Described by Stanislavsky as the 'heir' to his theatre, Meyerhold began as an actor and evolved into one of the most impactful directors in world theatre. You might wonder why Meyerhold is here when many people think of him as a director, rather than an actor-trainer. Given that he became Stanislavsky's immediate successor, I'd argue that it's worth seeing what he offered to acting processes to warrant that honoured position. Added to which, Meyerhold's work still forms a significant part of many acting syllabi in the UK (if less so in the USA), and for acting students in Moscow, the discipline of Meyerhold's Biomechanics is a critical part of their regular training.

Meyerhold's contact with Stanislavsky goes back to the opening season of the MAT, when he played Konstantin in Chekhov's *The Seagull*. Over the next four years, he performed eighteen roles, as well as serving as an assistant director. During that time, he fell in and out of favour with the management, leaving in 1902 to form his own company. Three years later, he was wooed back to the MAT to be director of the short-lived experimental Theatre-Studio, where he pursued his love of non-realistic dramas, emphasising tempo-rhythm over emotion. His career path then took a number of turns, including becoming the first director in 1921 of the State Higher Directing Workshop (the now world-famous Russian Academy of Theatre Arts, or GITIS. Look out for cross-overs with Grotowski). His training programmes here were always academic as well as practical, with Theory and Research featuring alongside singing, dancing, fencing, make-up classes, speech, movement and work on the imagination.

Stanislavsky simply couldn't let him go and in 1936, Meyerhold was wooed back again to lead Stanislavsky's Opera-Theatre Studio. Both directors spent their lives seeking an 'ideal' theatre, one which would combine delightful entertainment with thoughtful provocations, and they were inevitably drawn to one another. One year after Stanislavsky's death in 1938, Meyerhold was arrested as a spy. His wife, the actress Zinaida Raikh (1893–1939), was found dead shortly after, having been mutilated in their apartment; the neighbours heard her screaming, but thought she was rehearsing. After suffering brutal torture in prison, Meyerhold was shot in 1940.

## *MEYERHOLD ON THEATRE* (1969)

*Meyerhold on Theatre* (translated by Edward Braun) combines rehearsal commentaries, with speeches and reflections, spanning Meyerhold's colourful and intelligent career. What you'll find here is a collection of writings, rather than any kind of acting or directing primer. And the joy is that his range of references, his political and social engagement, his love of Oriental traditions, and his constant desire that theatre should be a pleasure, all resound throughout his words. His lively, intelligent personality shines forth.

## THE BENEFITS

For our particular purposes, the jewel of this book is Meyerhold's own elucidation of his main contribution to actor-training, **Biomechanics**. Fascinated by tempo-rhythm and the plastic body, Meyerhold was frustrated by actors who couldn't immediately do what he asked of them as the director. They seemed to waste so much energy and they had so little suppleness. While this is especially significant for the kind of physical theatre that fascinated Meyerhold at the time, the idea of physical relaxation and the appropriate use of energy are applicable to us all. So Meyerhold decided to look at science models, turning to *The Principles of Scientific Management* (1911) by the American industrialist Frederick Winslow Taylor (1856–1915). Using theories of time and motion, Taylor studied how men in factories could produce the greatest output with the least physical strain. He came up with a combination of 'work cycles' and 'motion economy' (including rest periods of as little as ten minutes). (Remember Laban's investigations in Manchester factories – Chapter 3?)

Meyerhold applied Taylor's study to the stage, his driving question being: 'If a factory worker could be efficient and effective simply by doing a series of actions in an order established by the conveyor belt, then couldn't actors be trained to be equally efficient with an appropriate order of actions?' He came up with the formula: Intention / Realisation / Reaction. Or to put it another way: I prepare for something (Intention); I do something (Realisation); and I regroup myself, ready for the next Intention (Reaction). It's a little like the Action-Reaction-Decision cycle that we looked at in Chapter 3, though it starts at a different place in the sequence. Rather than (1) Action / (2) Reaction / (3) Decision, Meyerhold's work cycle begins with (3) Intention (or Decision) / (1) Realisation (or Action) / (2) Reaction. Since the process is an infinity sign that weaves backwards and forwards, rather than a straight line thrusting from one partner to another, it's perfectly possible to come in on the sequence at varying points. The main thing is that we can see how Meyerhold and Stanislavsky were on a similar track; Meyerhold simply took an industrial model, while Stanislavsky took a behavioural model.

Using the Intention / Realisation / Reaction formula, Meyerhold devised a series of 22 exercises called Biomechanics. Each exercise consisted of a chain of simple actions, almost choreographies, with titles such as 'Shooting the Bow', 'The Leap on the Chest' and 'The Stab with a Dagger'. They combined psychology and physiology, biology and mechanics, making it very similar in principle to Stanislavsky's Method of Physical Actions and Active Analysis. The main difference was that it was predominantly a training process for unblocking an actor, rather than a rehearsal process for unlocking a text.

So what can Biomechanics offer to a twenty-first-century practitioner, when few of us are asked to leap onto our partner's chest?

Quite a lot, actually. I was amazed by the physical versatility of my Russian classmates during my time in Moscow. One demonstration they gave of their Biomechanics training was jaw-dropping in terms of their control, rhythm, collaboration, sense of risk and daring. These weren't actors who were intent on devoting their lives to physical theatre: they wanted to work in theatre and television like the rest of us. Yet, they revealed a fitness and stamina that put us Brits to shame.

Biomechanics offers us the means by which we can prepare our bodies, so that we can instantaneously execute whatever is needed at a moment's notice. The rigorous training requires the same four elements as Meyerhold had noted in the efficient factory worker: no unnecessary movement; a sense of rhythm; the correct positioning of the body; and stability. The pauses built into the mini-choreographies are the 'rest periods' that Taylor said were imperative in a work cycle.

Like Active Analysis, Biomechanics is fundamentally psychophysical: if you physically do the appropriate action, you'll feel the appropriate sensations. In other words, it's another way of awakening yourself to the impulses in your body and that delicate dialogue between inner experience and outer expression. With Biomechanics, you practise and practise until you have absolute 'reflex excitability': your body is so finely tuned that you can interact with complete plasticity of movement with anything on the stage – the set, the props, your fellow actors and the musical score.

However, as I said at the beginning of the chapter, we can't absorb a complicated training through reading a book. So what are the fundamental principles that we *can* immediately take from *Meyerhold on Theatre*? First of all, Meyerhold's belief in the inspirational power of theatre is infectious, as is his interest in the connection between actor and audience, and the liberating potential of a highly trained body. While in many ways, Meyerhold's ideas are not so very different from Stanislavsky's, you'll see how the aesthetic backdrop of the plays he chose – *commedia dell'arte*, **pantomime**, **grotesque**, tragic-farce and *cabotinage* – consciously expands the basics of Stanislavsky's 'system'.

You can also take a great deal of inspiration from the idea of being whole-hearted about everything you do when you step before an audience. For Meyerhold, preparing a role was like a sculptor standing before a piece of clay: how are you going to blend your soul with that of the playwright and reveal it to the audience through the character? You can only grip the spectator if you absorb the work of the director and the writer, and give of yourself freely from the stage in a generous live exchange.

## CAUTIONS

If there's any note of caution here, it's that ultimately Meyerhold's passion was for directing, rather than either acting or teaching. So, be aware that his desire that actors could do 'what the director wanted at a moment's notice' is not necessarily the best way to rehearse any more. Some of his writings, therefore, are about aesthetics and *directing* vision – inspiring in itself, but a different perspective from that of a young *acting* student. Also, as I've suggested, you obviously can't use Biomechanical exercises without some kind of preparatory training. It's no good thinking you can read *Meyerhold on Theatre* and then trying leaping onto someone's chest. (Although I remember vividly doing just such a thing as an undergraduate with Dr Robert Leach at Birmingham University – in the days before law suits and Health and Safety!) You can, however, easily take the philosophies of balance, musicality, tempo-rhythm, economy of gesture, plasticity of movement, and a sense of the body in space, without extensive knowledge of The Stab with the Dagger. And the idea of physical simplicity and dexterity is certainly very appealing.

## MICHAEL CHEKHOV (1891–1955)

Meyerhold and Chekhov share the fact that, despite having their moments of public glory in their Russian homeland, they were both eradicated from their country's records from some years (Meyerhold for fifteen, Chekhov for nearly fifty). Meyerhold was rehabilitated in 1955 (the year Chekhov died), but it wasn't until the 1980s that Chekhov's name could be discussed in Russian circles.

Mikail (Michael) Chekhov – nephew to the playwright, Anton – not only had a very colourful life, but he also knew how to write about it colourfully. Having lived in Russia, France, Italy, Germany, Latvia, Lithuania, United Kingdom and United States, he came into contact with many of the significant influences on twentieth-century acting, from Max Reinhardt (1873–1943) in Berlin to Alfred Hitchcock (1899–1980) in Hollywood. Described by Stanislavsky as the most gifted actor he'd ever worked with, Chekhov had his own attraction to both Stanislavsky and Meyerhold. While he appreciated Stanislavsky's passion for the psychologically true, Chekhov loved what he called Meyerhold's 'devilish' streak: Meyerhold saw everything in terms of mankind's sins and short-comings, revealing the darkest, cruellest, most unimaginable things – and Chekhov found this tremendously attractive.

In fact, his own life bore trademarks of darkness and cruelty, with a brilliant, but alcoholic father. Maybe as an escape from family life, Chekhov's passion was always for the theatre, and he made his debut at the First Studio in 1912 and remained with the MAT for the next fourteen years. Although he had many successes during that time, he also suffered a nervous breakdown – allegedly brought on by Stanislavsky's insistent use of affective memory. Chekhov found solace in the spiritual science of anthroposophy, gradually becoming more and more mystical in his teachings and talkings. This was his downfall. In 1927, he was denounced by the Soviet regime as an 'idealist' and a 'mystic' and, within a year, he was marked out for liquidation. Given thirty-six hours to leave the country with his second wife, Xenia, he was exiled in Europe for several. In 1935, he went to America, where he gave a series of lectures; in the audience was the actress, Stella Adler (see below). His serious teaching began when he ran the Chekhov Studio Theatre at Dartington Hall from 1936 to 1939, until the outbreak of war led to its relocation in Connecticut. A move to Hollywood in 1942 led to eleven movies, including Hitchcock's *Spellbound* (1945), for which he was nominated Best Supporting Actor in the Academy Awards. The first version of *To the Actor* was published in 1953, and two years later he died of a heart attack having dinner at home with Xenia. A very different ending to that of his compatriot, Meyerhold.

So you can see that Chekhov weaves Stanislavsky's 'system' with European theatre and Hollywood movies, as well as balancing acting and teaching almost in equal measure. *And* he wrote about it. This is a crucial combination in terms of taking acting processes forward: those who ply their trade, teach their craft, and commit their thoughts to paper.

## TO THE ACTOR (1953)

*To the Actor* (republished in 2002) is an extraordinary book, not least because it comes from a man who had the chance to work with Stanislavsky over many years; to see the changes in his practices and tastes; to be close to the life of Anton Chekhov; to collaborate intensively with Vakhtangov (whose style Chekhov understood to be midway between Stanislavsky's more realistic bent and Meyerhold's stylization); to tour Europe; to work at Dartington Hall during an extremely exciting period (remember, Laban was based there, too); to migrate from UK to US, and to hop between theatre and film. Added to which, Chekhov could speak English; so the words we receive through his book haven't been filtered through a translator.

Every chapter is a treasure, from the opening investigation of the actor's psycho-physicality to his detailed analysis of the composition of *King Lear*, and the Different Types of Performance (looking at tragedy, drama, comedy and clowning). With clowning in particular, he gives us a powerful understanding of the value of play and finding within us our creative 'inner child'.

## BENEFITS

There are instant gems to be plucked from *To the Actor*, as the style is so straightforward and the ideas are so inspiring. As Chekhov points out, the fundamental link between Stanislavsky, Meyerhold and Vakhtangov was the work on the imagination. And this is the creative seam that he himself mines. Where Stanislavsky's 'system' basically falls into (1) the actor's work on the self and (2) the actor's work on a role, Chekhov refocuses those into (1) Imagination and (2) Characterization.

Chekhov's emphasis on *Imagination* insists that you don't allow yourself to become enchained in your own personality. In some ways, he's reacting against a very specific, limited (and potentially unhelpful) interpretation of affective memory where you believe everything you invest in a character has to come from your own life experience. While, of course, you only have your own body, emotions, intellect, etc., you've also read books, you've been to movies, you've heard stories: your imagination will propel you into potential experiences based on what you've observed. And that's as valid as any actual experiences themselves.

*Characterization* is based on a similar ethos: Chekhov invites you to imagine your character has a body that's markedly different from yours. The difference might be as big as they're six inches taller, or it might be as small as they cock their head to one side in a way that you don't: the first will create an imaginative adaptation; the second will be a concrete, physical adaptation. Have you ever found yourself thinking that, unless you walk, talk, move as your character in exactly the same way as you do in everyday life, your performance won't be 'truthful'? If so, then Chekhov's work on Imagination and Characterization will guide you excitingly into new habits and experiences.

There are a couple of other useful tools to highlight, because they impact on you as a human being as much as an actor. The first is Chekhov's four types of movement: Molding, Floating, Flying and Radiating. Molding gives you a sense of the *space* (the sense that your body carves out spaces in a way that's as aesthetic as a sculpture). Floating gives you a sense of *poise* (the sense that your movements have a fluidity and grace). Flying gives you a sense of *lightness and easiness* (a sense that you're not leadenly bound by gravity). And Radiating gives you a sense of *freedom, happiness and inner warmth* (a sense of your inner being, as much as the outer being that molds the space). Put them all together and you'll probably have a pretty good 'inner creative state' ready to start your acting work. You may also find that you're a very happy, well-integrated individual. The underlying principle of Chekhov's method (and he does indeed call it a method – without either a capital M or parenthesis) is that everything you do as an artist should be with great joy. While his method is exacting and precise, the pleasure is paramount.

The second set of tools, allied to these four types of movement, comprises the four *qualities*: Ease, Form, Beauty and Entirety. The first two are accessible through the movements of Flying (*Ease*) and Molding (*Form*). *Beauty* essentially involves developing your sense of aesthetic: it's about inner beauty, not superficiality. (Part of Chekhov's way of freeing the actor is to assure you that whatever you do, right from the beginning of rehearsal, is already beautiful: you simply have to find the appropriate images and actions.) *Entirety* is connected to Chekhov's sense of perspective, in that you see each moment of creation in terms of a bigger picture; if you can sense the character's Entirety, you'll grasp its 'essence' right from the start, by appealing to your intuition as much as to your head-led analysis.

The four types of movement and the four qualities of movement (not dissimilar to Laban's Efforts: after all, they were both at Dartington Hall) are great ways of finding your own inner balance as an actor, but can just as usefully be applied to building a character and how they move through space.

### CAUTIONS

You should perhaps be cautious about how you approach the more mystical elements of Chekhov's ideas, even though he's generally very practical about his method in *To the Actor*. The caution lies in the fact that you need to have a rock-solid technique already in place. Chekhov said that Stanislavsky's 'system' is high school, while his own method is university. By that he means you won't be able to get the most out of his imaginative and esoteric work, until you've built a firm foundation of technique for yourself (such as the one available through Stanislavsky's 'system'). So don't read the book expecting a complete method: Chekhov's work springboards off Stanislavsky's, rather than being an alternative. Teachers who don't acknowledge the degree to which Chekhov is building on Stanislavsky's 'system' may leave their students in a potentially generalised place of preparation.

Chekhov made a huge impact on the American audience. In many ways, he's the real bridge between the Russian heritage and American practice, as he applied his work to film as much as theatre, in a way that neither Stanislavsky nor Meyerhold were able, and Vakhtangov died too young to try. After all, what happens in Hollywood impacts on the whole of the English-speaking acting fraternity. So now let's head to the States, starting with three giants, each of whom developed different aspects of Stanislavsky's 'system' and have already influenced more than one generation.

## THE AMERICAN CONTINGENT

There are myths and legends surrounding Lee Strasberg, Stella Adler and Sanford Meisner, all of whom worked together and knew each other very well. They were clearly three big personalities, each of whose temperaments inevitably coloured the particular strands of Stanislavsky that interested them and led them to spawn three different schools of acting in America. It's no longer useful to perpetuate the myths, dredging up who said what to whom and who was the best American interpreter of Russia's acting heritage. Underpinning all the debates and debacles would seem to be the question of: 'Who is the real heir of Stanislavsky?' And I'd suggest all of them are, so let's look at why.

## LEE STRASBERG (1901–82)

Lee Strasberg has probably been the most influential – and provocative – acting coach in America. Born in Austro-Hungary, he immigrated with his family to New York in 1909. In 1923, he was struck by the arrival of the MAT in America and the establishment in 1924 of the American Laboratory Theatre by Boleslavsky and Ouspenskaya. It was Boleslavsky who basically imported a written version of Stanislavsky's 'system' to the USA, first through a three-page article in 1923 and ten years later through his published lectures entitled *Acting: The First Six Lessons*. Those first six lessons were: Concentration; Memory of Emotion; Dramatic Action; Characterisation; Observation; and Rhythm. (Bear in mind that Stanislavsky's own book, *An Actor Prepares*, didn't appear until three years later.)

At the American Laboratory Theatre, Boleslavsky and Ouspenskaya focused on the tools of 'concentration' and 'affective memory' or 'emotion memory'. These then became the heart of Strasberg's own investigations into acting processes, although he was also heavily influenced by the writings of Stanislavsky and Vakhtangov. Through his work with the Group Theatre (1931–40), the Actors Studio (1949–82) and the Lee Strasberg Institutes of Acting (founded in New York and Los Angeles in the 1970s), Strasberg asked two crucial questions: (1) 'What are the blocks which prevent us as actors from contacting our inner landscapes?'; and (2) 'How can we access true emotions when building a character?' In other words, how do we create 'truthful behaviour' on the stage? Some argue that Strasberg focused on these two areas because he himself was emotionally restrained and so he was looking for a method that would loosen him up. (As we'll see, it was quite the opposite state of affairs with Stella Adler.) Whatever the driving forces behind his work, he made astounding headway in acting processes.

That said, he has often been misinterpreted. The reason may be partly to do with the fact that much of Strasberg's work evolved during the 1950s, when America was going through a national identity quest. Back in the 1920s, Boleslavsky had encouraged his students to find their own American way of interpreting Stanislavsky's ideas. Thirty years later, when it was politically desirable to break away from any sympathy with the Soviet Union, Strasberg followed Boleslavsky's suggestion – and he developed an American interpretation. The 1950s was a time of secrecy and introspection, and (wittingly or unwittingly) the Actors Studio encouraged that atmosphere. Because it was an exploratory laboratory rather than a producing theatre, Strasberg had no need to share publicly the intensely personal discoveries that his actors were making, as they confronted their inhibitions and tore down their social facades. The Method's heyday in the 1950s (when psychoanalysis and therapy hit big-time in America) perpetuated Strasberg's own reputation as a pseudo-therapeutic guru. Stories of people ripping off their clothes or beating each other up in a passionate frenzy added a further frisson to the Actors Studio's closed-door activities. To this day, you'll find some actors who only think they're being very 'truthful' if they can reduce themselves to tears in a scene, even if it doesn't really have much to do with the telling of the story. These contortions of the Method are a shame, because they can fuel unhelpful comments such as the one made by British actor, Bob Hoskins (1942–), in a British newspaper, saying that Method acting is 'a load of cobblers'.

## A DREAM OF PASSION: THE DEVELOPMENT OF THE METHOD (1988)

*A Dream of Passion* is far from being a 'load of cobblers'; there's a real intelligence in Strasberg's writing. The book is his first authentic description of what we've now come to call the Method, though he himself simply called it a 'method of work' (with a small 'm', like Chekhov did with his method). He began writing in 1974, and the first draft was edited by Evangeline Morphos a year after his death in 1983. What emerge through the thoughtful words are the clear stages involved in his method, as he sought truthful behaviour in actors.

As we approach the book's content, we should note that Strasberg wasn't offering comprehensive actor-training. In the Actors Studio and his own private teaching, he created a laboratory environment in which actors – who were *already* vocally and physically trained – could explore scenes and investigate characters through a structured series of exercises. While we'll look at the exercises in a moment, the main tools underpinning the method are: relaxation; concentration; affective memory; and improvisation.

### BENEFITS

The first, obvious benefit of this book is that it contains Strasberg's own words. We see very clearly how his investigations into affective memory take two specific avenues (sense memory and emotion memory), both of which involve a very structured and specific series of exercises.

The first set of exercises is designed to strengthen your ability to remember *simple sensory experiences* (beginning with easy tasks like drinking a cup of coffee, then moving on to studying yourself in an imaginary mirror, before recalling sharp pains, tastes, smells, etc., and finally imagining yourself in situations that affect your whole body, such as walking in the rain or taking a bath).

The second set of exercises is designed to strengthen your ability to remember more *complex emotional experiences*. You may start by focusing on the memory of *sensory* details (the colour of the coat, the volume of the music, the nip of the chill breeze), but ultimately you're using them to connect with the *emotional* details.

You certainly get the sense in *A Dream of Passion* that Strasberg's specific sequences of sensory and imaginative exercises are just as important as, say, the specialised voice exercises listed by Linklater or Rodenburg, and the rigour and order of the exercises is not to be ignored. (Ed Kovens makes this particularly clear in *The Method Manual*, 2006, which is a book worth reading in accompaniment to *Passion*). And you have to remember that, all the time, Strasberg was looking for the link between *feeling* something and *doing* something. How do you *behave* when you *feel* a certain emotion? In other words, affective memory is not self-reflective, it's an inducement to action. And this is where Strasberg's 'method of work' is sometimes misinterpreted.

Two other important aspects of the book are Strasberg's next stages in unlocking truthful behaviour on stage: *improvisation* (where the actors explore the physical actions of a scene), and *scene study* (where you look at the actor's body in action with the writer's text). These two stages tend to be overlooked by those who want to dismiss the Method exercises as psychologically dangerous, and yet *A Dream of Passion* includes some useful insights into both.

There are other gems in *A Dream of Passion*. The first features the value of working with imaginary props – not just to improve your mime technique, but also to build your faith in your own creations. If you can't even 'believe' that you're drinking an imaginary glass of ice-cold beer, then how can you believe you're seeing Banquo's ghost or that you've just murdered the king?

Two more gems are Strasberg's perspective on the Brecht–Stanislavsky juxtaposition drawn from his own interactions with Brecht: he brings the two practitioners far closer together than they're usually allowed to be. And Strasberg's inspiring belief that actor-training is actually applicable to all human beings: training our emotions and senses should be an essential part of all educational systems.

## CAUTIONS

You need to be cautious with the naivety of some of Strasberg's writing, as well as the fact that occasionally he misreads Stanislavsky. He possibly shoots himself in the foot when he confidently writes that, with practice, you can conjure up the effects of an emotion memory in *one minute*, or that only memories older than *seven years* will provide you with reliable material that won't be too distressing for you. The 'one-minute rule' could well be the case if you've trained your emotions, as we saw in Chapter 2, though Strasberg doesn't necessarily make that clear here. And how can you really be sure that a seven-year-old memory won't actually stir up some deeply affecting emotions? Isn't that why so many people go to therapy – to delve into the formative patterns of their childhood? Out of context, these timings can seem a little simplistic when you consider the complex nature of emotions that we touched on in Chapters 2 and 4, so don't give them too much weight.

You should also be cautious about how both Strasberg and Boleslavsky interpreted Stanislavsky's idea of 'living through' a role. We've touched on this already, but it's worth noting here that Stanislavsky (just like Strasberg) suffered incredible stage-fright; therefore, many of his experiments were geared towards channelling your performance adrenalin into the task in hand. So, 'living through' a performance is not just a question of understanding Othello's jealousy or Ophelia's pain. It's also a matter of listening to your partner, engaging your imagination, and allowing your dual consciousness of acting the role *and* attending to the technical demands to be part of your performance experience. 'Living through' your performance involves loving the experience of being on stage or in front of a camera, as much as whatever you're going through as the character.

Strasberg's compatriot, Stella Adler, on the other hand, had no qualms about performing.

## STELLA ADLER (1901–92)

'Aim high!' That was Stella Adler's motto as an actor-trainer. Born into a theatrical dynasty in 1901, key moments of Adler's acting evolution include her two-year training at the American Laboratory Theatre between 1924 and 1926, and her joining the Group Theatre in 1931. Three years later, she broke away, after spending five weeks studying with Stanislavsky in Paris. There she told him she'd grown to hate the theatre since encountering his 'system', mainly due to Strasberg's emphasis on affective memory. Unlike Strasberg, Adler was already emotionally volatile. The last thing she needed was a method that made her more so. When Stanislavsky asked her what she knew about superobjectives and tasks, she pleaded ignorance, at which point he shared with her the basis of the Method of Physical Actions. Armed with her new understanding of Stanislavsky's action-orientated processes (which in many ways suited her personality down to the ground), she returned to New York to alert the Group to this evolution. Certain ears were deaf and she quit soon after.

We shouldn't place too much emphasis on this meeting with Stanislavsky, as his account of the meeting is very brief and her account is rather colourful. Since the notes apparently taken during their five-week encounter have never been published, we don't know the details, and speculating doesn't help too much. What we do know is that Adler went on to work with Brecht and Reinhardt, she taught at Erwin Piscator's (1893–1966) Dramatic Workshop at the School for Theatre Research (where Marlon Brando was one of her devoted students) and she founded the Stella Adler Acting Studio (later renamed the Stella Adler Conservatory of Acting). Here she developed a comprehensive two-year training programme. In 1955, she participated in Michael Chekhov's lecture series in Hollywood, and in 1986, her Conservatory in Los Angeles was opened. Her experience of acting processes from all sides of the spectrum is unquestionable.

In many ways, you could say that Strasberg had picked out from Stanislavsky's 'system' the need for 'truthful' behaviour, while Adler picked out the tools of given circumstances and imagination. Both their perspectives are equally valid and vital.

## THE TECHNIQUE OF ACTING (1988)

*The Technique of Acting* has become an American classic, and in it you'll find some wonderful, visceral insights into acting, with Adler's underlying motive being to dignify the actor as a creative collaborator. She reacts (fairly or unfairly) against the 'stumbling, mumbling' brand of acting that she saw developing in the Method. (Though, ironically, her star pupil, Brando, could be held largely responsible for that label.) Instead, she urges you as an actor not to be afraid of creative magnitude and to embrace the universal wisdom inherent in us all.

In fact, one of the most exciting aspects of Adler's book is her philosophical, ethical outlook on acting. She asks you to take on 'psychic size', so that your character's personal crisis becomes a mirror of humanity's eternal dilemmas. You should rise to the size of the play, rather than bringing it down to street level. And that requires 'maximum acting', where you appreciate yourself as a *subject* aligned with Nature, rather than an *object* depreciated by society. The more you understand Nature, the greater your sense of compassion, and the stronger will be your ability to take responsibility for answering the moral questions underpinning a play. (There are arguably echoes of Michael Chekhov here.) She invites you to pursue an 'artistic way of life' – through your body (which should be worthy of being sculpted) and your voice (which should be worthy of being recorded). This is the fervour with which Adler writes: it's fightin' talk!

### BENEFITS

Although Adler draws on familiar tools, she adds some new colour, not least to Stanislavsky's notion of objective ('What am I doing?') and Vakhtangov's idea of justification ('Why am I doing it?'). For Adler, the main resources for answering these questions are the given circumstances, particularly 'Where am I?' (remember Viola Spolin and her emphasis on place?) and 'What's my job?' Taking her inspiration from her conversations with Stanislavsky, Adler pinpoints that *where* you are determines exactly how you behave; how you behave reveals what's important to you and how you go about getting it. 'What's my job?' will tell us about your relationship with money. This was significant for Adler, as she condenses the theme of most good dramas to the 'gimme instinct' versus the 'search for something higher'. Our relationship with material gains in a 'middle class' world (where we have few, common, spiritual values) often determines our choices. And for Adler, 'In your choices lies your talent'.

One of Adler's best pieces of advice is very practical and very pleasurable: it's to add an impediment to your work with props. Allow the way that inanimate objects can have a life of their own to be part of your realism. Let a watch chain be tangled. Let a wallet be so full of detritus that, as you pull out the twenty dollar bill, receipts fly everywhere. Complications like this – 'deliberate accidents' – can be great fun and can give your performance a healthy dose of appropriate imperfection.

A further great Adler wisdom is to fall in love. Fall in love with your text, fall in love with big ideas, fall in love with your craft, fall in love with humanity's complexities.

## CAUTIONS

However, I'd suggest that Adler's encouragement of love requires a little caution: at the end of a class, Adler reportedly would say to the students, 'Do you love me?' To which they would all chorus, 'Yes!' And this would be repeated a couple of times to increasingly fervent, 'Yeses!' The line between guide and guru may be a little too narrow for some. Indeed, for all the passion coursing through the book, there are some parts where you need to be particularly discerning.

For example, some of the verbs that Adler chooses for actions are self-reflexive, rather than forward-moving, and so may not be particularly helpful. 'To dream', 'to reminisce', and 'to confess' are in danger of producing generalised, self-orientated acting. Even her more direct actions, such as 'to unmask', 'to expose' and 'to reveal' are referred back to the actor, as in unmasking, exposing and revealing aspects of yourself. I'd suggest that trying to unmask, expose or reveal *your partner* are far more direct and dynamic actions than those geared towards yourself.

That said, it's wonderful how Adler brings right to the fore the importance of playing actions, and there's no question that she has influenced many theatre makers over the years and across the globe, not least Max Stafford-Clark, whose own brand of 'actioning' was discussed in Chapter 4.

It would be easy to fall into the Strasberg (Emotion) camp versus the Adler (Action) camp, but in some ways, they can't be compared. Strasberg wasn't offering a two-year comprehensive training system in the way that Adler was: his Actors Studio was a forum for ready trained professionals to investigate their craft. They were simply drawing on two equally valid aspects of our craft – and, as we'll see, our third American 'giant' drew upon another.

## SANFORD MEISNER (1905–97)

Born in New York, the key moment in Meisner's life as far as our story is concerned happened in 1931, when he became one of the original members of the Group Theatre. A personality equal in boldness and intelligence to his fellow actors, Adler and Strasberg, before long Meisner felt discontent among the company and in 1935, he began a life of teaching, both at the Neighborhood Playhouse (where he stayed for the best part of sixty years) and at the Actors Studio, where he was invited in 1947 to be one of their first actor-trainers. There's no question that Meisner *loved* teaching, and his desire to help actors train has spawned a training programme – the Meisner Technique – which is formidable in the States and over the last few decades has grown in popularity in the UK.

Again, I'd suggest we sidestep the personal comments that are made by each of the giants about each other, and unlock the way in which their training philosophies are ultimately highly complementary. The particular Stanislavsky tool that Meisner picked up and ran with was 'communion', with his technique channelling actors' energy into detailed observation of each other with the quality of dynamic listening that we've been discussing all along. Although I haven't trained extensively in Meisner Technique, I find Meisner's words strike so many chords with my own experience and understanding of Stanislavsky's Active Analysis, his principles are gold dust.

## *SANFORD MEISNER ON ACTING* (1987)

So, how does Meisner's book differ in style and content from what we've read so far? First of all, *Sanford Meisner on Acting* is written in

collaboration with Dennis Longwell. The narrative follows a thir-
teen-month course, during which time Meisner takes the students –
and the reader – through the basic exercises of his training, in a
specific order with specific intentions. Scattered through the narrative are references to his speaking machine (he'd already had two
operations on his larynx) and details of classroom in-jokes and
chuckles, not to mention trips to his office for his fur-collared coat.
In other words, this isn't a 'how to' like Adler's book; this isn't a
thought-through presentation like Strasberg's; this isn't a semi-
fictional class like Stanislavsky's; or collected thoughts like
Meyerhold's. This is a notated daily journey through an actor-
training programme with a man who says that he only enjoys
himself and feels free when he's teaching, and who understands that
the teaching of acting is an art-form in itself. What this means is the
energy of the classes, as well as the specificity of the exercises and the
real challenges to real students, pours through the pages. And by
the end, you can't help but like and respect him, because he loves
what he's doing and it seems to be for no other aggrandisement
than that of the art of acting.

## BENEFITS

The main message that leaps off the page is that the key to your
craft is your partner. The art of acting is *really* doing something, and
whatever you're doing is always in response to your partner,
because you're *really* listening to them. And this quality of attention
instantly achieves two things: your interaction with your partner is
incredibly alive, and you don't feel self-conscious because your
consciousness isn't on yourself.

Because Meisner's exercises are so simple, you can almost pluck
them out of the book and try them straightaway – as long as you
understand *what* the order is and *why* the exercises need to be in
that order, because otherwise you'll short-circuit the process.

The first exercise, the Word Repetition Game, simply involves
me making an observation about you: 'Your eyes are blue.' You
repeat back to me exactly what you heard: 'Your eyes are blue.' It's
a simple observation. The script is repetitive so it doesn't have to be
inventive. And the result of its simplicity and repetitiousness is that
we can tune into each other in a very direct, easy, and highly

connected way – because we've got nothing to worry about. The dialogue can be empty and inhuman, but it's very connected: i.e. it's the springboard to something else. Yet we have to be sure we've built the springboard before we can take the dive.

The second exercise, the Word Repetition Game from Your Point of View, means that you can now adjust what you hear to be truthful for you. 'Your eyes are blue.' 'My eyes are blue.' When the moment is right – and instinct will find that moment for you – the dialogue evolves. 'I said, your eyes are blue.' 'I know you said my eyes are blue.' 'You sound annoyed.' 'I sound annoyed?' 'Yes, you sound annoyed.' 'Well, I'm not.' 'You're not?' 'I'm not annoyed.' 'What are you then?' And so on. Instinct will change the dialogue for us if we pay absolute attention to each other, listening, observing, and opening ourselves up to whatever impulse is aroused in us by whatever you might say to me and whatever I might say in response. As long as we allow our instincts to respond (rather than our inner playwrights, telling us that there needs to be variety), then we'll remain absolutely connected to each other. And ultimately that's all that Meisner's technique is about.

*Sanford Meisner on Acting* is inspiring in its simplicity, its acuity and its accessibility. Meisner offers so many pithy sayings that instantly press your 'Aha!' button. 'Don't do anything unless something happens to make you do it.' 'What you do doesn't depend on you; it depends on the other fellow.' One of the most reassuring epithets is that a musician takes twenty years to become a master, and it's the same with actors. So if you're in Week 1 or Year 3 of your actor-training or Year 10 of your professional work, don't be afraid if sometimes you try something and it simply doesn't work. Acting takes years to master.

One final tool to pluck from this rich book is Meisner's focus on preparation. By this he refers to the state into which you come into a scene: you can never come in emotionally empty; you always have to have some condition of emotional aliveness. This equates to Stanislavsky's inner creative state that we've touched on throughout this book. As Meisner puts it, the text is the canoe, and the emotion of the scene is the river. You have to be sure you've put water in the river before you can float the canoe on it. That's what your preparation entails. You don't have to conjure up an emotion and hang on to it for five minutes until it's necessary for the dialogue: you have to put yourself in an inner creative state whereby you can react off your partners truthfully and instinctively once the scene begins.

## CAUTIONS

My main caution with *Sanford Meisner on Acting* is that he suggests you learn the words by rote without any emotional colouring. I understand that it's not until you encounter your stage partner and see how they behave towards you that you'll really know how to say your lines. And yet, if part of your preparatory work involves unlocking your character's thought processes: it can be very hard to *ever* say the lines without giving them an inner life. Otherwise, they feel like empty forms.

A second caution I have is with Meisner's emphasis on crying. For all his insistence that your emotions will come from the action and your partner, there are more than a dozen times in the book where he orders, 'Cry!' or 'Get hysterical!', goading his students into sobbing. This instruction makes sense only if you note carefully that right towards the end of the book he says, 'This is a classroom … And anything can happen in it which *might not happen if you were really on stage*' (p.245, my emphasis). Far too often, actors can fixate themselves on the crying and hysterical aspects of actor-training, applying them inappropriately to rehearsal room situations, not to mention performances. Be clear: the contents of Meisner's book focuses on *training*! It's a classroom. In their different ways, Strasberg, Adler and Meisner encourage you to be emotionally accessible as an actor; yet, as we saw in Chapter 2, that requires training. When it comes to a script that you're working on for a performance, you have to tell the writer's story, and often the story does *not* require sobbing and wailing, but just the opposite – the poignant containment of big emotions.

On the subject of writers, it's time to turn to our final American executor, who in fact spent some time training under Meisner at the Neighborhood Playhouse.

## DAVID MAMET (1947–)

'What's David Mamet doing here?' you may well ask. 'He's a director-playwright, not an acting coach.' The reason for including

Mamet is that his book, *True and False Heresy and Common Sense for the Actor*, has had a huge impact on actors, both sides of the pond. Although it's most certainly not a primer, the book often gives actors permission to make certain assumptions about acting, which are not necessarily helpful. And so I want to foreground both the benefits and the cautions of the book within the context of other actor-trainers.

As one of the most exciting and influential names in contemporary American drama, Mamet is renowned for pithy, poetic, raw, and highly structured dialogue, focusing primarily on male characters and often exposing the underbelly of modern, Western values. His Tony-nominated plays (including *Glengarry Glen Ross* [1984] and *Speed-the-Plow* [1988]) and Oscar-nominated screenplays (including *The Verdict* [1982] and *Wag the Dog* [1997]) reflect Meisner's repetition work in the very fabric and tempo-rhythm of their dialogue.

Mamet has also been a powerful voice in American actor-training. In 1983, he joined actor William H. Macy (1950–) to found the Atlantic Theater Company, which focused on studio actor-training. The company was affiliated to the Drama Department at New York University, where they both taught. Their programme became known as Practical Aesthetics, and was rooted in Meisner's own evolution of Method acting, though their other influences included Grotowski and Suzuki (see later in this chapter).

Mamet and Macy 'gave' their training to the first graduates of the NYU programme, who took over the now famous Off-Broadway theatre company in 1985. A year earlier, several students collaborated on a book outlining Mamet and Macy's training, entitled *A Practical Handbook for the Actor* (1986), now used extensively in the States.

## TRUE AND FALSE: HERESY AND COMMON SENSE FOR THE ACTOR (1998)

*True and False* has proved to be a very hot potato for actors on both sides of the Atlantic. In a major reaction against the more introspective elements of the American Method, Mamet argues passionately against almost everything that might be seen as fundamental acting processes. Perhaps his most quoted line is that the actor doesn't need to 'become' the character, because actually the phrase has no meaning: 'There *is* no character. There are only lines upon a page' (Mamet, 1998:9). The message throughout the book is that a character is nothing more than the dialogue written for you to speak, plus your own physical body (as we've noted several times in these chapters). All you have to do is learn the lines crafted by the writer, and basically get out of the way of the play. You can see the link between Mamet and Meisner in their shared belief that there's no need to focus on building a character *per se*: from your actions and your behaviour, the audience will figure out who your character is.

## BENEFITS

'Invent nothing. Deny nothing,' incites Mamet. Follow your impulses and get out of your own way. Like Grotowski's *via negativa*.

In fact, there are some spunky and provocative aspects to *True and False*, which has been seized hungrily by English-speaking actors across the globe. Mamet throws out Stanislavsky, ridicules any biography you might create for your character, and rails at affective memory as utterly irrelevant to the actor's task – that task being to walk out in front of the audience and tell the story. Mamet incites you to dive into the 'terrifying unforeseen' of performance and face the demons of nervousness and insecurity in all your creative nakedness. Courage is what the audience have come to see, not careful preparation and structured arcs to your character. The terrifying unforeseen is an invaluable concept.

So Mamet celebrates nerves, seeing the vulnerability of live performance as the absolute life-blood of acting. He healthily jibes at the acting gurus who make Big Cash out of appealing to the lonely actor's sense of insecurity. Don't get rid of that insecurity, he insists: it's the very pulse of your characterisation, as no one is without fears, doubts and uncertainties. The nearest you can get to 'truth' on the stage is to reveal those insecurities for what they are. In the moment of creating a role, you're given an extraordinary opportunity 'to be brave and simple in difficult circumstances'. What Strasberg calls a 'vulgar preoccupation' – i.e. the terror of performance – Mamet celebrates as the essential ingredient of vibrant, honest acting.

## CAUTIONS

*True and False* is also a very tricksy book. Mamet swipes at certain ideas, only to reclaim them later or to offer no alternative, and he dismisses actor-training in general. He freely bashes Stanislavsky, confusing his 'system' with specific aspects of the American Method in a detrimental way, revealing a limited knowledge of Stanislavsky, which is certainly very unhelpful. Especially as he pillages the main tools of objectives and actions, without referencing that these were just as important to Stanislavsky as affective memory was. He stresses that the actor needs a strong voice, superb diction, a supple body, and the ability to make exciting choices, without explicitly explaining that most of these are going to come from the very training he dismisses. Mamet's real beef seems to be with Strasberg and the Actors Studio, and Stanislavsky becomes a casualty on the way.

The crux of the book is that, without stressing it explicitly, Mamet is fundamentally addressing *performance*, rather than training or rehearsal. And herein lie the big differences between Strasberg, Adler, Meisner and Mamet. Adler offered a structured two-year training programme. Strasberg experimented intensively on one aspect of acting (i.e. how to free yourself from your emotional blocks and behave truthfully). Meisner developed an actor's ability to listen and commune with other actors. And Mamet, by contrast, heads straight for the jugular of performance, sidestepping training or rehearsal.

As you read *True and False*, you'll no doubt be highly charged and inspired. But be warned: many of Mamet's arguments seem to assume that all scripts are as good as his. Yet, as we all know – they're not. The thin-ness of many texts leaves us filling in more gaps than just the pauses written into the dialogue.

*True and False* is unquestionably exciting in its direct, full-on style, but it needs to be read with a hefty pinch of salt. For a theatre maker who actually founded an actor-training programme, he's hardly going to advocate that actors don't need any training at all. He's just wary of the kind of preparation that bears no resemblance to the task in hand. And that task is to listen dynamically to your partner, the story, the script and the audience, within the cold waters of the terrifying – and paradoxically addictive – unforeseen.

## THE EUROPEAN CONTINGENT: JERZY GROTOWSKI (1933–99)

While the Russian acting baton was clearly passed to the United States, it was also circulated in Europe, not least through the work of director-researcher Jerzy Grotowski. He referred to Stanislavsky as his 'personal ideal', and you can certainly see Stanislavsky's influence on Grotowski's life-long investigation into psycho-physicality, and his particular concern with how to reduce the time-lapse between your inner impulse and your outer expression so that impulse *becomes* expression. Grotowski also valued Stanislavsky's commitment to finding an appropriate score of physical actions, as well as developing the communion between actors, and deepening the relationship between actor and audience. At the same time, he was heavily influenced by Meyerhold's rigorous, physical training to place your body completely at the service of your director, the playwright and yourself. The cornerstones of Grotowski's training were spontaneity and discipline: without spontaneity your acting is dead and without discipline your performance is chaotic. Through total precision, you can be creatively free.

Born in Poland in 1933, Grotowski was a child of the Second World War. His father fought against Hitler as an officer in the Polish army, before immigrating to Paraguay and leaving behind his six-year-old son. You can see the rawness and decimation which underscored Grotowski's childhood making its impact on his performance ethos through the naked, confrontational style. He trained as an actor at the State Theatre School in Krakow and received a scholarship in 1955 to study directing in Moscow at GITIS (where Meyerhold had been a founding director). The combination of Stanislavsky's work on the actor and Meyerhold's work on the director, as well as Vakhtangov's visionary practices, made a huge impact on Grotowski's development as a theatre-maker.

Grotowski loved the mystical, often travelling like a nomad around the world. He journeyed deep into the human soul, and far across the planet. His travels into the inner realms of being human were always inspired by his search for what we might call 'being totally in the moment'. And over the years, he became more and more interested in human processes, and less and less interested in artistic results.

The question is: What can you take from Grotowski's work, when you're never going to acquire the psycho-physical acumen of his performers unless you're prepared to devote yourself to intense physical training for eight hours a day, six days a week, over several years?

## TOWARDS A POOR THEATRE (1975)

Actually, there are some very significant principles featured in *Towards a Poor Theatre*, which I believe you can apply to your work, whatever your training or whatever the task in hand. The book is a collection of insights, impressions, photographs and articles, rather than an acting guide. Yet there are some instant tools you can put in your kit.

### BENEFITS

The *via negativa* is a terrific concept, and it curiously connects with Mamet's 'terrifying unforeseen'. Grotowski stresses that his method (and, like Chekhov and Strasberg, he does call it a method) focuses on eliminating blocks, rather than acquiring skills. The idea of the *via negativa* was to abandon your bourgeois trappings and values, and return to a poor, rough, naked immediacy. Perhaps the most contemporary application of the *via negativa* is not to ask the question 'How do I do this?', but rather to ask 'What do I *not* do, in order to do this? How do I get out of my own way in order to trampoline over the obstacles thrown up by my psyche?' So the reason behind all the highly acrobatic physical training isn't necessarily to acquire corporeal excellence, it's to notice what gets in your way when you try to stand on your head or leap into a somersault. Is it physical fear? A battle with gravity? Lack of flexibility? He's really asking you: 'What's your relationship with your own body?' In fact, Grotowski teachers will often show you a series of headstands and somersaults, and then say: 'Now you do it!' Their objective is not to teach you where to put your hands and how to balance your butt; it's for you to find that out for yourself, by giving the moves a go and discovering what adaptations you need to make to work with and against gravity – to get out of your own way. As Lorna Marshall might say, 'Invite your body to the party.'

In effect, your body is the journey of your life: it's the expression of who you are right at this moment, and it's the tangible means by which the audience reads the signals, forms and spatial relationships you execute on stage. Because your body is your public instrument, you have to know it and love it (as we saw in Chapter 2). Basically, Grotowski has taken Stanislavsky's concept of psycho-physicality and pushed it to the Nth degree. He invites you to enjoy the flow of movement within your body, stripping away all the social clichés and paraphernalia, which have clogged up your creative arteries like cholesterol. (This sense of flow echoes Overlie's Viewpoints.)

To promote this ethos, he uses terms like 'self-penetration', 'self-revelation', 'self-research' and 'sacrifice' – all of which can sound rather terrifying. Yet, I'd suggest that, on some level as actors, we're doing it all the time. We're constantly addressing and assessing what we are and who we are, and how that self can be used in our profession to reveal the truths of a writer's text.

Where Grotowski's ideas become most useful is in making sure that we really listen to each other on stage or screen. He hits the nail on the head when he says that acting should be a 'total act', a genuine encounter between human beings. (A little like Meisner.) We live in an age where truth can be hard to come by: there often seems to be a hidden agenda in situations, and many people (particularly as I write in 2009 during a global economic meltdown) have shown that they're out for a fast buck. This makes genuine listening, genuinely hearing the truth about ourselves and others – and humanity in general – really hard to palate. But it's the only way humanity can move forward, and Grotowski incites us to stop cheating and start being 'authentic', as we tear off our masks and exteriorise all the anxieties, fears and desires, which actually link us all together.

## CAUTION

If there's a caution, it's 'Don't expect a manifesto'. Grotowski is a philosopher as much as a director, a poser of questions as much as a provider of answers. The pertinence and accessibility of the articles varies in *Towards a Poor Theatre*, but the illustrations are invaluable.

## EUGENIO BARBA (1936–)

At the centre of a kind of international vortex, Italian-born Eugenio Barba brings together many of the influences discussed throughout this book. He describes Stanislavsky as 'the primal father of modern Western theatre'. He draws upon Meyerhold's Biomechanics and Michael Chekhov's imagination work. He served as Grotowski's Assistant Director on *The Constant Prince* (1965). He trained in *kathakali* in the 1960s (when the West knew very little of Indian theatre and dance). Indeed, Barba's professional life has been devoted to combining Eastern (or what he calls 'North Pole') traditions with Western ('South Pole') traditions.

Born in Gallipoli in 1936, Barba (like Grotowski) was the son of an army officer, who died when Barba was ten. After joining a military school aged 14, he travelled to Norway three years later and served in the merchant navy. Since he couldn't speak Norwegian, he became expert at deciphering people's tiniest gestures and facial expressions, for which he coined the term **pre-expressivity** (i.e. the little meanings conveyed to another person, even before a word is spoken). He began to note where an impulse begins in the body, and what kinds of movements and gestures those impulses generate. This was to become the basis of his theatre research.

Barba's directing career began in earnest at Warsaw Theatre School, and three years were spent in the early 1960s with Grotowski in Poland, during which time he also travelled to India. There, he lived among villagers, who trained from a very young age in *kathakali*, learning to embody the ancient, codified theatre system, in the belief that you can't portray a god onstage unless you yourself believe in the gods. Acting is a priesthood, rather than a profession, requiring a complete way of living and faith.

Barba desperately wanted to be the Artistic Director of a theatre, but jobs were few and far between. So in 1964, aged twenty-seven, he founded his own company, the Odin Teatret, with a group of young actors. They were all drama school 'rejects' and therefore in the same position as he: they all yearned to make theatre but didn't have an outlet. Before long, he realised the Odin Teatret couldn't get very far until the young actors were trained, and yet he knew nothing about actor-training. And so began a fundamental practice in Barba's theatre. Each individual took responsibility for a particular aspect of training: the ballet dancer taught ballet, the gymnast researched and taught Biomechanics, and little by little, they shared skills so that each individual could build up their psycho-physical vocabulary, training for eight to twelve hours a day for six days a week.

In 1978, the actors were sent for three months to the far corners of the world to immerse themselves in other performance vocabularies. (Actress Else Marie Laukvik [1944–] went to Paris and took a clowning course with Jacques Lecoq. Watch the baton pass again.) When they all reconvened to share their newly acquired knowledge, Barba noted that, as each person began to show their work, they seemed to step out of their everyday bodies and take on a new one. Their weight and balance, their spines and eyes, were all used differently, and – whichever culture's work they were sharing – there seemed to be a sense of a special performance state. Barba adopted the term **extra-daily body** and applied his observations to the actor's working process.

## THE PAPER CANOE (1995)

*The Paper Canoe* is an invaluable addition to your library, not least because it's a challenging read. Barba is as interested in scholarly debate as he is in theatre practice, and he writes for both audiences. As you read it, you'll find yourself asking as an actor, 'What on earth has all this theory got to do with me?' At that very moment, he seems to read your mind, as he conjures up an imaginary actress who asks that very question: 'What use might all these analyses and examples be?' Barba answers that they're pipes and channels and reservoirs, but nobody can give you *your* water. As someone who straddles the Academy and the Industry, I'm personally very aware of the underlying tensions between performance theorists and practitioners: it's important that practitioners are seen to write in a scholarly way, even if it makes for a challenging read – so stick with it!

### BENEFITS

*The Paper Canoe* is packed with various philosophical perspectives on acting, and I want to pick just three of them here: (1) the importance of training; (2) the dialogue between theory/research and practice; and (3) the way in which Barba combines the highly structured techniques of Eastern practices with the less structured, more individualised practices of Western actor-training.

Let's take a look at each of these.

First of all, training requires your utter commitment: it's your chance to prove that you want to transform your dream about being an actor into actions that further your craft. You find in Barba's work that your training becomes a necessary lifetime pursuit, through which you keep addressing the daily obstacles that impede your communication skills. You also find it's a personal journey: there are no fixed routines. Each actor has a different temperament, and each exercise has a different temperature. Your personal training (drawing on both Eastern and Western principles) becomes your way of defining yourself. You actually dialogue with the training techniques themselves, as you assess the extent to which you're resisting or complying with whatever you choose to explore. The practice is very close to Grotowski's *via negativa*: you're getting ready to play with your own creative self. Training also includes some definite tools from Stanislavsky's kit: objectives (in that you need to know exactly why you're making a movement, training isn't just empty mechanics) and affective memory (you use very detailed, enriching images from your own life to motivate your sequences or 'scores'). Training becomes a very precise way to develop your 'presence'. For Barba, presence is a kind of dynamism, an 'energhia' which is all about being ready to produce creative work.

The second perspective to take from *The Paper Canoe* is how scholarly research is just as important as practice. Actors often run screaming to the hills at the idea of scholarship, though for Barba research is simply curiosity. The questions that preoccupy him are: 'Why act? What *is* the performer's presence? Is talent also a technique? How do I become an effective actor? Why do I choose to make theatre, and not something else? What am I going to accomplish through my theatre making? Who are the people for whom I'm making my particular brand of theatre?' Again, these are stimulating questions, applicable to us all as actors, whether for theatre or film.

The third perspective to take from *The Paper Canoe* is the Eastern–Western fusion, called here 'Eurasian' theatre. Barba points out that theatre is a land unbounded by geographical borders. So the concept of Eurasian is a mental/technical dimension, rather than a specific geography. During his time studying *kathakali*, Barba became fascinated by the way we can separate and activate different parts of the body using contradictory rhythms – maybe slow ankles and fast wrists. There's a total commitment demanded of Asian and Oriental (North pole) performers, which is summed up by Barba with the Japanese phrase spoken by audiences to actors after a performance: '*otsukaresama*' – 'you have tired yourself out for me'. As we saw in Chapter 2, Western (South pole) performers have a much harder time of it, as we have no stylised codes, no established repertoire of gestures and narratives, passed reverently down to us through the ages. Instead, our training is arbitrary, and the first point of departure is usually our own personalities. That's not to say that one 'pole' is better than the other; Barba simply invites us to evolve our own acting practice by studying and understanding others.

In addition to the philosophical perspectives in *The Paper Canoe*, there are also some great tools. I'm going to pick just one: the body-mind. Barba was amazed when he saw how an Asian or Oriental actor's coldly executed technique could actually arouse great emotions in their spectators. It led him to question the whole 'inner-outer/outer-inner' conundrum. The term 'body-mind' – as we've already seen – allows for inner and outer processes to exist simultaneously. Overthrowing Descartes' division of your inner processes from your physical expression, Barba describes every action as being like a garment with a lining (where the lining is usually invisible from the outside): 'Some performers prefer to begin with the lining, others with the garment. There is no lining-garment duality' (Barba, 1995:116). It doesn't matter whether your process begins from the inner work or the externals because, in the end, 'the lining and garment must be one entity: your body-mind'. This is a compact way of overcoming the turf war between the inner 'I have to feel it' school and the outer 'just do it' school. As far as Barba is concerned, there *is* no differentiation: your body-mind is your thoughts made physical, and your actions made imaginative. This could explain Meisner's repeated commands to his students in class: 'Cry! Just cry!' If they just do it, they'll probably feel it, as the muscle memory of sobbing will provoke the *experience* of sobbing. Maybe the baton passes more often than we notice.

## CAUTIONS

There aren't really any cautions beyond 'Stick with it'. For those of us who like the muscularity of Mamet or the accessibility of Adler, Barba's style is more oblique. Yet, given the subtle tension between 'Those Who Do' and 'Those Who Write about What Those Who Do Do', Barba makes a vital and dynamic contribution to the serious analysis of acting processes across academies and institutions, as well as across theatre styles and heritages. He pirouettes with paradoxes, just like Grotowski and others before him. Discipline versus freedom. Revolt versus submission. Accident versus necessity. Practice versus theory. Not to mention the very nuanced issue of how you avoid being narcissistic while also 'enamouring' your audience. They're all ideas worth wrapping your creative curiosity around.

Barba's references to Michael Chekhov, Grotowski, Stanislavsky, Copeau, Meyerhold, and numerous Eastern traditions (from Balinese dance to *kung fu*) reveal exactly how pivotal he is in both *taking* the baton and *passing* the baton of contemporary actor-training, not least in the contact both he and his actors have had with Lecoq.

## JACQUES LECOQ (1921–99)

Up until the day before he died, Jacques Lecoq devoted his life to actor-training, with a specific emphasis on gesture. We've already noted that our bodies learn by expressing themselves through gesture, finding out which gestures elicit what we need from those around us, and eliminating those that don't. By intensively observing people in different cultures, Lecoq noted the differences between gestures of *action* (which involve your whole body), gestures of *expression* (which reveal your emotional state) and gestures of *demonstration* (with which you punctuate speech to make a point or sustain a thought). Lecoq's driving principle was that your gestures emerge from stillness, just as your words emerge from silence.

Born in Paris in 1921, Lecoq spent much of his early adult life under German occupation. A keen gymnast, he joined the College of Physical Education in 1941, and six years later was teaching physical expression at an establishment for Education through

Physical Performance. Like Meisner, he seems to have been a natural teacher, going on to spend several years in Italy, working alongside (among others) Dario Fo and director Giorgio Strehler (1921–97). During his time in Italy, Barba devoured the art and traditions of *commedia dell'arte* and became impassioned by Greek tragedy and chorus work. These influences would significantly shape his training system and in 1956, he set up what's now known as *L'Ecole Jacques Lecoq* (The School of Jacques Lecoq). Here the emphasis is on developing 'the actor creator', rather than the 'actor interpreter'. (Remember Adler's emphasis on 'the actor as collaborator'?) Improvisation and mime are used to ignite your creative imagination, so that you can become the owner of your own art. (Remember Chekhov's use of the imagination so that you can 'own' your characterisation?)

Lecoq's influences were vast, bringing together a number of names, most of whom we've encountered already: Copeau, Stanislavsky, Meyerhold, as well as mime monarch Etienne Decroux (1898–1991), and the Eastern theatrical traditions of India, Bali, China and Japan. Lecoq's own influence on the development of European theatre over the last sixty years has been enormous. Two books of his writings have been published: the first is translated as *Theatre of Movement and Gesture*, in which he presents a host of philosophical ideas about gait, mime, the interplay between our bodies and our clothes, as well as practical technique. And the second is called in French *Le corps poétique* – 'the poetic body' – translated into English by David Bradby as *The Moving Body*.

## THE MOVING BODY (2001)

*The Moving Body* is a wonderful account of Lecoq's two-year training programme at his school. He vividly articulates the philosophical ethos behind particular classes, as well as their practical content. And it's in this respect that the book is extremely useful, especially if – like many young actors – you're considering this course of training, rather than a more conventional conservatory.

Year One begins with silent improvisations, in which the students replay particular real-life experiences. (Stanislavsky's Active Analysis begins with silent improvisations called 'silent *études*' and Strasberg's affective memory focuses on real-life experience. The baton passes.) Lecoq stresses that you don't need to worry about the audience in these improvisations, it's the faithful reliving of an experience that's key: the main reference point for all his training is simply 'life'. (Resonances here with Strasberg's 'truthful behaviour'?)

The focus of the second year is on what Lecoq calls 'geodramatic territories', where the key questions are: (1) 'What are the stakes being played for?'; (2) 'What's the best stage idiom or language for expressing these stakes dramatically?'; and (3) 'Which dramatic texts will most fruitfully explore this territory?' The six main territories for answering these questions are: melodrama (emphasising grand emotions and the pursuit of justice); *commedia dell'arte* (emphasising interactivity); **bouffons** (emphasising the caricatures of power and petty human struggles); tragedy (emphasising heroes and choruses); and clowns (emphasising child-like openness). (Remember Chekhov's emphasis on the importance of clowns in *To the Actor*?)

## BENEFITS

Though *The Moving Body* is rich in tools, we'll look at just five here: (1) the neutral mask; (2) working with mimed objects; (3) pushing and pulling; (4) clowning; and (5) the role of the audience.

For a heartfelt, practical understanding of the *Neutral Mask*, look no further than *The Moving Body*. As the central part of his teaching method, Lecoq uses the neutral mask to give you the opportunity to prepare your 'blank canvas', by finding within yourself a state of perfect balance and economy of movement. As well as human dimensions, the neutral mask is used to explore Nature – through earth, air, fire and water, and through colours, lights, sounds and spaces. Lecoq's training consciously seeks the 'universal poetic sense' in each of us (which echoes Adler's appeal to 'psychic size' and Grotowski's Theatre of Sources, which is all about the absolute 'sources' that bind us all on a deep level before our respective cultures shape us). These explorations are silent at first, though music and words are introduced later. In fact, Lecoq loved language: French, German, English, Spanish, Japanese and Italian all formed significant parts of his training. One delicious example is the difference Lecoq makes between the sound of the English word 'butter' (which, for Lecoq, remains in its packet in the fridge) and the French '*buerre*' (which has melted on your toast as soon as you purr the word). (Remember Chekhov's sensual playing with sounds?)

Lecoq's work with *objects* is also fascinating, involving great imaginative journeys (not unlike Adler). He draws out the personalities of objects: for example, a crumpled piece of paper or a sugar cube dissolving in your tea have 'tragic' qualities, as they're passive, they submit to their circumstances. Objects need not be real, of course, and mime is extremely important (as it was for Stanislavsky and Strasberg). As we've already suggested, if we can't even mime a familiar activity like drinking an ice-cold beer, how will we ever handle completely unknown objects such as Banquo's ghost or an imaginary dagger that I see before me? Imagination and physical exploration are intricately interwoven in Lecoq's training, with mime considered a vital part of every actor's education.

*Pushing and pulling* is the third tool we'll look at, and here *The Moving Body* is particularly inspiring is the way it combines technical work and imaginative work. Everything we do in life, Lecoq proposes, can be reduced to two actions: pulling and pushing. This is true of the specifics of 'action mime' (i.e. miming props, walls, ropes, activities, etc.), as well as the general undercurrents of human relationships. Lecoq suggests that pushing-pulling operates on three planes: on a *horizontal* plane, the push/pull is between two people. On the *vertical* plane, the push/pull is mankind's battle between heaven and earth. On the *diagonal* plane (like an axe into wood), the energy can fly off into all sorts of directions, creating who knows what? Personally, I find that this *physical* understanding of push/pull and its *metaphoric* resonances are incredibly useful when it comes to *feeling* the undercurrents of a relationship in a scene. In most dramatic scenes, you'll find that one character is usually 'major' (i.e. they're initiating the pulling or pushing) and the other is usually 'minor' (i.e. they're resisting or responding to that action). You could express pulling as 'Come over to my side and see the world from my perspective', and you could express pushing as 'Get away from me because we have nothing in common'. Alternatively, pulling could be expressed as 'I love you so much, let me embrace you into my life' and pushing could be 'You're a big boy now, you need to fly the nest'. You can instantly take the fantastic undercurrents of Lecoq's principle of action mime and apply them to all kinds of psychological scenarios – in traditional scripted dramas, as well as purely physical theatre.

The fourth tool I want to take from *The Moving Body* is Lecoq's understanding of *clowning*. For Lecoq, exploring the clown is a process of self-discovery, as you pit yourself against yourself. To be a successful clown, you have to be open, vulnerable and willing enough to share your weaknesses and folly. You can't hide behind a character – because there *is* no character: there's only you, in all your utter psychological and physical nakedness. The point of being a clown is that you fail, you flop, you mess up. You can't even dress yourself properly: your trousers are too short, your shoes are too big, your hat is too small, you have no sense of colour or style or design. You set yourself up from your first appearance to look ridiculous. With clowning, you almost have to visit the deepest fears of your childhood: fear of being alone, fear of not being picked for the team, fear of being too fat, too thin, too short, too tall, too geeky, too shy, too brainy, too stupid – whatever! Those deep-seated fears become the very source material for your clown. As Lecoq puts it, the clown 'brings out the individual in his singularity' (Lecoq, 2001:149). And the root of this singularity is making mistakes. Mistakes are the vital ingredient in life, they keep you moving forward and remaining endlessly curious. Clowning doesn't just embrace the mistakes – it *demands* the mistakes!

And finally: *the audience*. With clowning, you have to be connected to your audience, as your clown is dependent on the spectators' reaction. There's an innate sense of improvisation as you can never predict exactly how your audience will respond. At Lecoq's school, clown work only appears at the end of Year Two, when you're used to revealing yourself fully in front of everyone else. By then, you have a deep-rooted understanding that your connection with the audience *is* the reality of live performance – just as we saw in Chapter 5.

## CAUTIONS

As with several of the practitioners here, there are very few cautions with *The Moving Body*. It's an inspiration to all actors, whether you want traditional, script-based training or preparation for physical and devised theatre.

In fact, if you were to only take one tool from Lecoq's toolkit, it would have to be his emphasis on play. Play is essentially the quality of open listening that we've seen echoed through every training process. It's your ability to expand an idea to its physical and psychological extremes with utter conviction and without ever losing sight of the reality from which it evolved. Like Barba, Lecoq looked for that 'shine' which indicates 'presence' in a student. And it's the training of this presence which leads to the final passing of the baton – across Europe to the East.

## THE EASTERN REPRESENTATIVE: TADASHI SUZUKI (1939–)

I stamp. I stamp. I send the energy of my lower body into the ground and I sense the power of ancient energy that wards off evil and eradicates my ordinary sense of self. I stamp, and in so doing, I expand my performative presence.

Tadashi Suzuki is an extraordinary contributor to twenty-first-century stage aesthetics, in terms of his marriage of Eastern and Western philosophies and practices. While he shares this marriage with Barba, he applies it to reconstructing Western dramas (from Beckett to Shakespeare to Euripides to Chekhov) rather than creating new works as Barba does.

Born in 1939, Suzuki grew up in a country adapting to the humiliating defeat of the Second World War, while also trying to balance ancient values with sudden Westernisation. (Note how most of our 'executors' were affected by WWII in one way or another.) Having trained as a director, Suzuki worked intensively over the years with Kayoko Shiraishi (1941–) (considered one of the greatest actresses in the world), and in 1972, they were invited to the acclaimed Paris Festival, *Théâtre des Nations*. Suddenly, a whole aspect of Eastern actor-training was introduced to a Western audience, and so began Suzuki's influence on Europe and the States, leading to collaborations including that with Anne Bogart, which lasted for several years.

Another of Suzuki's great collaborations has been with architect Arata Isozaki (1931–). In 1976, they renovated a farmhouse in Toga-Mura village, outside urbanised Tokyo, to create a performance space that combined a sense of the natural with the expansiveness of an Ancient Greek amphitheatre. Suzuki worked with Isozaki for over twenty years, as he investigated the significance of a performance space and its architecture (a little like Lecoq did).

The space in which you perform is vital for Suzuki. After all, a traditional *Noh* theatre is a very special space: here, a specific troupe of actors, all highly skilled in a specific art form, shares with its audience the richness of humanity's beauty and experience. The troupe who have trained and grown up in a particular theatre get to know it extremely intimately in terms of its walkways, stage and pillars, not to mention its ritual grandeur. They could walk around it with their eyes closed. In fact, they'd find it difficult to perform anywhere else. Those of us working in the West have quite a different experience: we're used to touring from one venue to another, so that our bodies can never really be tuned to one particular playing space. Because most modern theatres have so few rituals or codifications, Suzuki believes that our Western bodies have no basic 'authority' in the same way that they do in traditional Japanese theatre. Every arbitrary change in the performance space weakens our creative body.

So, the essence of Suzuki's training is to interweave the sanctity and certainty of the ancient methods of *Kabuki* and *Noh* with contemporary practice, so that you can celebrate highly codified forms without losing any of your spontaneity.

## THE WAY OF ACTING (1986)

*The Way of Acting* (translated by Thomas J. Rimer) (or 'The Power of Transgression' in direct translation from the Japanese) is a little like Barba's *The Paper Canoe*. It contains philosophical perspectives rather than detailed exercises. That said, from the very first line, we get a flavour of Suzuki's influences as he cites the Moscow Art Theatre. Then, as the book unfolds, we begin to see how his fascination for the power of gesture and the body's means of communication has certain echoes with Lecoq. His study of the relationship between word and gesture is as intricate as both Grotowski's connection of impulse to expression and Stanislavsky's connection of thought to action. There are myriad cross-overs between our executors.

BENEFITS

Because *The Way of Acting* is philosophical as much as hands–on practical, its benefits lie in its poetry. That said, if there's one tool you can take straight from Suzuki's kit, it's the relevance of your contact with the floor.

1920's Japan saw a violent reaction against the formalised codes of *Kabuki*, and psychological realism began to revolutionise Japanese theatre. Suzuki's practice is basically a reaction against *that* reaction. He saw how the modernisation of acting had abandoned one of the most potent aspects of traditional theatre – the contact of your foot with the floor. Unlike the stilettos, sneakers, crocs, boots and myriad other footwear that you find in Western theatre costumes, *Kabuki* and *Noh* plays are performed in special socks, with the actors' feet being a significant part of the audience's entertainment. Because contemporary Western plays are performed in shoes, Suzuki believed the most basic aspect of acting becomes compromised. Modern theatre is 'tedious' as 'it has no feet'.

Since, for Suzuki, the performance begins when your feet touch the ground, this earthy contact must form the basis of your actor-training. After all, your contact with the floor affects the whole alignment of your spine, and (as Suzuki upholds) it also determines the strength and nuance of your voice.

To get us back in touch with our feet – and therefore our spine and voices – Suzuki has devised a series of set exercises (involving stamping, squatting, walking, vocalising and accessing different musical rhythms in the body). Working with posture and locomotion, he has four basic stamping patterns and ten walking exercises, which use the feet in different ways (all explained thoroughly in Paul Allain's *The Art of Stillness* [2002], an invaluable companion to *The Way of Acting*). These exercises are also designed to build our stamina, stability and concentration as actors.

CAUTIONS

While contact with the floor may sound easy and obvious, the stamping exercises are actually extremely strenuous, as you strike the ground with all your possible energy. However straightforward the exercises may seem, they do need training. That's not to say you shouldn't try them, especially as the key to the exercises is (paradoxically) stillness.

We've talked at various points throughout this book about stillness, in relation to relaxation and focus, so that you can act with pleasure and without fear. All these are very relevant here with the stamping. Just as Lecoq suggests that out of immobility comes gesture, for Suzuki stillness is the starting point for energy. That sense of stillness begins in your **hara** energy centre, which is located three or four centimetres below your navel. To find the strength and inner stillness to do the stamping and walking exercises properly, Suzuki suggests that you think of yourself as a puppet, imagining one string pulling you up from the crown, one string gravitationally pulling you down from the pelvis, one string pulling you forward through the *hara* (just below your bellybutton), and one string pulling you backwards from the small of your back (more or less opposite the *hara*). This equal pulling in four directions will help you create a sense of centredness. By radiating your energy out in all four directions from this still, centred place, he affirms that you'll find the 'presence' (see Lecoq and Barba) that magnetises the audience. Why don't you try it next time you're in a class or on stage and see what happens?

The paradox of stamping and stillness is just one of the counterpoints in Suzuki's work, as he dances in the gap between the mainstream and the marginal, the traditional and the modern. His training system is essentially psycho–physical: his physical exercises are designed to activate your body-mind, so that there's no disconnection between your body and your inner realm.

## BRINGING THEM ALL TOGETHER

Two subtle and recurring themes among most of our 'executors' are the spirituality of acting – some call it presence, others call it (dual) consciousness – as well as the shared experience of performance itself.

We live in an age in which there's no longer a belief in a collective god or gods. While that can be very all-embracing, in its own way it also throws up immense challenges for our global society. As Suzuki noted during his work around the world, especially in America, the more advanced Western civilisation becomes, the more our hearts become desolate and the more we seek some kind of spiritual prop. For an increasing number of young people, the art of acting and the process of performing somehow ignites a sense of magic, connection, self and presence, which can't necessarily be found in any other forum.

Theatre is a social form of artistic expression, where a community of people agree to meet at a specific time in a specific place and share the telling of a story. If there's one clear bond between our Eleven Executors, it's the belief that our task as actors is to pass on the collective experiences of humanity through story form, from one generation to the next. And we may choose to do that through film, television or theatre.

Each practitioner is searching for some kind of 'truth' – a truth that has nothing to do with style or genre, realism or absurdism. And if you read the books by each of the executors, you'll find a wonderful and inspiring sense emerging of different cultures sharing mutual interests with an urge to evolve acting practice.

## IN BRIEF

If we were to take one tool and one philosophy from each of the Eleven Executors, it might be as follows.

- Stanislavsky's 'psycho-physicality' and that we're fundamentally physical imaginations and thoughtful bodies.
- Meyerhold's 'reflex excitability' and that through our physical training we can be wonderful resources to ourselves, our directors and our audiences.
- Chekhov's 'types of movement' and 'qualities' and how they can feed your imagination, in everyday life and in your character work.
- Strasberg's 'use of imaginary props' and that emotional-imaginative training should be part of everyone's fundamental education.
- Adler's 'What's my job?' and that the given circumstances of each story address the 'gimme instinct' or 'the search for something higher'.
- Meisner's emphasis on communion through 'repetition' and really doing something to someone.
- Mamet's 'terrifying unforeseen' and that you have to have courage in the moment of performance.

- Grotowski's *via negativa* and that we should commit to the 'total act' of connecting with other people.
- Barba's 'extra-daily body' and that training in itself can be the pathway leading us to our own 'presence'.
- Lecoq's sense of 'play' and that by finding your clown, you find your performative freedom.
- Suzuki's 'stamping' and that codified form and chaotic spontaneity have much to take from each other.

## USEFUL WEBSITES

www.stellaadler.com
www.theactorsstudio.org
www.odinteatret.dk
www.michael.chekhov.org
www.cyberkerala.com

## AND FINALLY ...

Wow! That's quite some journey we've come on. We've gained insights into how acting processes have evolved over the centuries. We've understood how we can train our psycho-physical instruments. We've faced the mad challenges of auditions. We've looked at how we can build characters. We've greeted the camera and eyeballed the audience. And we've glimpsed at the legacies left by (and continually evolving from) eleven impressive practitioners. That's probably more than just the 'basics' – so bravo for staying the course!

Here are a couple of thoughts to close.

There's a huge and teasing paradox at the centre of our work. Our whole craft is based on artifice and deception, and yet we tell those 'lies' in order to unlock some fundamental human truths. We endeavour to take our audiences on a journey – be it on stage or on screen – at the end of which we hope they've been transformed in some way: through entertainment, enlightenment, curiosity and discovery. Our mission is fun, but serious.

If there's one overriding thought I'd like you to take from this journey, it's this:

We find ourselves in turbulent times at the start of the second millennium. And, as Suzuki alerts us, part of the problem is our ongoing (and often subconscious) fight to try and subjugate nature. We're so concerned with control. Understandably so. The world throws a lot of stuff at us. To hang on to some sense of control of our lives, we struggle to suppress the unexpected in our natural world – the landslide, the earthquake, the torrential rains, the droughts, and (as I sit writing in West Hollywood in the summer of 2009) the blazing fires. We try to suppress the big, natural Unexpecteds, as well as our own personal, metaphoric ones – and both seem as terrifying as each other. And yet for most of the practitioners in this book, it's exactly the unexpected moments in performance which *embody* the truth of your acting talent.

Before you shut this book, I want to offer you a huge invitation: if you can allow yourself – within the necessary boundaries set by our profession – to free your creative nature, listen to your partner, and let your imagination fly, then real 'presence' and 'communion' may exist in your acting. And then you may truly create magic.

# GLOSSARY OF TERMS

**Action**: Although the word has various definitions, arguably the most useful one for actors is determining what exactly it is that you are *doing* to others in a scene to try to achieve your *objective*. If your objective is what you *want*, your actions are how you go about getting it. It is connected with Aristotle's 'plot' and Stanislavsky's 'system'. Action can be inner (I educate you), verbal (I greet you: 'Hello!') or physical (I shake your hand).

**Actioning**: The breaking of a text into line–by–line inner actions, expressed as transitive verbs, such as 'I delight you', 'I belittle you', 'I threaten you', 'I nurture you'.

**Active Analysis**: Stanislavsky's rehearsal process, whereby you actively analyse a play through your body, in the space, and with a partner. It follows a sequence of readings, discussions, improvisations (which are usually silent at first) and further discussions.

**Affective memory**: A term introduced in the 1890s by Théodule Ribot, referring to the way in which your past-tense memory of an event (drawing on your sense memories of taste, touch, sound, smell and sight) can affect your present-tense state. Imagination also has a significant part to play.

**Alexander Technique**: A system realigning your spine and adjusting your awareness of movement, breath and posture, created by Frederick M. Alexander 'for the control of human reaction'.

**Anthroposophy**: Steiner's spiritual science, which respects the freedom of the individual, while also acknowledging that the spiritual in the individual can lead to the spiritual in the universe. His investigations took him into meditation, medicine, art, science and agriculture.

**Awareness Through Movement®**: Feldenkrais's invitation that you become increasingly aware of your own body's speed, rhythm and intensity of movement, so that you can dynamically change your motor behaviour.

**Body–mind**: The unity of body and mind, such that any duality between the two no longer exists. You are a thinking body and a physical mind, eliminating any idea that there's an inner-outer process or an outer-inner one.

*Bouffons*: A type of physical characterisation of exaggerated proportions, showing up the absurdities of human beings and their power struggles.

**Biomechanics**: Meyerhold's acrobatic training system, consisting of 22 *études*, developing an actor's physical efficiency, sense of rhythm and stability.

**Bits of action**: The breaking down of a scene into sizeable chunks (like carving up a turkey). Stanislavsky invites you to note where the river completely changes its course, rather than where there are smaller kinks in the banks.

*Cabotinage*: The tricks and gimmicks associated with strolling players and heightened, 'ham' acting of the nineteenth century.

**Cartesian dualism**: Descartes' notion that the soul resided in a gland in the brain from which it directed the body, like a driver in a car. The body was a moving machine, and the mind was a 'ghost in the machine'.

*Commedia dell'arte*: A form of improvisational travelling theatre, popular in Italy in the sixteenth century. Described by Jacques Lecoq as an art of childhood that highlights all the trickery of human nature.

**Communion**: Stanislavsky's concept of the exchange of energy between two or more human beings, through invisible rays. Allied to communion is 'grasp': as you and your fellow actors get each other 'in each other's grasp', the audience is magnetised towards the onstage action.

**Dual consciousness**: The ability to be both *in* the performance and *observing* the performance at one and the same time, so that you can deliver the story with all the heart required by the character and all the technical awareness demanded by the storytelling.

**Epic**: Referring here to Bertolt Brecht's interruption of narrative flow with placards, songs, projections and other devices which break the fourth wall and remind the audience they are watching actors in a theatre.

**Eight Laban Efforts**: Rudolf Laban's division of human movement into eight efforts of action (Pressing, Gliding, Punching, Dabbing, Wringing, Floating, Slashing and Flicking). Each of these comprises a combination of movement qualities based on the opposites of Direct/Flexible; Sudden/Sustained; Strong/Light.

**Emotion memory** (or emotional memory): The product of sense memory, based on Strasberg's evolution of affective memory By recalling of all the sensory details surrounding an emotional event, you can recreate psycho-physically your emotional experience of the original event.

**Extra-daily body (or self)**: A phrase adopted by Eugenio Barba to differentiate between your daily body (which uses minimum effort for maximum result) and the body you use in performance (which uses maximum commitment of energy for minimum result).

**Feeling of ease**: Michael Chekhov's phrase inviting you to execute any action on stage with a lightness of touch, regardless of how sombre the material might be.

**Feldenkrais Technique**: Feldenkrais's technique for increasing your awareness of your movement in the knowledge that body and mind are inseparable. If you change your attitude to one, you invariably change your attitude to the other.

**Forum theatre**: Boal's proposition that actors and spectators – spect-actors – come together in an arena where the actors pose good questions and the audience must supply the answers. Social discussion happens in a theatrical way, through the enactment of possible outcomes to situations.

**Functional Integration®**: An evolution of Feldenkrais technique which involves a trained practitioner applying contact to your body to enable you to correct your habits and train yourself to stand in a more healthy alignment.

**Given circumstances**: Stanislavsky's phrase for all the details that help you make choices about your characterisation. These can be facts from the play, research about the era, and the conditions of the production itself, not to mention how your director and fellow actors work.

**Grotesque**: A style of theatre essentially involving characters which inspire both pity and terror. Used by Vsevelod Meyerhold in relation to the Italian *grottesca* – a low comedy – mixing the opposites of the debased and the exalted. Used by Lecoq in reference to the physical comedy of the *bouffons*.

**Hara**: A Japanese word referring to an ocean of energy stored in your stomach, abdomen or belly, which expands throughout your whole body. By working with the *hara*, you can strengthen your whole psycho-physical energy.

**Humours**: Four humours or liquids believed, in the seventeenth century, to be stored in various organs of your body and characterised by sanguine, choleric, phlegmatic and bilious traits in your personality.

**Iambic pentameter**: An iamb is a 'foot' of verse, comprising two beats – the first unstressed, the second stressed (di-dum). Put five of them together and you have the basic poetic pulse underlying most Shakespearean verse.

**Inner psychological drives**: Stanislavsky's three centres of Thought, Feeling and Action.

**Invisible theatre**: Boal's practice of taking actors out into public places and enacting scenes of provocative social interest, without the public knowing they are acting and seeing how the public (spect-actors) then become involved. Its remit is to challenge – and change – social interaction.

**Kabuki**: Highly stylised, traditional Japanese dance-theatre from the seventeenth century, popular among townspeople. It is usually delivered in a monotone with the accompaniment of ancient instruments, and can last more than many hours.

**Kalarippayatu**: An ancient martial art from the twelfth century, stemming from Kerala, India. Training starts for children aged seven, and consists of a series of steps and postures.

**Kathakali**: An ancient Indian dance-drama originating in Kerala in the sixteenth century and using elaborate costumes, make-up, body movements and gestures.

**Little plus**: Stanislavsky's phrase for giving a stage action just a little too much emphasis; every little plus produces false theatricality, so he invites you to find the 'true measure'.

**Method of Physical Actions**: Stanislavsky's rehearsal process, developed towards the end of his life. Through a sequence of simple, easily executed tasks, actors work out a score of physical actions, which leads them to the fulfilment (or otherwise) of their objective. 'I switch on the kettle, I open the fridge, I take out the milk, I find a mug', etc.

**Naturalism**: A literary movement which flourished at the end of the nineteenth and beginning of twentieth century. Theatre productions strove to produce a 'slice of life', with the complete impression of reality. Actors were encouraged to identity with their roles, and playwrights wrote about gritty, earthy, non-aristocratic, 'real' people.

*Noh*: Originating in the fourteenth century, this combination of Chinese performing art and Japanese dance is the oldest traditional form. Originally the staple entertainment of the aristocracy, *Noh* operated within clearly established performance codes, with each *Noh* theatre comprising a stage, four pillars and a narrow bridge over which the actors enter.

**Objective**: The motivating drive or need which prompts your character into action in a scene and determines all the choices they make about what they do, what they say and how they say it, in order to have the appropriate affect on other people. Often translated as 'task'.

**Oratory**: The ancient Greek and Roman art of public speaking.

**Pantomime**: A silent performance style in which gestures are substituted for words. Very popular in the eighteenth and nineteenth century, pantomime is most closely associated with the figure of Pierrot, the white faced, moonish, silk-clad, skull-capped youth.

**Passions**: Two kinds of experiences based on the balance of humours within you, according to seventeenth-century philosophers and practitioners. Concupiscible passions were those aroused when you got what you wanted, leading to joy; and irascible passions were those aroused when you wanted to avoid something, leading to fear.

*Plastiques*: A series of physical exercises devised by Jerzy Grotowski exploring form and gesture, where you allow your body to respond spontaneously to the moment of movement, finding detailed structures and always being aware of the flow of energy inside you.

**Postmodernism**: A term that came into circulation in the mid-1980s referring to the arts, communication, technology, sociology and fashion. It rejects rigid narrative structures and distinctions between different genres. Instead, it celebrates dislocation, fragmentation, disintegration and ambiguous meanings.

**Post-dramatic theatre**: A term introduced in 1999 by German theatre researcher Hans-Thies Lehmann. Performances have no interest in plot. Instead, all the focus is on the relationship between the actor and the audience, and on the effect you're having rather than the story you're telling.

*Prana*: The Sanskrit term for radiating your energy from your body and communicating your emotions. Stanislavsky refers to *prana* in *An Actor Prepares*. It is also known as *Chi* in Chinese and *Ki* in Japanese, and it forms the root of many martial arts and meditative practices.

**Pre-expressivity**: Barba's phrase, essentially referring to how you organise your energy as a performer. Even before you begin to perform, you've prepared what Stanislavsky calls 'an inner creative state', which is different from than your everyday *modus operandi*.

**Psychological realism**: Essentially, the focus of the play or the characterisation is as much on the inner, unspoken life as the external, physical or vocal life. As audiences, we recognise that the script and the characters are operating on a number of levels simultaneously, because we ourselves do in everyday life.

**Psychoanalysis**: A therapeutic practice based on free association and stemming from Sigmund Freud's work in the late nineteenth and early twentieth centuries. It usually involved a couch and several sessions a week, so that you could try to dispel your psychoses.

**Psychology**: The 'study of the mind', coming from the word *psyche*, meaning breath, soul or spirit. Rooted in ancient Greece, Rome and China, its modern incarnation came into being in the mid-1700s.

**Psycho-physical**: A phrase made popular by Stanislavsky referring to his 'psycho-technique', in which the actor works as holistically as possible with body, mind, imagination, intellect and emotions.

**Realism**: A literary movement which is arguably broader in its definition than that of naturalism, where the emphasis was very specifically on the individual, and their heredity and environment. Realism allows for certain poetic symbols such as the breaking string in Chekhov's *The Cherry Orchard*. Naturalism was bound to a particular period at the turn of the nineteenth century: realistic writing still flourishes.

**Rhetoric**: The way in which you construct your speeches, the style, the language and the form, in order to persuade your listener to adopt a particular point of view.

**Sense memory**: The recollection of all the sensory details (sight, sound, taste, touch and smell) surrounding an event that was particularly affecting for you. When the sense memory is strong enough, it will arouse within you the emotions connected with the original experience.

**Sensibility**: The eighteenth-century ability to be open to and expressive with your emotions. Empathy and compassion were noble concerns.

**Sides**: The pages you're given to prepare for a television, film or theatre audition.

**Six Fundamental Questions**: Who? Where? When? Why? For what reason? and How? The answers to these six questions, according to Konstantin Stanislavsky, will springboard you into a character via the writer's script and your own imagination.

**Solar plexus**: A dense cluster of nerves between the stomach and the diaphragm.

***Spaß***: Brecht's idea of fun or amusement, which was very important in his theatre making.

**Subconscious**: In popular use, a level of perception or understanding beneath our cognitive awareness.

**Subtext**: A term devised by Stanislavsky and Nemirovich-Danchenko when trying to decipher Chekhov's *The Seagull*, referring to what goes on 'under the text', in the silences and beneath the words.

**Superobjective**: The overarching motive that links together all the fragments of a script. Sometimes applied to individual characters and their arc through the play. Sometimes defined as the reason why the writer wrote the play.

***T'ai chi chuan***: A series of solo Chinese physical forms and preparations harnessing martial arts, health considerations and meditation. It evolved through principles of Chinese philosophy and means 'the supreme ultimate fist'.

**Task**: The direct translation from the Russian, until now translated as 'objective': What is my task in this scene? What do I have to do to achieve my desired outcome?

**Tempo–rhythm**: The speed and the intensity with which we do something. Inner and outer tempos can differ: on the outside, I might look very calm (like a duck on the water) but inside I might be very upset (like the rapid webbed feet underneath).

**Tribunal theatre**: Distilling into stage form the actual words from important tribunals (such as the Hutton Inquiry and the accounts of Guantanamo, at the Tricycle Theatre, London, where collaborations often include director, Nicholas Kent and journalist, Richard Norton Taylor).

**Verbatim theatre**: The testimony of living people crafted into theatre productions. First popularised in the 1970s, they have had a resurgence in the UK in the late 1990s and early 2000s, with plays including Jonathan Holme's *Katrina* (2009) and *Fallujah* (2007), and David Hare's *The Power of Yes* (2009) and *The Permanent Way* (2003).

***Via Negativa***: The elimination of blocks, rather than the acquisition of skills in actor-training, as defined by Grotowski.

**Viewpoints**: Mary Overlie's six 'deconstructed' languages of Space, Shape, Time, Emotion, Story and Movement. Anne Bogart has built on Overlie's original idea in her own evolution of Viewpoints.

# SELECTED BIBLIOGRAPHY

Aaron, S. (1986) *Stage Fright: Its Role in Acting*, Chicago: University of Chicago Press.

Abbot, J. (2007) *The Improvisation Book*, London: Nick Hern Books.

Adler, S. (1988) *The Technique of Acting*, New York: Bantam Books.

Alfreds, M. (2007) *Different Every Night: Freeing the Actor*, London: Nick Hern Books.

Allain, P. (2002) *The Art of Stillness: The Practice of Tadashi Suzuki*, London: Methuen.

Annett, M. (1994) *Actor's Guide to Auditions and Interviews* (third edition), London: A&C Black.

Archer, W. (1957) *Masks or Faces?*, New York: Hill & Wang.

Arnold, M. B. (1968) *The Nature of Emotion*, London: Penguin.

Artaud, A. (1999) (trans. Corti, V.) *The Theatre and its Double*, London: Calder.

Babbage, F. (2004) *Augusto Boal*, Abingdon: Routledge.

Barba, E. & Savarese, N. (1991) (trans. Fowler, R.) *A Dictionary of Theatre Anthropology, The Secret Art of the Performer*, London: Routledge.

Barba, E. (1995) (trans. Fowler, R.) *The Paper Canoe: A Guide to Theatre Anthropology,* London: Routledge.

——(1999a) (trans. Barba, J.) *Theatre: Solitude, Craft, Revolt*, Aberystwyth: Black Mountain Press.

——(1999b) (trans. Barba, J.) *Land of Ashes and Diamonds: My Apprenticeship in Poland*, Aberystwyth: Black Mountain Press.

Barber, S. (1993) *Antonin Artaud: Blows and Bombs*, London: Faber and Faber.

Barker, C. (1977) *Theatre Games*, London: Eyre Methuen.

Barnes, J. (2000) *A Very Short Introduction to Aristotle*, Oxford: Oxford University Press.

Barr, T. (1997) *Acting for Camera*, New York: HarperCollins.

Barton, J. (1984) *Playing Shakespeare*, London: Methuen.

Bartow, A. (ed.) (2006) *The Training of the American Actor*, New York: Theatre Communications Group.

Beck, A. (1997) *Radio Acting*, London: A&C Black.

Ben-Ze'ev, A. (2000) *The Subtlety of Emotions*, Boston: Massachusetts Institute of Technology.

Benedetti, J. (1988) *Stanislavski: A Biography*, London: Methuen.

——(2001) *David Garrick and The Birth of Modern Theatre*, London: Methuen.

——(2005) *The Art of the Actor: The Essential History of Acting, from Classical Times to the Present Day*, Methuen: London.

Benedetti, R. (1997) *The Actor at Work*, Needham Heights: Allyn & Bacon.

Berry, C. (2000) *The Actor and the Text*, London: Virgin Books.

Black, L. C. (1984) *Mikhail Chekhov as Actor, Director and Teacher.* UMI Research Press.

Boal, A. (1979) (trans. Leal McBride) *Theatre of the Oppressed*, London: Pluto Press.

——(1992) (trans. Jackson, A.) *Games for Actors and Non-Actors*, London: Routledge.

——(1998) (trans. Jackson, A.) *Legislative Theatre*, London: Routledge.

Boleslavsky, R. (1933) *Acting: The First Six Lessons*, New York: Theatre Arts Books.

Bogart, A. & Landau, T. (2005) *The Viewpoints Book: A Practical Guide to Viewpoints and Composition*, New York: Theatre Communications Group.

——(2007) *And Then You Act*, New York: Routledge.

Brestoff, R. (1994) *The Camera Smart Actor*, Lyme: Smith and Kraus.

Brook, P. (1973) *The Empty Space*, London: Penguin.

——(1993) *The Open Door: Thoughts on Acting and Theatre*, New York: Anchor Books.

Bruder, M., Cohn, L. M., Olnek, M., Pollack, N., Previto, R., Zigler, S. (1986) *A Practical Handbook for the Actor*, New York: Vintage.

Bruehl, B. (1996) *The Technique of Inner Action: The Soul of the Performer's Work*, London: Heinemann.

Caine, M. (1990) *Acting in Film: An Actor's Take on Movie Making*, New York: Applause.

Calhoun, C. & Solomon, R. C. (1984) *What is an Emotion? Classical Readings in Philosophical Psychology*, Oxford: Oxford University Press.

Callery, D. (2001) *Through the Body: A Practical Guide to Physical Theatre*, London: Nick Hern Books.

Carnicke, S. M. (2009) *Stanislavsky in Focus: An Acting Master for the Twenty-First Century*, Abingdon: Routledge.

Chamberlain, F. (2004) *Michael Chekhov*, Abingdon: Routledge.

Chamberlain, F. & Yarrow, R. (2002) *Jacques Lecoq and the British Theatre*, London: Routledge.

Chekhov, M. (1985) *Lessons for the Professional Actor*, New York: Performing Arts Journal.

——(1991) *On the Technique of Acting*, New York: HarperPerennial.

——(2002) *To the Actor on the Technique of Acting*, London: Routledge.

——(2005) (eds. Kirillov, A. & Merlin, B.) *The Path of the Actor*, Abingdon: Routledge.

Christoffersen, E. E. (1993) (trans. Fowler, R.) *The Actor's Way*, London: Routledge.

Churcher, M. (2003) *Acting for Film: Truth 24 Frames a Second*, London: Virgin.

Cole, T. & Chinoy, H. (eds.) (1970) *Actors on Acting: The Theories, Techniques and Practices of the Great Actors of All Times as Told in their Own Words*, New York: Crown.

Coquelin, C. (1932) (trans. Fogerty, E.) *The Art of the Actor*, London: George Allen & Unwin.

Deer, H. & Dal Vera, R. (2008) *Acting in Musical Theatre: A Comprehensive Course*, Abingdon: Routledge.

Dennis, A. (2002) *The Articulate Body: The Physical Training of the Actor*, London: Nick Hern Books.

Diderot, D. (1994) (trans. Bremner, G.) *Selected Writings on Art and Literature*, London: Penguin Classics.

Donnellan, D. (2005) *The Actor and the Target*, London: Nick Hern Books.

Dychtwald, K. (1977) *Bodymind*, New York: Tarcher/Perigree.

Evans, D. (2001) *Emotion: A Very Short Introduction*, Oxford: Oxford University Press.

Evans, M. (2006) *Jacques Copeau*, Abingdon: Routledge.

Feldenkrais, M. (1990) *Awareness through Movement: Easy-to-Do Health Exercises to Improve your Posture, Vision, Imagination and Personal Awareness*, San Francisco: HarperSanFrancisco.

Ford Davies, O. (2007) *Performing Shakespeare*, London: Nick Hern Books.

Goleman, D. (1996) *Emotional Intelligence: Why It Can Matter More Than IQ*, London: Bloomsbury.

Goodall, J. R. (2002) *Performance and Evolution in the Age of Darwin: Out of the Natural Order*, Abingdon: Routledge.

Gordon, M. (1988) *The Stanislavsky Technique: Russia*, New York: Applause.

Gordon, R. (2006) *The Purpose of Playing: Modern Acting Theories in Perspective*, Michigan: University of Michigan Press.

Greene, D. (2001) *Audition Success: An Olympic Sports Psychologist Teaches Performing Artists How to Win*, New York: Routledge.

Grotowski, J. (1975) (ed. Barba, E.) (trans. Various) *Towards a Poor Theatre*, London: Methuen.

Guskin, H. (2003) *How to Stop Acting*, New York: Faber and Faber.

Haber, M. & Babchick, B. (1999) *How to Get the Part Without Falling Apart*, Los Angeles: Lone Eagle.

Hagen, U. (1973) *Respect for Acting*, New York: Wiley.

——(1991), *A Challenge for the Actor*, New York: Scribner.

Hodge, A. (ed.) (2000) *Twentieth Century Actor Training*, London: Routledge.

Hodgson, J. & Richards, E. (1979) *Improvisation*, London: Methuen.

Holdsworth, N. (2006) *Joan Littlewood*, Abingdon: Routledge.

Hornby, R. (1992) *The End of Acting: A Radical View*, New York: Applause.

Innes, C. (ed.) (2000) *A Sourcebook on Naturalistic Theatre*, London: Routledge.

Johnstone, K. (1981) *Impro: Improvisation and the Theatre*, London: Methuen.

Kanner, E. & Flinn, D. M. (2003) *How Not to Audition: Avoiding the Common Mistakes*

*Most Actors Make*, Los Angeles: Lone Eagle.

Keleman, S. (1986) *Emotional Anatomy: The Structure of Experience*, Berkeley: Center Press.

Konijn, E. A. (1997) *Acting Emotions*, Amsterdam: Amsterdam University Press.

Kovens, E. (2006) *The Method Manual for Teachers and Actors*, LaVergne, Tennessee.

Kumiega, J. (1987) *The Theatre of Grotowski*, London: Methuen.

Leabhart, T. (2007) *Etienne Decroux*, Abingdon: Routledge.

Leach, R. (1993) *Vsevelod Meyerhold: Directors in Perspective*, Cambridge: Cambridge University Press.

——(2003) *Stanislavsky and Meyerhold*, Amsterdam: Peter Lang.

——(2004) *Makers of Modern Theatre: An Introduction*, Abingdon: Routledge.

——(2006) *Theatre Workshop: Joan Littlewood and the Making of Modern British Theatre*, Exeter: University of Exeter Press.

Lecoq, J. (2006) (ed. Bradby, D.), *Theatre of Movement and Gesture*, Abingdon: Routledge.

——(1997) (trans. Bradby, D.) *The Moving Body: Teaching Creative Theatre*, New York: Routledge.

LeDoux, J. (1998) *The Emotional Brain: The Mysterious Underpinnings of Emotional Life*, London: Weidenfeld & Nicholson.

Lee, B. (1971) 'Liberate Yourself From Classical Karate', *Black Belt Magazine* (9), New York: Rainbow Publications Inc.

Leonard, C. (1984) *Michael Chekhov's to the Director and Playwright*, New York: Limelight.

Lewis, R. (1958) *Method – or Madness?*, New York: Samuel French.

Linklater, K. (2006) *Freeing the Natural Voice: Imagery and Art in the Practice of Voice and Language*, London: Nick Hern Books.

Lovell, A. & Krämer, P. (eds.) (1999) *Screen Acting*, London: Routledge.

Mamet, D. (1998) *True & False: Heresy and Common Sense for the Actor*, London: Faber and Faber.

Marowitz, C. (1978) *The Act of Being*, New York: Secker and Warburg.

Marshall, L. (2001) *The Body Speaks: Performance & Expression*, London: Methuen.

McKone, F. (2002) *First Audition: How to Get into Drama School*, Sydney: Currency Press.

McNaughton, N. (1989) *Biology and Emotion*, Cambridge: Cambridge University Press.

Meckler, E. (1989) *Masters of the Stage: British Acting Teachers Talk About Their Craft*, New York: Weidenfeld.

Meisner, S. & Longwell, D. (1987) *Sanford Meisner on Acting*, New York: Vintage.

Merlin, B. (2001) *Beyond Stanislavsky: The Psycho-Physical Approach to Actor Training*, London: Nick Hern Books.

——(2003) *Konstantin Stanislavsky*, London: Routledge.

——(2007) *The Complete Stanislavsky Toolkit*, London: Nick Hern Books

Meyerhold, V. (1995) (trans. & ed. Braun, E.) *Meyerhold: A Revolution in the Theatre*, London: Methuen.

Morris, E. (1988) *Acting from Ultimate Consciousness: A Dynamic Exploration of the Actor's Inner Resources*, Los Angeles: Ermor Publications.

Murray, S. (2003) *Jacques Lecoq*, Abingdon: Routledge.

Nachmanovitch, S. (1990) *Free Play: Improvisation in Life and Art*, New York: Tarcher/Penguin.

Olivier, L. (1982) *Confessions of an Actor*, London: Weidenfeld & Nicholson.

Pitches, J. (2003) *Vsevelod Meyerhold*, Abingdon: Routledge.

——(2006) *Science and the Stanislavsky Tradition of Acting*, Abingdon: Routledge.

Playfair, G. (1983) *The Flash of Lightning: A Portrait of Edmund Kean*, London: William Kimber & Co.

Pudovkin, V. I. (1935) *Film Acting*, London: George Newnes Ltd.

Richards, T. (1995) *At Work with Grotowski on Physical Actions*, London: Routledge.

Roach, J. R. (1993) *The Player's Passion: Studies in the Science of Acting*, Michigan: University of Michigan Press.

Rockwood, J. (1992) *The Craftsmen of Dionysus: An Approach to Acting*, New York: Applause.

Rodenburg, P. (1994) *The Need for Words: Voice and the Text*, London: Methuen.

——(1998) *The Actor Speaks: Voice and the Performer*, London: Methuen.

——(2005) *Speaking Shakespeare*, London: Methuen.

——(2009) *Presence: How to Use Positive Energy in Every Situation*, London: Penguin.

Rohrer, P. N. (2005) *Listen, Feel, Respond: A Workbook and Guide to Acting on Camera*, New York: iUniverse Inc.

Saint-Denis, M. (1976) *Theatre: The Rediscovery of Style*, New York: Theatre Arts Books.

Salt, C. (2001) *Make Acting Work*, London: Methuen.

Schechner, R. & Wolford, L. (eds.) (2001) *The Grotowski Source Book*, New York: Routledge.

Sedita, S. (2006) *The Eight Characters of Comedy: A Guide to Sitcom Acting and Writing*, Los Angeles: Atides Publishing.

Senelick, L. (ed.) (1992) *Wandering Stars: Russian Emigré Theatre 1905–1940*, Iowa: University of Iowa.

Sher, A. (2005) *Primo Time*, London: Nick Hern Books.

Shurtleff, M. (1978) *Audition: Everything an Actor Needs to Know to Get the Part*, New York: Walker and Company.

Slowiak, J. & Cuesta, J. (2007) *Jerzy Grotowski*, Abingdon: Routledge.

Sorrell, T. (1987) *Descartes: A Very Short Introduction*, Oxford: Oxford University Press.

Spolin, V. (1990) *Improvisation for the Theatre*, Evanston: Northwestern University Press.

Stafford-Clark, M. (1990) *Letters to George*, London: Nick Hern Books.

Strasberg, L. (1988) *A Dream of Passion: The Development of the Method*, London: Methuen.

——(1965) (ed. Hethmon, R. H.) *Strasberg at the Actors Studio*, New York: Vintage.

Strongman, K. T. (1996) *The Psychology of Emotion*, Chichester: John Wiley & Sons.

Styan, J. L. (1981) *Modern Drama in Theory and Practice 1: Realism and Naturalism*, Cambridge: Cambridge University Press.

——(1981) *Modern Drama in Theory and Practice 2: Symbolism, Surrealism and the Absurd*, Cambridge: Cambridge University Press.

——(1981) *Modern Drama in Theory and Practice 3: Expressionism and Epic Theatre*, Cambridge: Cambridge University Press.

Suzuki, T. (1986) (trans. Rimer, J. T.) *The Way of Acting: The Theatre Writings of Tadashi Suzuki*, New York: Theatre Communications Group.

Taylor, M. (1994) *The Actor and the Camera*, London: A&C Black.

Thomson, P. (2000) *On Actors and Acting*, Exeter: University of Exeter Press.

Toporkov, V. (1979) (trans. Edwards, C.) *Stanislavski in Rehearsal*, New York: Theatre Arts Books.

Tucker, P. (1994) *Secrets of Screen Acting*, New York: Routledge.

Turner, J. (2004) *Eugenio Barba*, Abingdon: Routledge.

Trussler, S. (2000) *Cambridge Illustrated History of British Theatre*, Cambridge: Cambridge University Press.

Vineberg, S. (1991) *Method Actors: Three Generations of an American Acting Style*, New York: Schirmer.

Wangh, S. (2000) *An Acrobat of the Heart: A Physical Approach to Acting Inspired by the Work of Grotowski*, New York: Vintage.

Watson, I. (ed.) (2001) *Performer Training: Developments Across Cultures*, Amsterdam: Harwood.

Whyman, R. (2008) *The Stanislavsky System: Legacy and Influence in Modern Performance*, Cambridge: Cambridge University Press.

Willett, J. (1959) *The Theatre of Bertolt Brecht: A Study from Eight Perspectives*, London: Methuen.

Wilson, S. (2004) *Humanity: An Emotional History*, London: Atlantic Books.

Zarrilli, P. B. (2008) *Psycho-Physical Acting: An Intercultural Approach after Stanislavski*, Abingdon: Routledge.

——(1995) *Acting (Re)Considered*, London: Routledge.

Zinder, D. (2002) *Body Voice Imagination: A Training for the Actor*, London: Routledge.

# INDEX

Aaron, Stephen 140, 143
accents 8, 43, 109
*Acting: The First Six Lessons* 176
*Acting Emotions* 118
acting types 146–7
action 11–12, 22, 65, 71, 85;
    executors 176, 180, 183, 197,
    203; performance 141, 149;
    rehearsals 96–8, 108–11, 117, 129
action mime 200
action-centre 121–3
actioning 110, 183
Actions 100, 112, 120, 189, 196
Active Analysis 11, 28, 98, 121–3,
    163, 169, 183, 198
*The Actor (Le comédien)* 18
*An Actor Prepares* 98, 162, 164–6,
    176
*Actor's Guide to Auditions and
    Interviews* 77, 86
Actors Studio 176–7, 183, 189
*An Actor's Work* 99, 164–6
adjustment 114
Adler, Stella 11, 45, 101–2, 110,
    172, 175–6, 179–84, 186, 189,
    197–200, 206

aesthetics 16, 23, 31, 122, 145, 153,
    155, 170, 174, 187, 202
affective memory 5–6, 11, 25, 63,
    66; executors 163, 171, 173,
    176–8, 180, 189, 198; rehearsals
    103, 111, 113, 115; training
    68–9
affectivity 135
afflictions 45
agents 76–7, 82, 89
Alexander, Frederick M. 44–5
Alexander Technique 44–5
Alignment 43–4, 204
American Academy of Dramatic Art
    36
American Laboratory Theatre 175–6,
    180
Americans 7–10, 12–14, 32, 36, 38;
    executors 160, 163, 168, 175–89;
    realism 122; rehearsals 95, 106,
    109; training 43, 48, 52, 60, 71
Ananyev, Vladimir 104–5
anatomy 14, 54
angst 139, 142
animal improvisations 50–1
Annett, Margo 77, 86

anthroposophy 29, 171
anticipation 38
antithesis 125
Antoine, André 7, 23, 25
anxiety 90, 129–30, 142, 149, 192
Archer, William 10, 30
architecture 6, 45, 49, 202–3
Aristotle 11–12, 14
*The Art of the Actor* 27
*The Art of Stillness* 204
Artaud, Antonin 29, 160
articulation 53–6, 71, 137
as if 113–15
assimilation 39
assistant directors 193
Atlantic Theater Company 187
atmosphere 76, 82, 88, 94, 96, 100, 150
attention 166
audience 58, 71, 134–7, 139, 142, 188–90, 192, 197, 199, 201, 203–5
*Audition* 86
auditions 72, 75–92
auditoria 128–9, 135–8, 143
authenticity 31–3, 72, 192
automated dialogue replacement (ADR) 15
Awareness Through Movement (ATM) 44

backstage 136
balance 20, 61
Barba, Eugenio 41, 71, 193–7, 202–3, 205, 207
Barker, Clive 61–2
Barton, John 124–5
beats 108–9
Beckett, Samuel 124, 202
being in the moment 58, 106
being yourself 81–2
Belasco, David 24
believability 33
Benedetti, Jean 99, 163–4, 166
Benedetti, Robert 43, 52, 71
Bernhardt, Sarah 23

Berry, Cicely 40, 52–3, 55, 124–5, 137
*Beyond Stanislavsky* 121
bile 15
biofeedback 44
Biomechanics 167–70, 193–4
bits of action 108–11, 149, 165
black bile 15
bleeds 109
blocking 95–6, 98, 122, 129
blocks 22, 31, 37, 50–1, 53, 59, 62, 143, 176, 189
Boal, Augusto 8, 62–3, 160
body 38, 40, 49–50, 53–4, 60, 188–9, 191–4, 196–8, 202–3, 206; auditions 82, 87, 90; executors 164, 168–71, 173, 178, 181; extra-daily 194; performance 136, 141, 144; rehearsals 96, 99, 121–3, 131; training 62–3, 68, 70–1
body-mind 196, 205
Bogart, Anne 36, 48, 202
Boleslavsky, Richard 7, 108, 112, 162, 175–6, 179
*bouffons* 199
Brahms, Otto 23
brain 63–5, 67, 98, 115, 130, 155
Brando, Marlon 9, 180–1
breath 12–13, 38, 40–1, 44, 51–3, 55–6, 63, 70–1, 131, 138
breathing gym 53
Brecht, Bertolt 3, 8, 28, 136, 160, 178, 180
Bristol Old Vic 71
British 9, 18, 26, 31, 40; auditions 77; executors 160, 163, 169, 177; performance 140–1; rehearsals 93, 109, 134; training 52, 57
Brook, Peter 57, 160
Buddhism 29
building character 87, 93–133, 147, 151, 174, 188
*Building a Character* 164

*cabotinage* 170
Caine, Michael 149, 151

CalArts 71
callbacks 80, 84
camera acting 144
camera crew 130, 151–2
*The Camera Smart Actor* 153
Cannon, Doreen 161
cardiovascular system 14
Carnicke, Sharon M. 121, 163
Cartesian dualism 16
casting directors 79, 81, 84, 88
castings 75–8, 80–1, 83–5, 89–90
Central School of Speech and
    Drama 71, 160
chambers of sound 54
character 11–12, 20–1, 23–5, 27,
    30–3; auditions 76–8, 81, 85–8,
    90, 93–134; building 87, 93–133,
    147, 151, 174, 186, 188; close-
    ups 153; executors 174, 186, 188;
    film acting 145, 147, 155;
    performance 137, 139; stage fright
    142–3; training 35, 38, 41–2, 45,
    48, 56, 60
characterization 173, 176
charisma 18
Chekhov, Anton 9, 24, 102, 114,
    120, 126, 136, 167, 171–2
Chekhov, Michael 3, 10, 28–9, 31,
    45, 49–50, 55–6, 162, 171–5,
    177, 180–1, 191, 193, 197–200,
    202, 206
Chekhov Studio Theatre 172
Chekhov, Xenia 172
chest 54
choleric traits 15
choosing monologues 85
Cibber, Susannah 21, 56
cinematographers 152
La Clairon 21–3
Classic Hollywood Style 153
classical era 11–14, 27
Close, Glenn 131
close-ups 100, 119, 148–9, 152–4,
    156
clothes 83, 198
clowning 50, 172, 194, 199, 201, 207

co-ordination 42
coaches 12, 21, 37, 67, 72; auditions
    78, 82–3; executors 175, 186;
    performance 144, 147, 150;
    rehearsals 129, 131
collaboration 36, 38, 62, 111, 143;
    executors 169, 172, 184, 187,
    198, 202; performance 146–7,
    150–1, 153
College of Physical Education 197
comedy 13, 80, 172
*commedia dell'arte* 170, 198–9
commercials 83, 89
communication 41–2, 51, 54, 62;
    auditions 80; executors 165–6,
    195, 203; performance 146–7;
    rehearsals 96, 98–9; unconscious
    70–1
communion 71, 143, 165–6, 190,
    206, 208
*The Complete Stanislavsky Toolkit* 109
complication 153
complicity 138–9
concentration 20, 166, 176–7, 204
concupiscible passions 15, 64
conditioning 37, 63, 67–70, 112
confidence 63, 72, 81, 148, 150
consistency 87
consonants 54–6, 137–8
*The Constant Prince* 193
continuity 152, 155–6
control 65, 76–7, 81, 119, 141–2,
    146, 169, 208
Copeau, Jacques 10, 30–1, 62,
    197–8
Coquelin, Benôit-Constant 10,
    27–8, 135
costume 83, 127–8, 204
Crawford, Joan 145
crying 119–21, 186
cue-to-cue run 127
CVs 72, 81–2, 156

Dabbing 47–8
Dartington Hall 45, 172, 174
Darwin, Charles 7, 23

De Niro, Robert 6, 106, 156
deconstructed languages 48
Decroux, Etienne 198
Dennis, Anne 42
dénouement 153
Descartes, René 16, 25, 64, 99, 196
design 42–3, 45
desire 16
diaphragm 40, 53–4
Diderot, Denis 10, 20, 27
diphthongs 55
Direct 46–7
directors 9–10, 22–3, 36–7, 48, 57–8;
    audience 134; auditions 78–80,
    82, 84; executors 190, 192, 202;
    film acting 144–5, 149, 151, 153–4,
    156; rehearsals 94–6, 98, 100,
    105, 109–12, 121–2, 130–1; run-
    throughs 127; screen acting 146–7;
    stage fright 142; technical
    rehearsals 128; television acting
    157–8; training 61
directors of photography (DOP)
    100, 145, 149, 152
discipline 190, 197
drama schools 30, 37, 61, 81, 84, 91,
    164, 193
Drama Studio 160
Dramatic Workshop 180
A Dream of Passion 177–9
dress rehearsals 128–9
dressing rooms 76, 136
Drury Lane 21
dual consciousness 20, 27, 135–6,
    179, 205
dualism 16
Dumesnil, Marie Françoise 21–3
Duse, Eleanora 23
dynamic listening 3, 35, 58–9, 71,
    96–9, 106, 122, 143, 145, 153,
    189
dyskrasia 15

easiness 173–4
Eastern theatre 36, 193, 195, 197–8,
    202–5

L'Ecole Jacques Lecoq 198
Ecole Supérieure d'Art Dramatique
    30
efforts of movement 45–8, 50
The Eight Characters of Comedy 127
Eight Laban Efforts 46, 48
eighteenth century 17–22, 26, 30,
    119
Ekman, Paul 16, 32, 64
The Eleven Executioners 160
elision 55
emotion 13, 17–18, 21, 25–8, 32,
    183, 185–6, 189, 196, 199;
    auditions 81, 85, 88; centre 108,
    111–21; charting 150; executors
    167, 176, 178–80; film acting
    145; memory 20, 25, 66–7, 70,
    115, 165, 176–7, 179;
    performance 136–7; rehearsals
    111–13, 129, 131; takes 154;
    training 38, 48–50, 53–4, 60–1,
    63–72
empathy 18, 24–5, 77, 94, 108, 111
The End of Acting 119
energhia 195
energy 124–5
energy centres 205
Enlightenment 17
ensembles theatre 23
entirety 174
environment 8, 10, 24, 40, 53–4;
    auditions 75, 79, 81, 84; rehearsals
    95, 108, 112; training 65
epic plays 8
ethics 17
eukrasia 15
Euripedes 202
Evans, Dylan 69, 115
exercises 177–8, 184–5, 204–5
exhalation 41
exposition 153
expression 190, 196–7, 203, 206
The Expression of Emotions 7, 25
external actions 22
extra-daily body 41, 194, 207
extras 145

faces 29–31, 64, 82, 137
farce 135, 170
fear 37–8, 40, 59, 64, 69, 90, 140–4, 191, 201, 205
feeling 18, 28, 62
Feldenkrais, Moshe 43–5
Feldenkrais Technique 43–4
Fettes, Christopher 161
film acting 144–56
film crews 150–1
final cuts 156
final moments 88–9
first assistant directors (first AD) 151–2
first public read-throughs 100–1
first readings 99
First Studio 162, 171
first/second self 27
Fitzmaurice, Catherine 52
flexibility 42–3, 46, 52, 70, 78, 81, 131, 165, 191
Flexible 46–8
Flicking 48
Floating 47, 173
Florentine, Isaac 131
fluffing lines 155
flying 173–4
Fo, Dario 8, 198
focus 135, 152, 166, 205
foolishness 142–3
for what reason 101, 104–6
Ford Davies, Oliver 124, 126
form 135–6, 174
forum theatre 8
frames 145–6, 152
Free Play 57
Freeman, Morgan 154
Freie Bühne 23
Freud, Sigmund 7, 29
fun 28
function 104
Functional Integration 44
fundamental questions 101–6

Galen 14–15
games 57–8, 60–2

Games for Actors and Non-Actors 62
gamesercises 62
Garrick, David 10, 18–19, 21, 26
geodramatic territories 199
German Expressionism 122
gestural codes 13, 17, 27, 36, 196–7, 203–4, 207
Ghosts 25
GITIS see Russian Academy of Theatre Arts
given circumstances 60, 101–2, 111–13, 116, 120, 131, 150, 180–1, 206
Glengarry Glen Ross 149, 187
Gliding 46, 48
goals 107
Goethe, Johann Wolfgang von 22
Goldsmith, Oliver 104
The Graduate 82
grasp 71
gravity 191
Greeks 6, 11–12, 14, 198, 203
Green Room 76
Greene, Don 90
grotesque 170
Grotowski, Jerzy 3, 29, 31, 37, 49–51, 167, 187–8, 190–3, 195, 197, 199, 203, 206
Group Theatre 120, 176, 180, 183
guidelines 148
Gurdjieff, G.I. 29
Guskin, Harold 106

Haber, Margie 83
Hagen, Uta 10, 114
Hamlet 14–16, 50, 87
hara centre 205
Hart, Roy 51
Hartley, David 17
head 54, 99
heart 118, 139, 141
heredity 8, 10, 24
Hill, Aaron 21, 28
Hitchcock, Alfred 171–2
hitting the mark 130–1, 136, 145, 152, 158

Hollywood 71, 79, 83, 147, 153, 171–2, 175, 180, 208
Hornby, Richard 119, 122
hot sets 130
Houseman, Barbara 52
how 101, 106
humours 14–15, 17

iambic pentameter 125
Ibsen, Henrik 24–5, 140
identification 24
imaginary emotions 119
imagination 12–14, 20–1, 25–8, 38, 49–51; auditions 87–9; executors 165, 173, 179–80, 193, 198, 200, 206, 208; film acting 145; performance 136–7; rehearsals 102–6, 112–13, 115–16, 120–1, 124, 131; training 56–63, 66–7, 69–71
imitation 20
*Impro* 61–2
improvisation 28, 30, 50–1, 57–9, 62, 71, 83, 89, 121–2, 177–8, 198–9, 201
*Improvisation for the Theatre* 60
impulse 190, 193, 203
inconsistencies 86–7
indicating 123
inhalation 41
inhibition 95, 176
inner improvisation 28
inner psychological drives 98–9, 111–12, 117, 146, 165
instincts 52–3, 55, 58, 61, 63, 96–7, 106, 185, 206
*Institutes of Oratory* 12
intelligence 18–19, 38
Intention 168–9
interaction 62, 68, 70, 199
intercostals 53
interruptions 87–8, 139
interviews 77, 79, 93, 118, 158
intuition 57–8, 71, 80, 94, 99, 122, 155, 174
invisible theatre 8

irascible passions 15, 64
irresistible weeping 18, 119
irreverence 38
Irving, Henry 27
Isozaki, Arata 202–3

jaws 53
Jeet Kune Do 4
Johnstone, Keith 61–2
Jouvet, Louis 10, 31–2
judgement 57
Juillard School Drama Division 30
Jung, Carl 29
justification 114

kabbalah 29
*Kabuki* 36, 203–4
*kalarippayatu* 36, 51
*kathakali* 36, 193, 196
Kayoko, Shiraishi 202
Kazan, Elia 9
Kean, Edmund 26
Kershaw, Baz 134
Knebel, Maria 121
Konijn, Elly A. 118–19, 139
*Konstantin Stanislavsky* 109
Kovens, Ed 178

Laban, Rudolf 6, 45, 50, 168, 172, 174
LAMDA 160
larynx 53
*A Laughing Matter* 56
Lautvik, Else Marie 194
learning lines 149–50, 186, 188
learning monologues 87
Lecoq, Jacques 6, 51, 71, 194, 197–203, 205–6
Lee, Bruce 4
Lee Strasberg Institutes of Acting 176
Leris, Clair *see* La Clairon
Lessing, Gotthold 22
*Letters to George* 110
Lewes, George Henry 26–7
Lewis, Robert 120

Light 46–8
lighting 127–9, 145, 152
lightness 173
lines 84, 149–50, 155, 186, 188
linguistic energy 124–5
Linklater, Kristen 52–3, 55, 178
lips 53–5
listening 62, 71, 95–9, 120, 122;
    executors 179, 185, 189, 192,
    202, 208; performance 143, 145,
    153, 155
little plus 123
Littlewood, Joan 61, 160
living the part 28, 112–13
love scenes 86, 101
lures 111–15

Macy, William H. 187
magic if 113–14
make-up 83, 128, 152, 155
Malmgren, Yat 161
Mamet, David 9, 72, 106, 144, 149,
    186–9, 191, 197, 206
Marowitz, Charles 95, 120, 134, 138
Marshall, Lorna 41–3, 191
masks 29–31, 50, 54, 62, 102, 192,
    199
master shots 152–3
maximum acting 181
Mehrabian, Albert 41–2, 62
Meisner, Sanford 3, 12, 59, 71, 76,
    94, 96, 106, 114, 175, 183–6,
    188–9, 192, 196, 198, 206
Meisner Technique 183
melancholic traits 15
melodrama 122–3, 135, 199
metaphor 125, 137, 200, 208
Method 160, 176–8, 181, 187, 189,
    191
The Method Manual 178
Method of Physical Actions 22, 163,
    169, 180
Meyerhold on Theatre 167–71
Meyerhold, Vsevolod 10, 31, 45, 162,
    166–73, 175, 190, 193, 197–8,
    206

mid-shots 153
Miller, Arthur 116, 126
mime 123, 178, 198, 200
mind-body link 16, 25–6, 28–9, 32,
    40–1, 44, 99, 123, 196, 205
mise-en-scène 122
Mitchell, Katie 109
molding 173–4
moments of decision 96–8
monologues 84–9, 118, 148
monosyllables 125
monster of expediency 95–6
mood congruence 69–70
Morphos, Evangeline 177
Morris, Eric 38
Moscow Art Theatre (MAT) 7, 23,
    96, 108, 120, 162–3, 166, 171,
    175, 203
motivation 114, 195
motive forces 98
mouth 54–5
movement 23–4, 45–50, 61–2, 71,
    192–3, 199, 206
The Moving Body 198–202
Mowrer, Orval Hobart 64, 116
multi-cameras 158
muscle memory 20, 196

Nachmanovitch, Stephen 57–8, 71,
    142
National Theatre 14, 56, 104
naturalism 7, 23–4, 124–5
Nature 181, 199, 208
need for emotions 65–6
need for training 35, 38–9
negative path see via negativa
Neighborhood Playhouse 183, 186
Nemirovich-Danchenko, Vladimir
    7, 9
nerves 143–4, 188
nervous system 14, 17, 26, 141
neutral masks 199
New York University 71, 187
nineteenth century 22–3
Noh theatre 36, 203
nonverbal communication 41–2

Northwestern University 60
Number One/Two Self 27, 135–6, 142

objectives 48, 103–5, 107–8, 110–13, 115–17; executors 165, 181, 189, 195; performance 137, 139, 143, 149, 155; rehearsals 120
objects 200
observation 20–1, 68, 70, 88, 120, 135, 142, 176, 184–5, 194, 197
*Observations on a Book* 19
*Observations on Man* 17
Odin Teatret 193
Old Vic Theatre School 30
Olivier, Laurence 8, 140, 144
on-set rehearsals 129–30
opening beats 88
oratory 6, 12, 17, 27, 38
*The Origin of Species* 7
Original Anarchy 49
Osborne, John 9
Oscars 120, 187
Ouspenskaya, Maria 96, 108, 112, 138, 175–6
over-the-shoulder shots 152–3, 156
Overlie, Mary 48–50, 63, 192

pantomime 170
*The Paper Canoe* 194–7, 203
paradox 19–20
*The Paradox of the Actor* 20, 27
Paris Festival 202
particularisation 114
partners 59–60, 72, 80, 86–7, 89; executors 179, 184, 186, 189, 208; performance 135, 143, 146; rehearsals 97–8, 102, 106, 108, 110–12, 116–17, 120
passions 15–17, 20, 22–3, 25, 29; auditions 86–7; executors 182; history 32; performance 135; rehearsals 117, 123; training 45, 64
*The Passions of the Soul* 16
performance 9–10, 20–1, 23, 25–8, 31–3; auditions 75, 83–4, 89;

executors 172, 179, 186, 188–90, 194, 196, 201–2, 204, 206, 208; film acting 145, 156; final cuts 156; performance 136, 139; practices 134–59; rehearsals 94–5, 105–6, 112, 118, 120–2, 128–9, 131; stage fright 140–1, 143; television acting 157–8; training 36–7, 39, 44, 72
personality 23–4, 29–30, 40, 48, 51–2, 80, 89, 173, 180, 196
philosophy 10, 12, 16–18, 23, 28; executors 161, 181, 183, 192, 194, 196, 198, 202–4, 206; rehearsals 119; training 39, 60
phlegm 15
phlegmatic traits 15
physicality 12–13, 41–3, 62–3, 69
physiological stage fright 141–2
physiology 13, 17
Piscator, Erwin 180
Pisk, Litz 43
place 88
plastic body 168
plastic imagination 21
*plastiques* 49
play 28–9, 32, 37–8, 40, 51, 56–8, 72, 172, 195, 202, 207
pleasure 64, 66, 87, 116, 119, 174, 205
plot 11–12, 28
poetry 124–5, 204
points of view (POV) 100
post-dramatic 33
postmodernism 33
posture 44, 204
power of acting 13–14
power of repetition 93–4
Practical Aesthetics 187
*A Practical Handbook for the Actor* 187
*prana* 29
pre-expressivity 193
preparation 20, 75–6, 83–5, 88, 106, 110, 112, 146–7, 149–50, 175, 185, 188–9
presence 71, 202, 205–8

Pressing 46–8
*The Principles of Scientific Management* 168
process 26, 38, 57, 70, 76; actioning 110; auditions 80; executors 196–7; performance 143, 151; rehearsals 93–133
producers 79–81, 146, 156
professionalism 10, 21, 77–9, 118–19, 147, 155
prompts 83, 88, 150
props 76, 89, 127–8, 130, 145, 153, 170, 178, 182, 200, 206
psyche 29, 43, 52, 71, 191
psychoanalysis 7, 177
psychologists 25, 32, 41, 64, 66, 69, 90, 115, 118, 141
psychology 15, 17, 20, 24, 26; auditions 83, 91; challenges 75–7; executors 164–5, 201–2, 204; history 29; performance 146, 153; realism 24–5, 33; rehearsal 98–9, 111–12, 117; stage fright 141; subtext 125–6; training 36, 45–6, 53, 58
public read-throughs 100–1
public speaking 14
pulling 200
Punching 47–8
punctuation 126–7, 197
puns 125
purging 28–9
pushing 200
Pushkin, Mike 121

qualities of movement 46, 174, 206
Quintilian 12–15, 20, 38

radiating 173–4
Raikh, Zinaida 167
reaction 85, 96–8, 117, 129, 148, 153, 168–9, 186
read-throughs 93, 100–1
reading 34, 73, 83–4, 91–2, 99, 121, 132, 159, 161; realism 8–9, 24–5, 33

reflex excitability 106, 169
rehearsal rooms 76, 93, 98, 121, 128, 135, 166, 186
rehearsals 9–11, 27, 30, 39–40, 49; auditions 80; dress 128–9; executors 163, 167, 189; film acting 147, 151; on-set 129–30; performance 135, 146; processes 93–134; technical 127–9
rehearsing, camera 129–31
Reinhardt, Max 171, 180
relaxation 37, 40–1, 53, 56, 61; auditions 81, 84, 96, 113, 120; executors 168, 177, 205; performance 147–8; rehearsals 96, 113, 120; training 67
reliability 147
repertory theatres 84
repetition 21, 37, 39, 71, 93–4, 106, 187, 206
representation 27
research 41, 63–4, 82–3, 106, 145, 162, 167, 193–5
resonance 106, 134–6, 138
resonating ladder 54
resonators 53–4, 56
respect 38
responses 148
rest periods 168–9
Restoration comedies 135
rhetoric 6, 12
rhythm 82, 88, 97, 99–101, 104; executors 169, 176, 196, 204; performance 135, 149; rehearsals 109, 125, 130; shots 153; takes 154
ribcage 53, 68
Ribot, Théodule 25, 66
Riccoboni, Antoine-François 22
Riccoboni, Luigi 22
Richardson, Ralph 124
Rimer, Thomas J. 203
risks 37–8, 57, 89, 94, 100, 123, 131, 169
ritual 6, 29, 71, 99, 135, 203
Roach, Joseph 32

Rodenburg, Patsy 52, 54, 56, 124, 126, 137–8, 143–4, 178
roles 28, 31, 35–6, 41, 72; auditions 76–8, 81–5, 90–1, 93; rehearsals 93, 99, 105, 114, 127, 131; television acting 158
romance 86–7
*Romeo and Juliet* 101–2, 104
round-the-table work 101, 110
Royal Academy of Dramatic Art (RADA) 36, 71, 160
Royal Court Studio 61
Royal Dramatic School 36
Royal Scottish Academy for Music and Drama 71
Royal Shakespeare Company 140
*Rules for Action* 22
run-throughs 118, 127
Russian Academy of Theatre Arts (GITIS) 167, 190

Saint-Denis, Michel 6, 30–1, 61–2
Sainte-Albine, Pierre de 18
Salvini, Tommaso 117
*Sanford Meisner on Acting* 183–6
sanguine traits 15
Saratoga International Theatre Institute (SITI) 36
Saxe-Meiningen group 23
scenes 86–8, 97, 100, 107, 109–10; rehearsals 117, 120, 124; run-throughs 127; stage fright 141; study 178; takes 154
Scenic Movement 50
School for Theatrical Research 180
scores 20, 110, 123, 170, 190, 195
screen tests 83–4
scripts 57, 75, 80, 82–4, 89; actioning 110; executors 184, 186, 189; film acting 147, 149, 156; learning 149–50; performance 136; rehearsals 97–9, 101, 103, 109, 115, 121, 123, 130; stage fright 142; supervisors 130, 152; television acting 157

*The Seagull* 9, 114, 167
second assistant directors (second AD) 151–2
second plans 105
Sedita, Scott 127
sensations of sound 55–6
sense memory 25, 66–7, 177–8
senses 64, 68, 103, 178–9
sensibility 17–18, 20–1
sets 127–8, 130, 145, 170
seventeenth century 14–16, 25, 32, 135
Shakespeare, William 12, 31, 79, 101–2, 116, 124–7, 138–9, 202
Shape 48–50
Sharp, Craig 141
shattered time 49
Shaw, George Bernard 24
Shchepkin, Mikhail 24
*She Stoops to Conquer* 104
Sher, Anthony 140
shock 115
shots 153
Shurtleff, Michael 78, 86–7
sides 82
silence 143, 166, 197
simplicity 30
Six Fundamental Questions 85–6, 101–6, 111, 139, 191–2, 195, 199
Slashing 47–8
slowness 39–40
solar plexus 54
soliloquies 87, 138–9
solitude in public 20
sound 39, 53–4, 127–8, 138, 145, 156
sound mixers 151
Southern California University 71
space 6–7, 43, 45–50, 59–60, 62, 146, 173–4, 203
speech 51–2, 54–5
*Speech and Drama* 56
speeches 84–8, 110, 118, 124, 126
*Speed-the-Plow* 187
*Spellbound* 172

spirit 38, 70–1, 96, 126, 131, 166, 205–6
spiritual resonance 134–5, 138
split focus 135
Spolin, Viola 60–2, 181
spontaneity 27–8, 30, 57–9, 62, 89; executors 190, 203, 207; performance 135, 146, 154; rehearsals 112, 131, 134
Stafford-Clark, Max 93, 110, 127, 183
stage directions 99
stage fright 139–44, 179
*Stage Fright: Its Role in Acting* 140
stage pictures 122
stage schools 37
stamina 42, 52
stamping 202, 204–5
*Stanislavsky in Focus* 121, 163
Stanislavsky, Konstantin 3, 7, 9–12, 20, 22–3, 27–8, 31, 36, 40, 45, 50, 59–60, 71, 90, 96, 98–9, 101, 105, 108–9, 111–13, 117, 121, 123, 161–7, 169–76, 178–81, 185, 188–90, 192–3, 195, 197–8, 200, 203, 206
Stanitsyn, Viktor 120
star system 23
State Higher Directing workshop 167
State Theatre School 190
Status 62
Steiner, Rudolf 29, 56
Stella Adler Acting Studio 180
Stella Conservatory of Acting 180
stillness 154, 205
stomach 54
Story 48–50
storyboards 89
storytelling 42, 60, 62, 88, 93; executors 177, 206; performance 141–2; rehearsals 99–101, 105, 127–9, 131, 134
Strasberg, Lee 11, 31, 38, 45, 50, 70, 96, 112, 175–80, 183–4, 186, 188–9, 191, 198–200

strategy 63, 89–91, 110, 127, 141, 146, 156
*A Streetcar Named Desire* 9
Strehler, Giorgio 198
strength 42, 52
Strindberg, August 24
Strong 46–7
structure of rehearsals 98
style 135–6
subconscious 16, 137
sublime 18, 20
subliminal messages 62
subsiding emotions 26
substitution 114–15
subtext 9, 115, 117, 125–6, 148, 157
Sudden 46–8
suitability for roles 77–8
Sulerzhitsky, Leopold 165
superobjectives 104, 126, 180
Sustained 46–7
Suzuki, Tadashi 36, 41, 187, 202–5, 207–8
symbolists 71
system 7, 11, 20, 36, 160, 162, 164, 170, 172–5, 180, 189
*t'ai chi chuan* 36
takes 154–5
talents 77–81, 94, 155, 195
task-emotions 118–19
tasks 165
Taylor, Frederick Winslow 168–9
tear sticks 119–20
tears 119–21
technical rehearsals 127–9
technique 119–21, 134, 137–8, 147, 174, 195–6
*The Technique of Acting* 181–3
teeth 54–5
telegraphing 123
television acting 157–8
temperament 10–11, 23, 45, 78, 80, 82, 97, 195
tempo-rhythm 49, 127, 167–8, 170, 187
tension 42–4

terrifying unforeseen 72, 191, 206
testing boundaries 123
text 39, 52, 56, 84, 87; auditions 91;
    executors 178, 185, 189; owning
    122; performance 138, 148–9,
    154; punctuation 126; rehearsals
    94, 96, 101–2, 105, 109–11, 121,
    123–4, 127
text analysis 106, 109
theatre 23, 93, 134–5, 151, 160
*Théâtre des Nations* 202
*Theatre Games* 61
*Théâtre Libre* 7, 23
*Theatre of Movement and Gesture*
    198
Theatre of Sources 199
Theatre Workshop 61
Theatre-Studio 162, 167
*Thérèse Raquin* 24
thought-centre 99–111, 116, 121
thoughts 57, 62, 87, 97–8, 122,
    139, 148–9, 186, 196, 203, 206
*Three Sisters* 102, 136
time 46, 48–50
time-and-motion studies 168
*To the Actor* 172–5, 199
tone of voice 42
tongue 55–6, 64
total immersion 27
touch of sound 52–3
*Towards a Poor Theatre* 191–2
tragedy 117, 172, 198–9
training 35–74
trance 62
transference 114
transformation 24, 31, 65–6
tribunal drama 8
tricycle Theatre 8
*True or False Heresy and Common
    Sense for the Actor* 187–9
trust 59–60, 72, 81, 131
twentieth century 28–31, 71, 160,
    171
twenty-first century 32–3, 71, 160,
    166, 169, 202
two-shots 152–3

unconscious 70–1, 83
understanding of character 77–8
units 108–9, 165
University of California, Davis
    36

Vakhtangov, Yevgeny 114, 160,
    162, 172–3, 175–6, 181, 190
vaudeville 24
verbatim drama 8, 123
verse 125
vertical traditions 36
*via negativa* 37, 50, 188, 191, 195,
    207
Victorian melodramas 135
Viewpoints 48, 50, 63, 192
vocal cords 52–3
vocal range 54
vocal relaxation 53
vocational training 63
voice 8, 12–13, 27, 38–40, 42;
    executors 181, 189, 204; film
    acting 156; performance 137–8;
    training 51–6, 63, 70–1
voice coaches 10, 40
vowels 54–6
vulnerability 37–8, 57, 90, 95, 148,
    158, 188, 201

*Waiting for Godot* 124
Wangh, Stephen 71
warm-ups 41, 49, 51, 68
warmth 174
Warsaw Theatre School 193
Warwick University 61
*The Way of Acting* 203–5
websites 34, 73–4, 92, 133, 159,
    207
Wedekind, Frank 8, 160
weeping 119–21, 136
weight 46–8, 61
Weisman, Sam 80
West End 6, 9, 35, 101
*The West Wing* 33
when 101, 103
where 60, 101–2, 181

who 101–2
why 101, 103–4
Williams, Tennessee 9
wings 136
Word Repetition Games
    184–5
work cycles 168
working class 9

Wringing 47–8
wrinkled time 49

yellow bile 15
yoga 29, 165

Zarrilli, Phillip B. 36, 40, 51
Zola, Émile 7, 10, 24

# Shakespeare: The Basics

Second Edition

## Sean McEvoy

'Engaged and engaging, informed and accessible, critically up-to-date but not doctrinaire, this is the best bridge to an understanding of Shakespeare that I know.'

Rob Pope, *Oxford Brookes University and author of*
The English Studies Book

*Shakespeare: The Basics* is a refreshingly clear and insightful introduction to Shakespeare's work, helping to demystify the plays and the ways in which they have been interpreted. Topics covered include:

- Shakespeare's language
- the cultural and political contexts of the plays
- early modern theatre practice and the plays in performance
- the major genres
- Shakespeare on film.

This second edition has been fully updated and discusses more recent criticism and performance. It is an essential resource for anyone interested in Shakespeare.

978-0-415-362-467

Available at all good bookshops
For ordering and further information please visit www.routledge.com